HomeGuard: CyberSecurity

Digital Empowerment for Families

By: Drew Ighorewo

Table of Contents

Introduction

This book has been written as a service to my community. The word community is being used in a broad context because we live in a global village. Information security is now fashionably called cyber security, but the practice has been here as long as computer networks have existed. The information being presented is not new. It is simply the most recent available. I ensured this by using AI technology to gather and capture the information used to write this edition.

Cyber security is a mindset that requires you to be present, aware, vigilant, and creative. Armed with awareness, we are less vulnerable to tactics being used to compromise our freedom, safety, and security. Teaching our children critical thinking at an early age allows them to assess information with a healthy skepticism that will keep them safe. Being vigilant is the opposite of being fearful. Vigilance empowers us to be present when doing things on the internet. In a world full of multi-tasking and instant gratification, it reminds us to breathe before clicking the next button labeled I Accept or I Agree.

Having a security mindset means looking at the world through a lens where "rules" are not absolute. Don't get me wrong; clearly, we need systems and rules. However, the circumvention of systems and rules is how attacks occur. These rules are not just being circumvented and manipulated by hackers and cybercriminals. Privacy and data sovereignty laws are also being manipulated by governments and corporations. Our digital footprints are being weaponized against us for profit and power. It is important to examine all rules to determine who and what they serve. This knowledge is critical in order to recognize attacks and prepare a defense.

We must empower our communities, families, children, and the elderly to navigate this digital landscape with creativity and confidence. The contents of each chapter are presented as a series of checklists followed by a summary. The checklist format lays out different attacks and the tools we can use to mitigate them.

This information will be of little value if we do not first cultivate a cyber security mindset. The best antivirus, EDR, XDR, and firewall technology in the world cannot save us from our own negligence.

EDR stands for Endpoint Detection and Response. Think of it as a security system for your computer or other devices. It constantly monitors what's happening on your device, looking out for unusual or suspicious activity. If it spots something that could be a threat, like a virus or a hacker trying to break in, it alerts you and can take action to stop the threat. It's like having a security guard who keeps an eye on your device all the time, ready to respond if something goes wrong.

XDR stands for Extended Detection and Response. It's like an advanced version of EDR but with a broader focus. While EDR mainly protects individual devices, XDR integrates and coordinates security across multiple layers of your IT environment, including your network, cloud services, and endpoints.

Think of XDR as a more comprehensive security system that brings together information from various sources to give a more precise and complete picture of threats. It helps in detecting and responding to security issues more effectively by providing a unified view and automatic responses across all your security systems.

Definition of Cybersecurity

Cybersecurity, or information security, refers to the practice of protecting computer systems, networks, programs, and data from digital attacks, unauthorized access, damage, or theft. It involves strategies, technologies, and practices designed to safeguard the confidentiality, integrity, and availability of digital information. The primary goal is to ensure that your computer systems and data are secure from potential threats, such as:

- Hackers
- Malware
- Ransomware
- Phishing attacks

And other forms of cybercrime. Learning and implementing simple measures can help you prevent, detect, respond to, and recover from security incidents. Every individual can create a secure and resilient digital environment.

Importance of Cybersecurity at Home

We should expand on the concept of the CIA triad and what it means to the individual. In the realm of information security, the acronym CIA stands for:

- Confidentiality
- Integrity
- Availability

The triad is like a stool with three legs. When all three legs are strong, there is balance and stability. If one of the three is compromised, the system is no longer safe, reliable, or useful. It topples over broken. Confidentiality is closely related to privacy. It is the notion that everything you communicate on your digital device is between you and the recipient. The recipient can be another individual, group, or organization. The message or action should only be observed by the intended recipient of said message or action. The message is not meant to be seen or heard by the public, the government, or any corporate interests.

Modern digital communications are no longer confidential. We can illustrate this loss of confidentiality. When you use a search engine, the results are cached on millions of servers. An algorithm reads the results and then sends you targeted advertising that you see in the margins of your browser. Your phone is sitting next to you on the table when you discuss purchasing a new refrigerator with your spouse. Ads for new appliances appear on your phone the next time you pick it up. It does not matter whether the eavesdropper is a corporation that wants your money, a government that wants your vote, or a hacker. The end result is an invasion of your privacy. Integrity is closely related to truth and trust. When we store information for future use, we expect it to remain unaltered. If the information is tampered with or altered, it has lost its integrity. When we seek information, we expect to find relevant results in our search. If our search is redirected to a fake website or the search results are filtered, the integrity of that information has been lost. If data loses its integrity, we can no longer have trust and confidence that what we are seeing is the truth.

To safeguard the integrity of our systems, we scan them with antivirus software. In countries where the government censors internet access, citizens often use VPN services. A VPN, or Virtual Private Network, is like a secure tunnel for your internet connection. When you use a VPN, it hides your online activities and keeps your data private by routing it through a special server. This makes it harder for others, like hackers or even your internet service provider, to see what you're doing online. Plus, a VPN can help you access websites and content that might be restricted in your location by making it look like you're browsing from a different place.

Availability is fundamental in that if a resource is unavailable, we cannot access or use it. Anybody who has been hit by an attack that renders your system unusable can relate. The computer slows to a crawl and becomes unresponsive to your commands. Files used for system operation may have become corrupted, encrypted, or damaged and can no longer be read by the operating system.

The best way to make sure that your computer is available is by backing up your data. In the event of a security breach, restoring your data from the most recent backup is the shortest path to recovery.

What follows is a brief diagram that illustrates layers of the digital landscape where data is secured. The diagram is not exhaustive but covers the most important scenarios.

Defense in Depth: Layered Security

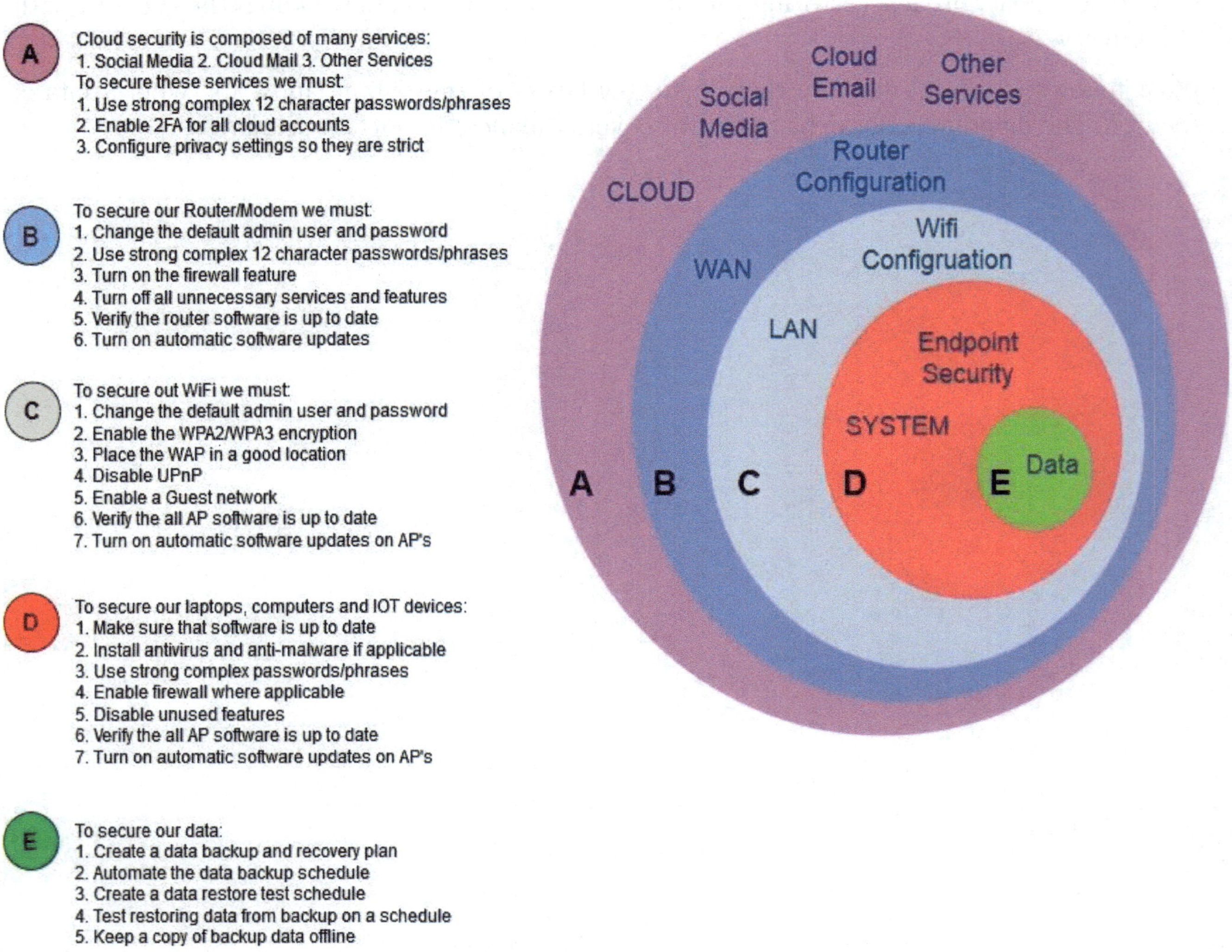

Defense in depth is a cybersecurity strategy that involves implementing multiple layers of security controls throughout our infrastructure to protect against potential threats. It is derived from military strategy, where multiple layers of defense are employed to prevent adversaries from advancing on the battlefield.

Cultivating a security mindset means understanding that no single security measure is foolproof. We need to configure controls at each layer for a resilient and robust security posture. These layers typically include:

Cloud Security: Enabling MFA (Multi-Factor Authentication) for all our cloud-based email and social media accounts. Ensuring we have configured strict privacy settings for our social media accounts.

WAN (Wide Area Network) Security: This is the outermost layer of your home's physical network. Typically, your firewall configuration and intrusion prevention systems (IPS). The firewall can be configured to prevent unauthorized access to our home network.

LAN (Local Area Network) Security: This layer involves securing internal networks and communication channels. Network segmentation using Guest networks and VLANs, virtual private networks (VPNs), and network access control (NAC) solutions.

Endpoint Security: Endpoint devices such as desktops, laptops, smartphones, and servers are often targeted by attackers. Endpoint security solutions such as antivirus software, host-based intrusion detection systems (HIDS), and endpoint detection and response (EDR) tools help protect these devices.

Data Security: This layer focuses on protecting sensitive data from unauthorized access, theft, or manipulation. Create a data backup and recovery plan. Store a copy of the Backup data offline. Encryption, data loss prevention (DLP) solutions, and data masking techniques are also used to secure data.

By implementing defense in depth, families can mitigate the risks associated with cyber threats more effectively. Even if one layer of defense is compromised, other layers can provide protection, reducing the likelihood and impact of a cyberattack.

To Prevent Identity Theft

Preventing identity theft starts by protecting our personally identifiable information(PII). Our homes contain a wealth of personal information stored on devices and online accounts. Home networks can be targeted by cybercriminals seeking to steal personal information for identity theft. Cybersecurity measures help safeguard sensitive data such as financial records, medical information, and personal communications. Implementing Cybersecurity practices can mitigate the risk of unauthorized access to a family member's PII that could result in identity fraud.

To Protect Financial Information

Many individuals conduct financial transactions online, from banking to online shopping. In fact, web-based financial transactions are so common that we no longer stop to weigh the potential risks. Without proper Cybersecurity awareness, our financial information becomes vulnerable to theft, potentially leading to financial loss. Cybercriminals frequently employ scams and phishing attacks that convince victims to click links in emails or in pop-up windows, redirecting them to counterfeit websites that look official. The scheme involves tricking victims into providing sensitive information or making fraudulent payments. Cybersecurity awareness helps us recognize and avoid falling victim to such scams.

To Protect Family Members

In a connected home, family members use many devices, and children and the elderly may be particularly susceptible to online threats. The internet is a tool that gives us access to immense amounts of content. It is our responsibility to train our family members in the use of this tool. We would not hand our child a sharp knife, axe, or chainsaw without extensive safety training.

Yes. We should view internet platforms such as Facebook and Instagram in the same way we view other dangerous yet useful tools. To take this analogy one step further, each member of the family should take one internet self-defense course. Sharing this book helps them adopt a security mindset encouraging them to make mindful choices online. Our children are not ready to receive all the information being offered on the internet. It's important to ensure that our children are viewing age-appropriate content. Another concern is the amount of time that children spend consuming online content. There is a wealth of information online that can be used for learning purposes. There is also a bottomless bucket of online games that display violence and sexual innuendo. Not all content is suitable for the consumption of minors. Managing children's screen time is good parenting.

Limiting screen time reminds our children to interact with real people in the family and our communities. It also encourages them to stay involved in physical and artistic activities that don't involve screens and keyboards. Cybersecurity measures protect our most vulnerable family members from malicious content, cyberbullying, and online predators.

Home Network Security

Home networks are increasingly interconnected with the rise of smart devices. In many homes, family members and home appliances are connected to the internet. These devices have been labeled with the term "smart" and are often referred to as IoT (Internet of Things) devices. Common examples of IoT devices include:

- Televisions
- Security cameras
- Fridges
- WiFi Access Points
- Digital assistants

Homes are targeted by criminals for a variety of reasons. In a ransomware attack, the objective is to extortion. However, it may be to compromise other devices in your home to gain command and control of them for a botnet. I know what you are thinking right now...why would anybody want control of my fridge? Typically the devices in a botnet have been infected by malware. The malware turns the devices into "zombies" so that they can be used by criminals to launch attacks. Cybersecurity safeguards the home network from unauthorized access, protecting personal information and connected devices.

Maintaining privacy in the digital age can be difficult. Cybersecurity measures help ensure that personal conversations, online activities, and digital behavior remain private and protected from unauthorized surveillance. Family photos, videos, and other digital assets are often stored on personal devices. Cybersecurity measures, including regular backups, help preserve these digital memories and protect against data loss.

To Protect Peace of Mind

A home with robust cybersecurity measures in place provides peace of mind. We can navigate the digital landscape with confidence, knowing that our personal information and digital assets are secure. Cybersecurity at home is vital for protecting personal and financial information. It ensures family safety, prevents financial loss, preserves digital assets, and maintains the integrity of home networks.

Chapter 1: Understanding Your Digital Footprint

Personal Data Online

Think of your digital footprint as the breadcrumbs you leave behind as you traverse the internet. An individual's digital footprint consists of various types of data that collectively form a digital representation of their activities, behaviors, and personal information on the internet.

It had been a rough few days at Evan and Clarice's house. The burglary had shaken up the whole family. Clarice's purse was stolen, and inside were her ID, bank cards, and even her phone. What worried her the most wasn't losing those things but the fact that her personal information could now be misused.

After dinner, the family gathered in the living room, sitting tensely in a circle, not sure what to do next. Clarice had already taken the first steps–reporting the theft to the police, blocking her bank cards and credit cards, and deactivating her phone. But deep inside, her worries were far from over. She couldn't help but think about how easily the thief could access her email, her shopping accounts, and even her social media and how fast things could go out of control.

Shannon, their tech-smart daughter, was quick to step in. "Mom," she said, "I think it's time we all talk about our digital footprints. What happened to you could just as easily happen to any of us. We're not being careful enough."

Clarice looked around at her family: her husband, Evan, trying to hide his worry; her teenage son Idris, who was glued to his phone; and even little Aditsan, who spent hours playing games online. Her thoughts wandered to elderly parents Margaret and Hannibal, who had adopted technology without fully understanding its risks. Clarice knew it wasn't just her information that was at risk; it was the whole family.

Shannon took a deep breath and began explaining, her voice steady but urgent. "We need to understand what happens when we share things online. Mom's purse getting stolen is bad, but what's even worse is how much personal information could now be exposed. What we post or even look at online leaves behind a trace–a digital footprint."

We can break the footprint down into two types of data. Active and Passive:

1. **Active digital footprints** consist of data a user leaves intentionally. The user is also aware of the digital trace they leave behind because they have deliberately submitted information. Examples include posting text, images, or videos on social media, online banking, fitness apps, subscribing to newsletters, and applying for credit. In all cases, we leave a digital history that we are aware of.

2. **Passive digital footprints** A passive digital footprint is created when information is collected about the user without them being aware that this is happening. Essentially, data a user leaves behind unintentionally on the internet. Website visits and actions,

searches, and online purchases are among the online activities that add passive data traces to a digital footprint. Passive information is collected when a site, app, or service records how many times a user visits the user's location and IP Address. This is a hidden process, making passive footprints harder to track because they are collected without user consent. When a hacker collects data about a targeted system, it is known as **footprinting or fingerprinting**.

After explaining these concepts, Clarice's family realized that it is much easier to limit the data they share than to go back and try to scrub it from the internet.

Clarice emphasized the importance of being mindful. With her family's support, they discussed strategies for managing their digital footprint effectively, like using browser incognito mode, regularly updating privacy settings, and only sharing essential information online.

What we post or share online is, in many ways, permanent and accessible to many entities. Aspects of our digital footprint, such as uploaded photographs, blog comments, YouTube videos, and Facebook posts, may be dated and may not portray current values.

It is now standard practice for employers, universities, and government agencies to check an individual's digital footprint prior to making hiring, admission, and application approval decisions. Employers can check our digital footprints, particularly social media, before hiring. Colleges and universities check their prospective students' digital footprints before granting admission. We need to keep these things in mind before posting personal information and opinions on social media.

After discussing types of footprints, the family brainstormed ways to effectively manage their digital footprints. Let's dive deeper into this topic and explore other important aspects.

Managing Our Footprint

Here are a few ways we can manage our digital footprint:

- Close old or unused email accounts
- Browse the internet in incognito mode to avoid cookies
- Unsubscribe from unwanted email newsletters
- Limit the information we share on social media
- Keep our personal email address private
- Regularly update our browser and privacy settings

- Use virtual private networks (VPN) to stop web browsers from accessing our IP address and other data
- Set age-based internet safety restrictions for children
- Regularly update passwords used online

Read privacy policies and terms of use. Before downloading an application or using a service, understand the types of information being collected and how it will be used. What security measures are in place to protect personal information?

Disable cookies and monitor settings, if possible. Even when not actively sharing information on applications and websites, your data is still traced through your device, IP address, and network. Configure the application's privacy and security settings with the highest and most restrictive settings available.

Do not browse unencrypted sites and install browser privacy extensions (e.g., ad-blocker). Make sure you're transacting with a secure website – the URL should start with https:// and have a padlock icon in the address bar. The padlock and https:// in the URL- indicate that the site has a security certificate. Don't make purchases or share confidential information on unsecured sites.

Permit access to only those needing to know and classify data based on the level of sensitivity. This can be done using your social media account privacy settings. Review these settings and ensure they are set to a level you are comfortable with. For example, Facebook allows you to limit posts to friends and make customized lists of people who can see certain posts. However, bear in mind that privacy settings only protect you on the relevant social media site.

Remove metadata from photos before sharing online. Information stored in an image file can expose personal details (i.e., date, times, and location):

1. Navigate to the folder holding the images you want to edit.
2. Select the file (or files) you wish to delete metadata from.
3. Right-click and select **Properties**, then **Details**.

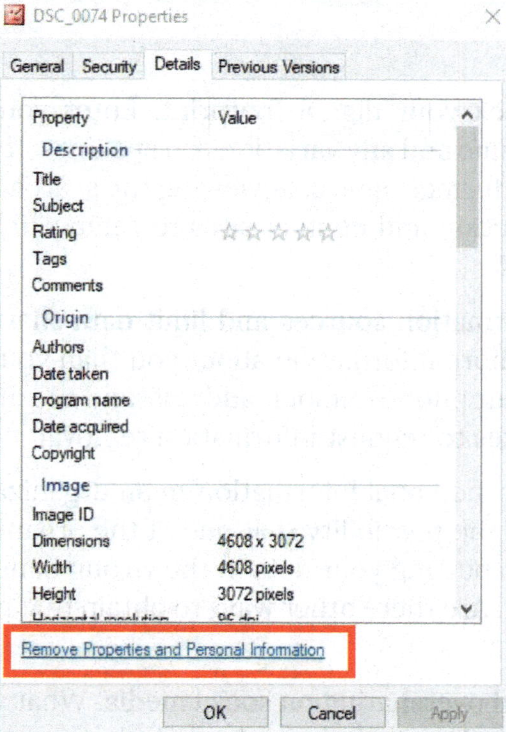

4. Click Remove Properties and Personal Information.

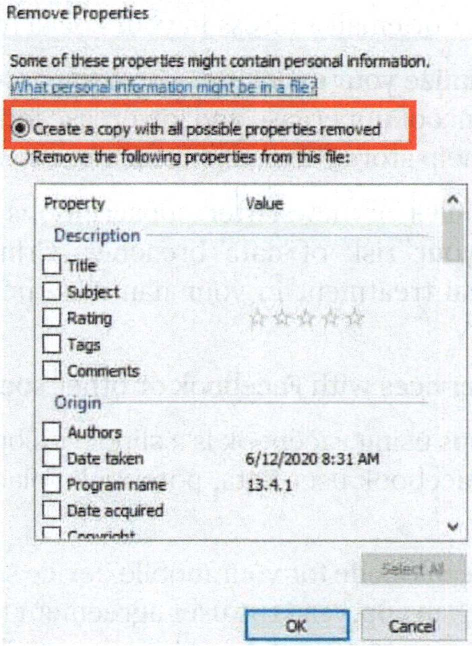

5. Click Create a copy with all possible properties removed.

6. Click OK

Use search engines to check your digital footprint. Enter your name into search engines. Include your first and last name and any variations on spellings. If you have changed your name, search for both current and former names. Reviewing the search results will let you know what is publicly available. Take action and contact sites to remove information that should not be disclosed.

Reduce the number of information sources and limit data sharing. Real estate websites and whitepages.com may have more information about you than you may wish. These can include personal information like your phone number, address, and age. If you are not comfortable with this, you can contact websites to request information removal.

Every time you provide your personal information to an organization, you expand your digital footprint. You also increase the possibility that one of the organizations storing your data will misuse it or suffer a breach, putting your data in the wrong hands. So, before you submit that form, consider if it's worth it. Are there other ways to obtain that information or service without sharing your data?

Think before you post: Avoid oversharing on social media. What you post or say online sends a message about who you are. This includes uploaded photographs, blog comments, YouTube videos, and Facebook posts. They might not portray the image you desire. Create a positive digital footprint by posting only those things that contribute to the image of you that you want others to see (this may seem disingenuous, but think about the alternative).

Social media makes it easy to connect with others but can also make oversharing easy. Think twice before revealing your location, travel plans, or other personal information, and avoid disclosing your phone number or email address in your social media bio.

Use strong passwords & Minimize your exposure. A strong password is long, ideally made up of at least 12 characters with a mix of uppercase and lowercase letters plus symbols and numbers. Use a password manager to help store them, and remember to rotate passwords regularly.

Delete old social media profiles or newsletter subscriptions you no longer use. Reducing dormant accounts lowers your risk of data breaches. Criminals can use your personal information to obtain medical treatment in your name, so periodically review your medical records for suspicious activity.

Do not log into third-party services with Facebook or other social accounts.

Logging into websites and apps using Facebook is a slippery slope. When you do this, you allow the company to mine your Facebook user data, potentially placing your personal information at risk.

Review your mobile use. Set a passcode for your mobile device so that other people can't access it if you lose it. When installing an app, read the user agreement to understand what information they collect. These apps may mine personal data like your email, location, and online activities. Check that you are comfortable with the information being shared before you use the app.

Act fast after a breach and use a VPN for added security. If your data is compromised, take immediate action. Report financial losses to your bank or credit card provider and change any exposed passwords across your accounts. Using a virtual private network, or VPN, can help safeguard your digital footprint. This is because VPNs mask your IP address and encrypt all data transfer between your device and the VPN server. It makes your online actions more difficult to trace and prevents man-in-the-middle attacks (MITM), data sniffing, and cookies that track your internet browsing history.

Avoid disclosing private data on public Wi-Fi. A public Wi-Fi network is inherently less secure than your personal one since you don't know who set it up or who else might be watching. Avoid sending personal information when using public Wi-Fi networks. If this cannot be avoided, use a VPN.

Typical data comprising an individual's digital footprint include:

Social Media Activity

Posts, comments, likes, and shares on platforms like Facebook, Twitter, Instagram, LinkedIn, etc. Personal and professional connections and networks.

Online Profiles

Usernames, profile pictures, and personal information on social media, forums, and other online platforms. Bios and description details on various websites.

Search Engine Queries

Search terms entered into search engines, revealing interests, concerns, and information-seeking behavior.

Location Data

Geotagged posts, check-ins, and location information shared through mobile devices, social media, or location-based services.

Email Communication

Email addresses, communication patterns, and the content of emails. Contacts and interactions within email accounts.

Browsing History

Websites visited, pages viewed, and time spent on different online platforms. Online shopping history, if applicable.

Online Purchases

Transaction details from online shopping, including items purchased, payment methods, and shipping information.

Digital Identity Information

Usernames, passwords, and security questions used across various online accounts. Digital identifiers, such as device fingerprints or IP addresses.

Content Creation

Blogs, articles, or other content created and shared online. Multimedia content, such as photos, videos, and audio recordings. Reviews and ratings left on e-commerce websites, apps, or other platforms. Feedback and comments on products, services, or experiences.

Employment and Educational History

Professional profiles on platforms like LinkedIn, including work history and educational background.

Public Records and Directories

Information available in public records, directories, or online databases. Participation in online forums and discussion groups.

App Usage

Applications installed on devices, usage patterns, and permissions granted. Data collected by mobile apps and third-party services.

Cloud Storage

Files and documents stored in cloud services. Sharing and collaboration history within cloud platforms.

Online Subscriptions

Subscriptions to newsletters, mailing lists, or online services. Preferences and interests indicated through subscribed content.

The nature of your digital footprint varies based on your activities. It is constantly evolving, emphasizing the need for privacy awareness and responsible online behavior.

Risks of Oversharing

Sharing personal information online can expose individuals to various risks, and it's crucial to be aware of these potential dangers. Our social media profiles often contain details about our lives, relationships, interests, and even our location. Without proper privacy safeguards, this personal information becomes vulnerable to misuse, data breaches, identity theft, and unwarranted surveillance.

Here are some risks associated with sharing personal information on the internet.

Phishing & Identity Theft

Sharing personal information online increases the risk of falling victim to phishing attacks, where malicious actors attempt to deceive individuals into providing sensitive information through fraudulent emails, messages, or websites. Criminals use personal information, such as names, addresses, and social security numbers, to commit identity theft and engage in fraudulent activities. This information can be used to gain unauthorized access to financial accounts, leading to unauthorized transactions, credit card fraud, or other forms of financial exploitation.

Loss of Privacy & Location Tracking

Excessive sharing of personal details online makes it easier for others to track an individual's activities, preferences, and locations. Location data shared through mobile devices or check-ins on social media can be exploited to track an individual's movements, posing potential safety and privacy concerns. It can contribute to an overall feeling of being constantly monitored or invaded, affecting one's sense of personal space and security. Details shared on social media or other online platforms can be used by malicious individuals for harassment, stalking, or cyberbullying.

Social Engineering Attacks

Attackers use gathered personal information to manipulate individuals into revealing sensitive data or performing actions that compromise their security. This information is used by scammers to craft convincing schemes to perpetrate fraudulent activities or financial scams.

Employment and Reputation Risks

Inappropriate or compromising information shared online could negatively impact an individual's professional reputation, job opportunities, or relationships.

Targeted Advertising and Profiling

Personal information is often used for targeted advertising, which can lead to a loss of online privacy and potentially contribute to unwanted surveillance and profiling. Companies and third parties collect personal data to gain insights into consumer behavior, preferences, and demographics without explicit consent.

Data Breaches

Organizations storing personal information may experience data breaches, exposing individuals' data to unauthorized access and potential misuse. Weak or reused passwords and answers to security questions can lead to unauthorized access to various online accounts, compromising personal and sensitive data.

To mitigate these risks, practice responsible and intentional online behavior. Limit the amount of personal information shared online, and be cautious about the platforms you trust. Be clear about what and why you are posting. Stay informed about privacy settings and security measures.

Importance of Privacy Settings

Privacy settings are critically important when using online apps and services. Most social media platforms offer privacy settings that allow you to control who can see your posts, profile information, and contact details. Take the time to review these settings and customize them according to your comfort level.

Control Over Personal Information

Privacy settings allow users to control what personal information is shared and with whom. Robust privacy settings help prevent unauthorized access to personal accounts, reducing the risk of identity theft, fraud, and other cybercrimes. This control is crucial for maintaining the privacy of sensitive data.

Mitigate Risks & Harassment

Privacy settings reduce risks by limiting exposure to phishing attacks and social engineering. We can customize sharing preferences based on the sensitivity of our information, ensuring that only desired audiences have access to specific content. Adjusting these settings can help manage who can interact with our content, reducing the risk of harassment, cyberbullying, and unwanted attention. It allows us to control our online image, helping to manage our reputation by restricting the visibility of certain content.

Limit Data Collection & Increase Privacy

We can use privacy settings to limit the amount of data collected by apps and services, reducing the risk of personal data misuse and targeted advertising. We can control the sharing of location data, reducing tracking and protecting individuals' physical privacy. Some apps and services may have data-sharing agreements with third parties. We can opt out of such agreements in privacy settings, preserving our data privacy.

Protect Family and Children From Solicitations

Parents can use privacy settings to create a safer online environment for their children by controlling who can interact with them and limiting exposure to inappropriate content. It is essential for maintaining the security and confidentiality of personal and sensitive data, preventing it from falling into the wrong hands. Correctly setting this tool protects contact information and other details. It reduces the likelihood of receiving unwanted solicitations, spam, or phishing attempts. Use it to manage your online presence and share information on your own terms.

In summary, managing your digital footprint is about more than just keeping your privacy safe; it's also about being aware of the dangers of oversharing. As we spend more time online, it's important to have control over our personal information and what we share. By learning about active and passive footprints, using protective measures, and being careful about the information we give out, we can protect ourselves and maintain a safe online presence. The main point is to stay informed and take steps to make sure our digital footprint truly represents us without risking our security or privacy.

Chapter 2: Common Cyber Threats

A few days had passed since the family's talk about digital footprints, and they were starting to get back to their normal routines. Clarice had reactivated her accounts with better security, Evan was using stronger passwords, and even Idris was being more careful with his social media.

After the burglary at their home, the family had been talking about how easily personal information could be stolen and misused. Their conversation about digital footprints had opened their eyes to the dangers of cyber threats, and it wasn't long before another real-life incident brought these concerns even closer to home.

Evan trusted his office's computer network security, believing the IT team had everything covered. His job required him to work with sensitive financial data, but he never thought much about cybersecurity. That all changed one Monday morning when he arrived at work and found total chaos. The company had been hit by a ransomware attack over the weekend. Employees couldn't access their accounts, and all the important data was locked. The attackers were demanding money to release the files.

It became clear that the company wasn't as prepared as they thought. Their security protocols were outdated, many employees, including Evan, were using weak passwords, and they had no reliable backup system. The ransomware had entered through a phishing email, which one employee had mistakenly clicked, exposing the company's weaknesses.

Management immediately brought in cybersecurity experts, who quickly implemented stronger defenses. Employees were required to use unique, complex passwords and set up two-factor authentication. Sensitive data was encrypted, and an automated backup system was installed.

For Evan, this was a wake-up call. He realized how easily his own carelessness could have contributed to the breach. The attack disturbed the company's operations and led to financial losses, but it also taught them a valuable lesson: cybersecurity wasn't something they could afford to ignore.

When Evan got home later that day, he shared what had happened at work with his family.

"We're lucky the company didn't lose everything," Evan said as he sat at the dinner table. "It was all because one person clicked on a link in a phishing email. It opened the door for the ransomware to get in."

Shannon looked up from her plate. "So, it's like what we've been talking about, right? Always being careful with emails and links?"

"Exactly," Evan replied. "We need to be careful. I didn't think it could happen at work, but it did. And now I see how easily it could happen to us at home, too."

Clarice, still shaken from the burglary, nodded. "That's why I keep worrying about our accounts and what we share online. It's all connected, isn't it?"

"It really is," Evan agreed. "At work, the company didn't have proper security measures. They didn't have strong passwords or two-factor authentication. I thought I was safe, but I wasn't paying attention."

Evan's experience with the attack at his office highlighted some of the most common cyber threats individuals face at home and at work:

Social Engineering & Phishing Attacks

Cybercriminals often use deceptive emails, messages, or websites to trick individuals into revealing sensitive information, such as passwords or financial details. Attackers use psychological manipulation to trick individuals into divulging confidential information. Often posing as trustworthy entities or exploiting personal relationships scraped from social media, etc.

Malware & Ransomware

Malicious software, including viruses, ransomware, and spyware, can infect devices and compromise data, leading to loss of control over the system or unauthorized access. Ransomware encrypts files and demands payment for their release. Individuals may lose access to important data unless a ransom is paid.

Identity Theft & Data Breaches

Cybercriminals may steal personal information to impersonate individuals for fraudulent activities, access financial accounts, establish false credit lines, or commit other crimes. Large-scale breaches on online platforms may expose sensitive data, putting individuals at risk of identity theft.

Password Attacks

Brute force attacks, credential stuffing, or password spraying are methods used by attackers to gain unauthorized access to accounts by exploiting weak or compromised passwords.

Unsecured Wi-Fi Networks & Device Vulnerabilities

Inadequately secured Wi-Fi networks can be exploited by attackers to intercept data, launch attacks, or gain unauthorized access to connected devices. Outdated software, operating systems, and applications may have vulnerabilities that attackers can exploit. Regular updates are essential to patch security flaws.

Online Scams & Social Media Threats

Fraudulent schemes, such as fake online shopping sites, lottery scams, or tech support scams, aim to deceive individuals and extract money or personal information. Cybercriminals may use social media to gather personal information, launch phishing attacks, or impersonate individuals to spread misinformation.

Online Predators & Eavesdropping

Individuals, especially children, may encounter online predators who exploit vulnerabilities to manipulate or exploit them. Attackers may exploit vulnerabilities in devices or use advanced techniques to eavesdrop on conversations or conduct unauthorized surveillance.

Insecure IoT Devices

Internet of Things (IoT) devices with weak security can be targeted, leading to unauthorized access to personal data, home surveillance, or even control of smart home systems.

To mitigate these threats, individuals should practice good cybersecurity hygiene, such as using strong and unique passwords, keeping software updated, being cautious with email and online communications, securing Wi-Fi networks, and staying informed about the latest cyber threats and protective measures.

We will address the tools and strategies available to mitigate these challenges in the chapters that follow. Beginning with the most fundamental. Do you have a backup and restore strategy?

Chapter 3: Data Backup Strategies

The importance of having a good backup plan became clear to everyone in the office after the ransomware attack. While the IT department started putting stronger security measures in place, the next big task was ensuring they could quickly restore their data if another cyberattack happened. As a security consultant, I've seen many organizations fail to set up a backup plan, which led to serious financial losses. Backing up data is very important because it helps keep information safe and available. A solid backup and restore strategy is more valuable than an insurance policy. It is the ultimate insurance that allows the restoration of systems and data without the need to acquiesce to an attacker's demands.

The company's new plan included local and cloud backups to guard against possible attacks. The best way to protect against data loss from things like corruption, accidental deletion, malware, or ransomware is to have a copy stored offline. Backups that are connected to the network can be targeted and damaged during an attack. So, the team looked at different backup strategies to ensure they were well-protected against future threats.

Evan watched as the IT team worked hard to put the new backup strategies in place. They started by checking the current systems to see what needed protection. "We need to understand our data before we can secure it," said Sara, the IT manager, during a meeting. Knowing their data was key to creating a strong backup plan.

"Evan, we need your help to explain these changes to the rest of the staff," Sara said. "Everyone must know why backups are important." Evan agreed, realizing that as a financial manager, it was his job to help raise awareness about cybersecurity in the office.

While preparing a presentation for his colleagues, Evan thought about his family's talks about digital footprints and online threats. He wanted to connect his work knowledge to how families could protect themselves at home. "If we can understand these threats at work, we should do the same at home," he thought.

The room was filled with questions and conversations as coworkers showed interest in learning more about keeping their personal and work data safe. Evan felt proud to see how his colleagues' attitudes had changed. They were no longer indifferent; they were now eager to discuss cybersecurity. He left the meeting feeling motivated to share these important lessons at work and home.

Let's look at different data backup strategies that can protect both companies and families. While this can be used on company backups, it is crucial to understand that these strategies can be used to secure personal data at home. These strategies are beneficial for many scenarios.

Choosing A Backup Strategy

The strategy you select will ensure data integrity and determine your recovery timelines. Each strategy offers varying levels of protection, ease of recovery, and recovery timelines. Here's an overview of different backup strategies, along with a table and flowcharts that illustrate how each strategy impacts recovery timelines:

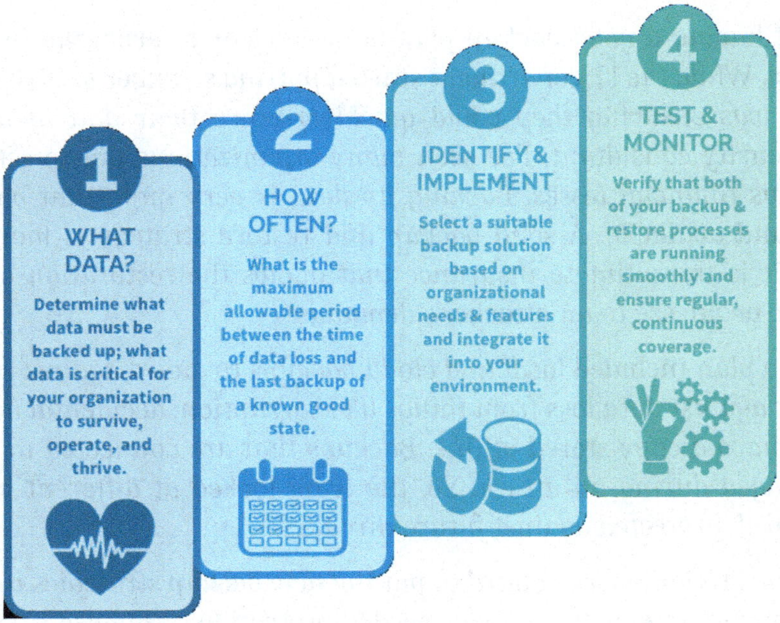
1
WHAT DATA?
Determine what data must be backed up; what data is critical for your organization to survive, operate, and thrive.
2
HOW OFTEN?
What is the maximum allowable period between the time of data loss and the last backup of a known good state.
3
IDENTIFY & IMPLEMENT
Select a suitable backup solution based on organizational needs & features and integrate it into your environment.
4
TEST & MONITOR
Verify that both of your backup & restore processes are running smoothly and ensure regular, continuous coverage.

Backup Strategy	Description	Pros	Cons	Recovery Timeline
1. Full Backup	A complete backup of all data at a specific point in time.	Simplifies recovery as all data is available in one backup set.	Time-consuming and requires significant storage space.	Quick; minimal processing is needed.
2. Incremental Backup	Only saves changes made since the last backup (full or incremental).	Reduces backup time and storage requirements compared to full backups.	Recovery can be slower as it requires the last full backup and all subsequent increments.	Moderate to high; multiple backups must be processed.
3. Differential Backup	Saves changes made since the last full backup.	Faster backup times than full backups and quicker recovery times.	Backup size increases over time until the next full backup.	Moderate; only the full backup and last differential backup are needed.
4. Mirror Backup	An exact copy of the source data without compression or encryption.	Immediate access to files in their original format.	Higher storage requirements and no historical versioning.	Very fast; data is readily available in its original state.
5. Synthetic Full Backup	Combines a full backup and subsequent incremental backups to create a new full backup.	Reduced time for creating full backups and efficient storage management.	Requires more sophisticated software and infrastructure.	Fast; appears as a full backup.
6. Continuous Data Protection	Automatically saves a copy of every change made to the data in real-time.	Allows for ear-instant recovery to any point in time.	High storage and resource requirements; more complex to manage.	Very fast; can be restored to the exact point before failure.
7. Hybrid Backup	Combines local and cloud backups for comprehensive protection.	Offers quick local recovery and offsite cloud-based disaster recovery.	Higher costs and more complex management.	Variable: local recovery is fast, but cloud recovery may depend on bandwidth and data size.

Backup Process

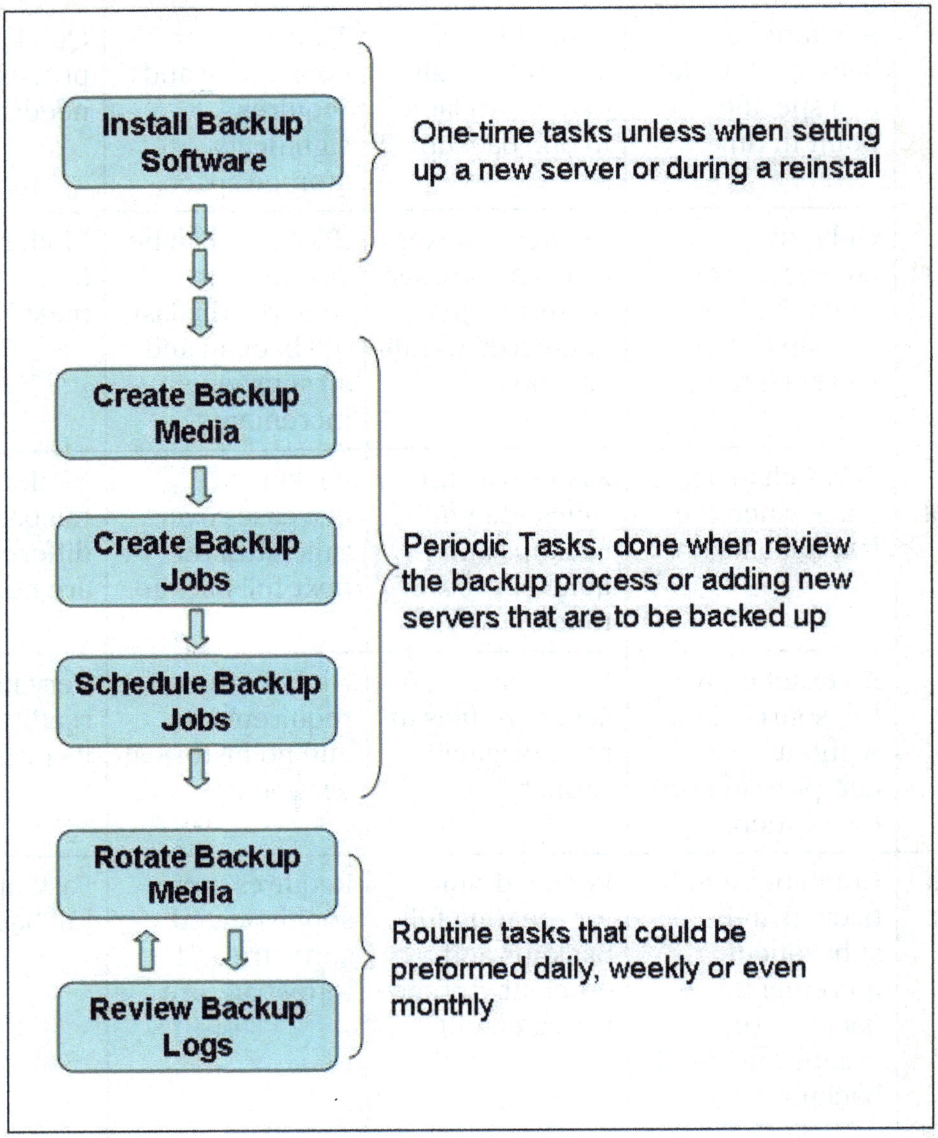

Recommended 3-2-1 Backup Strategy for Families

- Perform a full backup once per week (on a day and at a time with the least activity).
- Perform incremental backups on all other days.

Use three external drives to accomplish the local backup. Here's how:

1. Use Drive 1 to take a full backup.

2. Use Drive 2 for incremental backups throughout the remainder of the week.

3. Use Drive 3 to take a second full backup at the end of the first week.

One full backup will always remain offline to ensure data protection in case the online media is compromised.

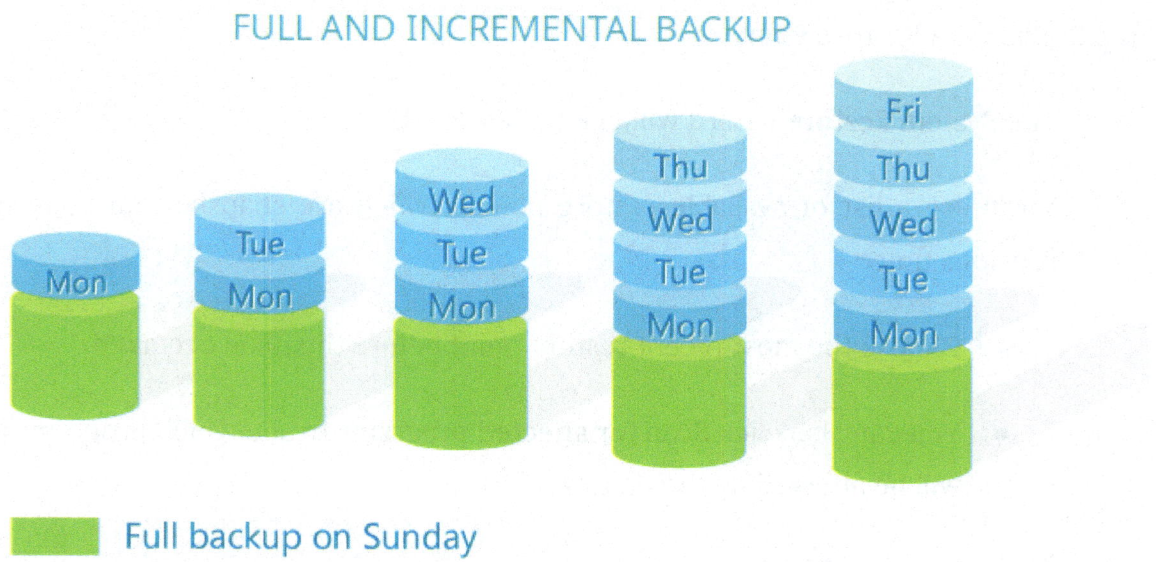

Restoring Windows Systems

Method 1: Restore Last Known Good Configuration via System Restore

System Restore allows you to revert your computer's settings to a previous point in time, which is similar to the older **Last Known Good Configuration.**

Step 1: Boot into Advanced Startup

1. **Access the Advanced Startup** options:

   - **Windows 10/11**: Go to **Start** > **Settings** > **Update & Security** > **Recovery**. Under the **Advanced Startup** section, click **Restart now**.

   - Alternatively, restart your PC and press the **F11** or **Shift + F8** key repeatedly during startup to enter recovery mode (this may vary depending on your hardware).

2. **Once your PC restarts, you'll see the Advanced Startup menu.**

Step 2: Open System Restore

1. In the **Advanced Startup** options menu, select **Troubleshoot** > **Advanced options** > **System Restore**.
2. Choose your user account and enter your password if prompted.

Step 3: Choose a Restore Point

1. The **System Restore** wizard will open. Click **Next**.
2. You'll see a list of available restore points, which are snapshots of your system at a previous time.
   - Choose the most recent restore point before the issue occurred.
   - You can also click **Scan for affected programs** to see which programs and drivers will be affected by the restore.
3. Click **Next**, then **Finish** to start the restoration process.

Step 4: Complete the System Restore

1. Your computer will restart, and the system will be restored to the selected point. Check if the issue has been resolved.

Method 2: Use Safe Mode to Resolve Issues

Safe Mode is a diagnostic mode that starts Windows with a minimal set of drivers and services, allowing you to troubleshoot issues. This can sometimes mimic the effect of **Last Known Good Configuration**.

Step 1: Boot into Safe Mode

1. Restart your computer and press **F8** (on older systems), or hold **Shift** and click **Restart** from the Start menu (Windows 10/11).
2. In the **Advanced Startup** menu, select **Troubleshoot** > **Advanced options** > **Startup Settings** > **Restart**.

3. After restarting, you'll see a list of options. Press **4** or **F4** to start your PC in **Safe Mode**.

Step 2: Resolve the Issue

- Once in Safe Mode, you can perform tasks like:
- Uninstall problematic drivers or software.
- Use **System Restore** from within Safe Mode.
- Run **Startup Repair** from the **Advanced Startup Options** menu.

Method 3: Startup Repair

If **System Restore** or **Safe Mode** doesn't fix the issue, you can try **Startup Repair**.

Step 1: Boot into Advanced Startup

1. Follow the steps above to access the **Advanced Startup** menu.
2. Go to **Troubleshoot** > **Advanced options** > **Startup Repair**.
3. Windows will attempt to automatically fix startup issues.

Backup Procedure

Windows System Backup Procedure

The procedure here uses FREE tools that are standard on all Windows-based systems. The only purchase is the external drive you will be backing up to.

The examples assume that data is being copied to Drive D:. Please alter the drive letter given in the example to match your situation. Your backup drive may be E:, F:, or G: depending on how many drives you have.

Using Windows Backup

Requirements:

- An **external drive** or another storage location, such as a network location or a second internal drive.
- **Administrative privileges** on your Windows machine.

Steps to Create a Backup Using Windows Backup:

1. Open the Backup and Restore Tool

- Open the **Control Panel**.
- Under **System and Security**, click on **Backup and Restore (Windows 7)**.
  Note: Even on Windows 10 and Windows 11, the Backup tool is still referred to as "Backup and Restore (Windows 7)."

2. Set Up Backup

- In the **Backup and Restore** window, click on **Set up Backup**.
- Windows will search for available backup devices, such as external drives or network locations.

3. Select a Backup Destination

- Choose where you want to save your backup:
    - **External drive**: Select the connected external USB, Thunderbolt, or other compatible drives.
    - **Network location**: You can also choose a network drive by clicking on **Save on a network...**, entering the network path (e.g., \\Server\Share), and providing login credentials if required.
- Click **Next** once the destination is selected.

4. Choose What to Back Up

- You will be given two options:
    - **Let Windows choose**: Windows will automatically back up the files in your libraries (Documents, Pictures, Music, and Videos), the desktop, and the system image. This is recommended if you're not sure what to include.
    - **Let me choose**: This allows you to manually select specific folders, libraries, or system images you want to back up.
- Select the appropriate option and click **Next**.

5. Review Backup Settings

- Review the backup settings to ensure everything is correct.
- If you selected "Let me choose," you can specify whether to include a **system image**. This is a complete copy of your system, including the operating system, programs, and

settings.

- Click **Save settings and run backup** to start the backup process.

6. Configure Backup Schedule

- During the setup process, you'll have the option to **schedule** backups to occur automatically.
- Click on **Change Schedule** to customize the frequency (e.g., daily, weekly, monthly) and the time when the backups should run. Scheduling ensures that your data is backed up regularly without manual intervention.
- Ensure that the **Run backup on a schedule (recommended)** checkbox is selected if you want automatic backups.

7. Start the Backup

- After configuring the settings, Windows Backup will start the initial backup process. Depending on the amount of data and the speed of your storage drive, this could take some time.
- You can monitor the backup progress in the **Backup and Restore** window.

8. Check Backup Status and Logs

- Once the backup is complete, you'll see a status message in the **Backup and Restore** window.
- You can also click **Manage Space** to check the backup disk usage or delete older backups to free up space.

Restoring from Backup

1. Open Backup and Restore

- Open the **Control Panel**.
- Go to **System and Security** > **Backup and Restore (Windows 7)**.

2. Restore Files

- Click **Restore my files** under the **Restore** section.
- You can search for files or browse your backup to locate the specific files or folders you want to restore.
- Once found, click **Next** and choose the location where the files should be restored (either to their original location or a new one).
- Click **Restore** to start the process.

3. Restoring the Entire System (System Image)

- If you need to restore your entire system, you'll need to use the **system image** created by Windows Backup.
- Boot your computer into the **Advanced Startup Options** by:
  - Holding **Shift** and restarting the computer.
  - Selecting **Troubleshoot** > **Advanced options** > **System Image Recovery**.
- Follow the on-screen instructions to restore your system image.

Microsoft link providing pc backup and restore instructions: [Back up your Windows PC - Microsoft Support]

Advanced: Using RoboCopy

1. Open Command Prompt with Administrative Privileges

- Search for cmd in the Windows search bar.
- Right-click on the "Command Prompt" and select "Run as administrator."

2. Choose the Source and Destination Directories

- **Source directory**: This is the folder or directory on your system you want to back up. For a full system backup, this may include directories like C:\Users or other important directories.

- **Destination directory**: The backup location. This could be an external drive, another partition, or a network location (e.g., D:\Backup or \\NetworkShare\Backup).

Run the Robocopy Command

The basic syntax for using **Robocopy** is:

robocopy <source> <destination> [options]

Sample System Backup Command:

robocopy C:\ D:\SystemBackup /MIR /Z /R:5 /W:5 /XJ /FFT /LOG:D:\BackupLogs\backup_log.txt /V /NP

Sample Backup of a Single Directory i.e., Documents:

robocopy C:\Users\YourUsername\Documents D:\SystemBackup\Documents /MIR /Z /R:5 /W:5 /XJ /FFT /LOG:D:\BackupLogs\backup_log.txt /V /NP

Automating the Backup Process

You can automate the backup by creating a batch file and scheduling it to run periodically.

- **Create a Batch File**:
  - Open Notepad.
  - Enter your Robocopy command.
  - Save the file as backup.bat.
- **Schedule the Batch File Using Task Scheduler**:
  - Open "Task Scheduler" (search for it in the Windows search bar).
  - Select "Create Task."
  - Under the "Actions" tab, browse to your .bat file.

- Under the "Triggers" tab, set a schedule (e.g., daily, weekly).
- Complete the setup, and your system will automatically back up at the scheduled time.

Check the Backup Logs

- After the backup is complete, open the log file specified by /LOG to review any errors or skipped files:

Notes and Tips

- **Restartable Mode**: Using /Z ensures that the copy process can resume if interrupted.
- **Mirror Mode (/MIR)**: Be cautious when using /MIR, as it deletes files in the destination that are not in the source.

Mac Backup Procedure

The procedure given here uses FREE tools that come standard on all Mac-based systems. The only purchase is the external drive you will be backing up to.

The examples assume that data is being copied to Drive D:. Please alter the drive letter given in the examples to match your situation. Your backup drive may be on an alternate system path.

Using Time Machine

Requirements:

- **An External Drive**: This can be a USB, Thunderbolt, or FireWire drive, or a network drive (like a NAS).
- **macOS**: Time Machine is available on macOS Leopard (10.5) and later.

Steps to Set Up and Use Time Machine for Backup

1. Connect the External Drive

- Plug in the external drive to your Mac via USB, Thunderbolt, or FireWire.
- If the drive isn't already formatted for macOS, Time Machine will prompt you to format it.

2. Choose the Drive for Backup

- Once the drive is connected, you'll likely see a prompt asking if you want to use it as a Time Machine backup. Select **Use as Backup Disk**.
- If you don't get a prompt, open **Time Machine Preferences** manually:
    - Go to **Apple Menu** > **System Settings** (or **System Preferences** in older macOS versions).
    - Click **General** > **Time Machine** (or directly **Time Machine** in older versions).
    - Click **Add Backup Disk** and choose the external drive.

3. Select Backup Options

- **Automatic Backups**: Once you've selected the disk, Time Machine will automatically back up your system. You can choose to disable automatic backups if you prefer manual control.
- **Encryption**: You have the option to encrypt your backups. This adds an extra layer of security by password-protecting the backup.

4. Start the First Backup

- After selecting the backup disk, Time Machine will start the first full backup of your system. The time depends on the amount of data and the speed of your drive.
- To manually start the backup, go to **Time Machine** preferences and click **Backup Now**.

5. Regular Automatic Backups

- After the initial backup, Time Machine will automatically create incremental backups every hour, daily backups for the past month, and weekly backups for previous months. These backups continue until your backup disk is full.
- Once the drive is full, Time Machine will automatically delete the oldest backups to make space for new ones.

6. Excluding Files from Backup

You can exclude specific files or folders if you don't want them included in your backup:

- Open **Time Machine** preferences.
- Click **Options**.
- Click the **+** button to add folders or files to exclude.
- Click **Save** when done.

7. Restoring Data from Time Machine

- To restore individual files or your entire system:
    - Click the **Time Machine** icon in the menu bar and choose **Enter Time Machine**.
    - Use the timeline on the right side of the screen to navigate through different points in time.
    - Select the files you want to restore and click **Restore**.
- **To restore the entire system**:
    - **Restart your Mac while holding down Command + R to enter macOS Recovery.**
    - **Choose Restore from Time Machine Backup from the recovery options.**

8. Verifying Backups

- Time Machine automatically verifies your backups. If issues arise, you are notified with instructions to resolve them.

Additional Tips:

- **Backup Schedule**: Time Machine automatically creates backups every hour, but if you want to manually initiate backups, simply click **Back Up Now** from the Time Machine menu.

- **Multiple Backup Disks**: You can add multiple backup disks, and the Time Machine will rotate between them. This can be useful if you want to have one backup at home and another in a separate location for redundancy.

- **Monitoring Backups**: To check the status of your backups, click the **Time Machine** icon in the menu bar.

Linux Backup Procedure (Ubuntu)

The procedure given here uses FREE tools that come standard on all Ubuntu Linux-based systems. The only purchase is the external drive you will be backing up to.

The examples assume that data is being copied to Drive D:. Please alter the drive letter given in the examples to match your situation. Your backup drive may be on an alternate system path.

1. **Deja Dup**: A graphical tool that comes pre-installed in Ubuntu for backing up files and directories.

2. **Rsync**: A command-line utility for syncing files and directories, useful for manual and scheduled backups.

3. **Timeshift**: A tool designed for system snapshots, similar to Time Machine for macOS.

4. **Tar**: A built-in utility that creates compressed archives of your files.

5. **Cloud Backup**: Using services like Google Drive or Dropbox with tools like **rclone**.

Method 1: Backup Using Deja Dup (GUI)

Deja Dup is a user-friendly tool for creating regular backups, supporting encryption, incremental backups, and scheduling.

Step 1: Open Deja Dup

1. Press **Super (Windows key)** and search for **Backup**. Open the **Backup** tool (Deja Dup).

Step 2: Set Up Backup Location

1. In the Backup tool, go to the **Storage Location** tab.
2. Choose where to store your backups:
    - **Local Folder** (an external hard drive, network share, or another location).
    - **Network Location** (FTP, SSH, etc.).
    - **Cloud Services** (e.g., Google Drive or Nextcloud).

Step 3: Select Folders to Back Up

1. Go to the **Folders to save** tab.
2. Add the folders you want to back up by clicking **Add Folder**.
3. If you want to exclude any directories, go to the **Folders to ignore** tab and add them.

Step 4: Schedule the Backup

1. In the **Scheduling** tab, you can choose how frequently the backup should run (e.g., daily, weekly).
2. Enable automatic backups.

Step 5: Perform the Backup

1. Go back to the **Overview** tab and click **Back Up Now** to start the backup process.
2. You can also encrypt your backups by setting a password when prompted.

Step 6: Restoring Data

1. To restore data, go to the **Restore** tab in the Backup tool.
2. Select the backup location and choose the date to restore from.
3. Follow the prompts to restore the files to their original or a new location.

Method 2: Full System Backup Using Timeshift

Timeshift is designed for system snapshots, similar to Deja Dup, but focused more on system files rather than user data. It is helpful in creating system-level backups that can restore your entire system in case of a failure.

Step 1: Install Timeshift

Open a terminal window and type the following commands:

```
sudo apt update

sudo apt install timeshift
```

Step 2: Set Up Timeshift

1. Run **Timeshift** from the applications menu or via terminal:

   ```
   sudo timeshift-launcher
   ```

2. Choose the snapshot type:
   - **RSYNC**: Default and recommended for most users.
   - **BTRFS**: If you're using a BTRFS file system.

Step 3: Select Backup Location

1. Choose the drive where you want to store the backups (it’s recommended to use an external drive).
2. Configure the snapshot schedule (e.g., daily, weekly, monthly).

Step 4: Create a Backup

1. Click **Create** to generate a system snapshot.

2. Timeshift will create a snapshot of your system's root directory (not user files unless specifically configured).

Step 5: Restore the System

1. In case of system failure or issues, open Timeshift and select the snapshot you want to restore.

2. Click **Restore**, and your system will be reverted to the selected state.

Method 3 is Advanced: Creating a Compressed Backup with Tar

Tar is useful for creating compressed archives of your files, allowing you to back up large directories in a compressed format.

Step 1: Create a Backup Archive

To create a tar archive of your home directory. Open a Linux terminal and type:

```
tar -czvf backup.tar.gz /home/username
```

CMD Explanation

-c: Create a new archive.

-z: Compress with gzip.

-v: Verbose output (show the process details).

-f: Specify the archive file name.

Step 2: Store the Backup Archive

Move the created archive (backup.tar.gz) to an external drive or network location. Open a Linux terminal and type:

mv backup.tar.gz /path/to/external/storage/

Step 3: Restore the Backup

To extract the backup archive. Open a Linux terminal and type:

tar -xzvf backup.tar.gz -C /path/to/restore/

Method 4 is Advanced: Backup Using rsync (CLI)

rsync is a powerful command-line tool for syncing files and directories, often used in scripts for automated backups.

Step 1: Install rsync

Open a terminal window and type the following commands:

sudo apt update

sudo apt install rsync

Step 2: Basic rsync Command

To back up your home directory to an external drive

rsync -avh --delete ~/ /path/to/backup/location/

CMD Explanation:

-a: Archive mode (preserves permissions, symlinks, etc.).

-v: Verbose (show the process details).

-h: Human-readable output.

--delete: Removes files in the destination that no longer exist in the source.

You can find a comprehensive list of rsync commands by typing

man rsync at an Ubuntu terminal or by going here:

https://manpages.ubuntu.com/manpages/trusty/man1/rsync.1.html

Step 3: Automate rsync Backups with Cron

You can schedule rsync backups to run automatically using **cron**.

1. Open the cron file for your user

   crontab -e

2. Add a cron job to run rsync daily at 2 AM:

   0 2 * * * rsync -avh --delete ~/ /path/to/backup/location/

You can find a comprehensive list of cron commands and how to manage the crontab file by typing man crontab at an Ubuntu terminal or by going here:

https://www.digitalocean.com/community/tutorials/how-to-use-cron-to-automate-tasks-ubuntu-1804

https://manpages.ubuntu.com/manpages/focal/en/man5/crontab.5.html

Method 5: Backup to Cloud with rclone

rclone is a command-line program used to sync files and directories to various cloud storage services like Google Drive, Dropbox, and OneDrive.

Step 1: Install rclone

sudo apt install rclone

Step 2: Configure rclone

1. Run the configuration tool:

   rclone config

2. Follow the prompts to set up your cloud service (e.g., Google Drive or Dropbox).

Step 3: Sync Files to the Cloud

Use rclone to sync files to your cloud storage:

```
rclone sync ~/Documents remote:/Backup/Documents
```

Replace remote in the sample command with the name of the remote storage you configured.

Key Benefits of a Data Backup

Data Loss Prevention

Accidental deletion, hardware failure, software glitches, or even malicious activities like malware or ransomware attacks can lead to the loss of important data. Regular backups act as a safety net, allowing you to restore your information. Human errors, accidental deletions, or data corruption can occur at any time. Backups allow you to recover the data to a point before the error or corruption took place.

The Ultimate Ransomware Insurance

With the increasing prevalence of cyber threats such as ransomware, having up-to-date backups is essential. In case your data becomes encrypted or compromised, you can restore it from a clean backup, minimizing the impact of the attack.

Hardware & Software Failures

Hard drive failures, server crashes, or other hardware issues can lead to data loss. Backups stored on separate devices or in the cloud protect against the loss of data due to hardware failures. Software updates or installations that go wrong can sometimes lead to data corruption or loss. Backups provide a way to revert to stability before software-related issues occur.

Peace of Mind

Knowing that your data is backed up provides peace of mind. It reduces the stress associated with potential data loss, allowing individuals to focus on their work without the constant fear of losing valuable information. Backups often include versioning, allowing you to restore data to a specific point in time. This can be valuable in situations where you need to access a previous version of a file or document.

Fires, floods, earthquakes, or other natural disasters can damage physical infrastructure and storage devices, leading to data loss. Offsite backups or cloud-based solutions ensure that data remains accessible even if the primary location is affected. When you buy new systems, having backups simplifies the data transfer. You can quickly restore your data onto the new computer or device without the risk of losing critical information.

Facilitating System Recovery

In the event of system failures or crashes, having a backup of your operating system and applications allows for a quicker and smoother recovery process. Some data, such as family photos, personal documents, or unique creative works, may be irreplaceable. Backing up this data ensures that it can be preserved for future generations.

Cost Savings

Whether personal files or critical business assets, backups protect valuable information and assets from unforeseen events. While initial costs may be associated with implementing backup solutions, the long-term cost savings from avoiding data loss and downtime far outweigh the investment.

Choosing A Reliable Backup Solution

Choosing a data backup solution requires careful consideration of your specific needs, budget, and the type of data you want to protect. We will not be comparing or contrasting any commercial backup solutions in this section. Chapter Three contains a dedicated section with clear instructions on how to create backups. The instructions provided in Chapter Three use the free tools provided with each major operating system. If you opt to employ a third-party solution, here are key factors to consider when selecting a data backup solution:

Type of Data

Consider the types of data you need to back up. This includes files, databases, system images, and other critical information. Ensure that the backup solution supports the specific data types you want to protect.

Backup Frequency and Schedule

Determine how often you need to perform backups and whether you require automated scheduling. Some solutions offer real-time or continuous backup options, while others may have scheduled backup intervals.

Data Retention and Versioning

Check if the backup solution supports data retention and versioning. This allows you to keep multiple versions of files over time, enabling you to restore data to specific points in case of errors or data corruption.

Scalability

Consider the scalability of the backup solution. Ensure that it can accommodate the growth of your data over time without significant disruption. Scalable solutions are essential for businesses and individuals with expanding storage needs.

Ease of Use

Choose a backup solution that is user-friendly and easy to set up. Look for intuitive interfaces and straightforward configuration processes to simplify the backup and recovery tasks.

Backup Storage Location

Decide where you want to store your backups. Options include local storage, external hard drives, network-attached storage (NAS), or cloud storage. Consider the advantages and limitations of each storage option based on your requirements.

Security Features

Ensure that the backup solution includes robust security features. Look for encryption (both in- transit and at rest), secure access controls, and authentication mechanisms to protect your data from unauthorized access.

Cost Considerations

Assess the cost of the backup solution, including any upfront fees, subscription costs, and additional charges for storage usage. Compare pricing models to determine the most cost-effective solution for your needs.

Platform Compatibility

Ensure that the backup solution is compatible with your operating system and platforms. Check if it supports Windows, macOS, Linux, or specific server environments that you may be using.

Support and Documentation

Look for backup solutions with reliable customer support and comprehensive documentation. This is important for troubleshooting issues, understanding features, and ensuring a smooth user experience.

Testing and Recovery Features

Assess the testing and recovery features of the backup solution. The ability to perform periodic tests to ensure data recoverability and the speed and reliability of recovery processes are critical considerations.

Reviews and Reputation

Research reviews and feedback from users who have experience with the backup solution. Pay attention to the provider's reputation in terms of reliability, customer support, and responsiveness to security concerns.

Trial Periods or Free Versions

Consider solutions that offer trial periods or free versions. This allows you to test the functionality, user interface, and compatibility with your systems before committing to a paid subscription.

Disaster Recovery Capabilities

Evaluate the disaster recovery capabilities of the backup solution. Look for features such as bare-metal recovery, which allows you to restore an entire system, including the operating system, applications, and data.

Automatic Backups and Notifications

Automatic backups and notification features can simplify the backup process. Look for solutions that can perform backups automatically according to your chosen schedule and notify you of any issues or completion.

By carefully evaluating these factors, you can choose a data backup solution that aligns with your specific requirements and provides a reliable and secure means of protecting your valuable information.

Creating a Backup Schedule

Creating a data backup schedule is essential to ensure that your important information is regularly backed up, reducing the risk of data loss. The schedule you choose will depend on factors such as the type of data you have, how frequently it changes, and your specific needs. Here's a step-by-step guide to help you create an effective data backup schedule:

Assess Your Data

Identify the types of data you have and categorize them based on their importance and frequency of change. For example, critical business documents may require more frequent backups than static reference materials.

Determine Backup Frequency

Decide how often you need to perform backups based on the nature of your data. Common backup frequencies include:

**Daily Suitable for data that changes frequently.

**Weekly Appropriate for data with moderate changes.

**Monthly Ideal for static or rarely modified data.

Balance Frequency and Resource Usage

Find a balance between backup frequency and the impact on system resources. Frequent backups may consume more resources, potentially affecting system performance. Adjust your schedule to minimize disruption.

Prioritize Critical Data

Prioritize the backup of critical data that is essential for business operations. This ensures that the most important information is backed up more frequently, reducing the risk of data loss in case of an incident.

Create a Written Schedule

Document your backup schedule in a clear and accessible format. Include details such as the types of data being backed up, the frequency of backups, and the time each backup will occur. This written schedule serves as a reference for all involved parties.

Consider Full and Incremental Backups

Depending on your needs, incorporate a combination of full and incremental backups. Full backups capture all selected data, while incremental backups only capture changes since the last backup. This can optimize storage space and backup duration.

Set Backup Window Times

Define specific time windows during which backups will occur. Choose times that minimize impact. Consider overnight and early morning hours, which are times of lower system activity. Consider the time it takes to transfer data to the backup destination. If your backup solution involves transferring data over a network, ensure that the backup schedule allows sufficient time for completion.

Automate the Backup Process

Whenever possible, automate the backup process using scheduling features provided by backup tools. Automation reduces the likelihood of human error and ensures consistency in your backup schedule.

Perform Test Restores

Regularly review and update your backup schedule. Changes in data volume or technology may necessitate adjustments to the backup frequency or timing. Periodically perform test restores to ensure that your backups are valid and can be successfully restored. This practice helps identify any issues with the backup process and ensures data recoverability.

Offline Backup

Consider incorporating offline backups into your schedule for additional data protection. Offline backups protect against network events, such as ransomware hardware or software failures.

Monitor and Audit

Implement monitoring and auditing processes to track the success and efficiency of your backup schedule. Regularly check the backup report to confirm that there are no problems. If there are errors in the report, address them immediately.

By carefully planning and implementing a data backup schedule that aligns with your family's needs, you can establish a robust data protection strategy that minimizes the risk of data loss and ensures the availability of critical information when needed.

Chapter 4: DATA ENCRYPTION

What is Data Encryption?

The process of converting plain, readable data (plaintext) into a coded format (ciphertext) to prevent unauthorized access. This transformation uses algorithms and an encryption key, which is known only to authorized users. Without the correct key, the data is unintelligible, ensuring its confidentiality even if intercepted or stolen.

DATA AT REST VS. DATA IN FLIGHT

DATA AT REST: Stored Data

Encryption of data at rest refers to the process of protecting stored data by converting it into an unreadable format using cryptographic algorithms. Data at rest typically includes information stored on hard drives, databases, cloud storage, mobile devices, and other storage systems. Encrypting data at rest is a critical security measure that often involves the use of encryption keys, which must be managed securely to ensure only authorized parties can decrypt the data.

For example:

- Full Disk Encryption (FDE): Encrypts the entire storage device.
- File-Level Encryption: Encrypts specific files or folders.
- Database Encryption: Secures data within databases.

DATA IN FLIGHT: Data in Transit

Encryption of data in flight (also known as encryption of data in transit) refers to the process of securing data as it moves between devices, networks, or systems. When data is transmitted over the internet or other communication channels, it is vulnerable to threats such as eavesdropping, man-in-the-middle attacks, or packet sniffing. Encrypting data in flight protects it by converting it into an unreadable format that can only be decrypted by the intended recipient using the appropriate key.

Common methods for encrypting data in flight include:

- Transport Layer Security (TLS): Used for secure web browsing (e.g., HTTPS).
- Secure Shell (SSH): Encrypts remote terminal sessions.
- Virtual Private Networks (VPNs): Create encrypted tunnels for secure communication.

- Encrypted Email Protocols: Such as S/MIME or PGP.

Data encryption is crucial for maintaining the confidentiality and integrity of sensitive financial data, personal details, and authentication credentials being transmitted.

Encryption: Using Free Tools

Windows Bitlocker: Drive Encryption

Prerequisites

1. **Windows Edition:** Ensure you are using a Windows version that supports BitLocker (e.g., Windows 10 Pro, Enterprise, or Education).

2. **Trusted Platform Module (TPM):** Most modern devices have TPM, which BitLocker uses for secure key storage. If your device lacks TPM, you may need to enable BitLocker without TPM by using a USB drive for the startup key.

3. **Backup:** Back up important files before starting. Encryption issues can lead to data loss.

Steps to Enable BitLocker

1. Access BitLocker

Open the **Control Panel**.

Navigate to **System and Security** > **BitLocker Drive Encryption**.

Or press the windows key + s and type "bitlocker" in the search window.

2. Select the Drive to Encrypt

Identify the drive you want to encrypt (C:, D:, E: etc)

Right-click the drive and select Turn on Bitlocker

3. Choose How to Unlock Your Drive

For a **System Drive (C:)**

Select an authentication method:

- **TPM with PIN or Password:** Set a PIN/password to enter during startup.
- **USB Key:** Insert a USB drive that stores the startup key.

For **Data Drives** (non-system drives):

Choose to unlock with:

Password: Set a password to unlock the drive.

Smart Card: Use a compatible smart card and reader.

4. Backup Your Recovery Key

- Save the recovery key in case you forget your password or lose your USB key:
  - Save to a **cloud account (recommended).**
  - Save to a **USB Drive**.
  - Save to a **File**.
  - Print the recovery key.
- Store this key securely, as it is vital for accessing your data if needed.

5. Choose How Much of the Drive to Encrypt

- Encrypt used disk space only (faster): Encrypts only the current data. Recommended for new drives.
- Encrypt the entire drive (slower): Encrypts all data, including free space. Recommended for drives with existing data.

6. Choose the Encryption Mode

- **New Encryption Mode (XTS-AES):** Best for internal drives.
- **Compatible Mode:** Use this if the drive may need to be used with older versions of Windows.

7. Start Encryption

- Click **Start Encrypting**.
- Allow the process to complete.

After Encryption

- **Verify Encryption:**
    - Go back to **Manage BitLocker** to confirm the drive shows as "BitLocker On."
- **Optional Settings:** Change your PIN/password or manage your recovery key through the **BitLocker settings**.

Windows EFS: File and Folder Encryption

Encrypt Files or Folders Using EFS

1. Locate the File or Folder to Encrypt

- Open File Explorer and navigate to the file or folder you want to encrypt.

2. Access File or Folder Properties

- Right-click the file or folder.
- Select **Properties** from the context menu.

3. Enable Encryption

- In the Properties window:
  - Go to the **General** tab.
  - Click **Advanced.**
- In the Advanced Attributes window:
  - Check the box for **Encrypt contents to secure data.**
  - Click **OK.**

4. Apply Changes

- Back in the Properties window, click **Apply.**
- Choose one of the following options:
  - **Apply changes to this folder only:** Encrypts only the selected folder.
  - **Apply changes to this folder, subfolders, and files:** Encrypts the folder and all its contents.

5. Confirm Encryption

- The folder name and its files may now appear with green text in File Explorer, indicating they are encrypted.

Disabling Encryption

1. Right-click the encrypted file or folder.
2. Select **Properties** > **Advanced.**

3. Uncheck **Encrypt contents to secure data**.

4. Apply changes to decrypt the file or folder.

Managing Your EFS Encryption Certificate

1. Backup Your Encryption Certificate and Key

- Open **Control Panel** > **System and Security** > **BitLocker Drive Encryption** (or use the search bar to find **Manage File Encryption Certificates**).
- Click **Back up your file encryption certificate and key**.
- Follow the wizard to export the certificate and private key:
    - Save the certificate to a secure location, such as an external USB drive.
    - Protect the backup with a strong password.

2. Restore the Certificate if Needed

- If you ever lose access to encrypted files, import the backed-up certificate through the Certificate Manager.

Important Notes

- **EFS Encryption Scope:** EFS encrypts files at the user level. If you switch to another account or reinstall Windows, you'll need your encryption certificate to access the data.
- **Data Loss Prevention:** Always back up your EFS certificate. Losing it makes encrypted files permanently inaccessible.
- **Compatibility:** EFS works only on NTFS-formatted drives. It won't function on FAT32 or exFAT drives.

VeraCrypt: Open Source Drive Encryption (Windows, Linux, MacOsX)

Prerequisites

1. **Download VeraCrypt:**
   - Visit the VeraCrypt official website: www.veracrypt.fr
   - Download and install the latest version suitable for your operating system.
2. **Backup Your Data:**
   - Back up all important files on the drive to avoid data loss during the encryption process.
3. **Understand Scope:**
   - VeraCrypt can encrypt entire drives, partitions, or create virtual encrypted volumes.

Steps to Encrypt a Hard Drive

1. Install VeraCrypt

- Run the downloaded installer and follow the prompts.
- Accept the license agreement and choose either a standard installation or portable mode (for use without installation).

2. Launch VeraCrypt

- Open VeraCrypt from the Start Menu or Desktop shortcut.

3. Select Encryption Scope

- Click **Create Volume** to open the Volume Creation Wizard.
- Choose **Encrypt a Non-System Partition/Drive** for data drives or **Encrypt the System Partition/Drive** for your operating system drive.

Encrypting a Non-System Drive or Partition

Step 1: Choose Encryption Type

- Select **Standard VeraCrypt volume** unless you require a hidden volume for additional security.

Step 2: Select the Drive or Partition

- Choose the drive or partition you want to encrypt from the list.

Step 3: Encryption Options

- **Encryption Algorithm:** The default (AES) is secure and widely used, but you can select others like Serpent or Twofish for specific needs.
- **Hash Algorithm:** Stick with the default (SHA-512) unless you have specific requirements.

Step 4: Password Setup

- Set a strong password or passphrase. Use a combination of uppercase, lowercase, numbers, and special characters.
- For enhanced security, use a keyfile (optional).

Step 5: Randomness Collection

- Move your mouse randomly within the VeraCrypt window to generate cryptographic randomness for the encryption keys.

Step 6: Choose Filesystem

- Select a filesystem for the encrypted drive (e.g., NTFS, FAT, or exFAT). NTFS is recommended for large files and Windows compatibility.
- You can also choose **Do not format** if you don't want the data on the drive to be erased during encryption.

Step 7: Start Encryption

- Click **Encrypt** to begin. Confirm the operation.
- The process will take time, depending on the size of the drive and your system performance.

Encrypting A System Drive

Step 1: Select the System Drive

- From the VeraCrypt Volume Creation Wizard, choose **Encrypt the System Partition or Entire System Drive.**

Step 2: Whole Drive vs. Partition

- **Encrypt the whole drive** (recommended for maximum security).
- Alternatively, encrypt only the Windows system partition.

Step 3: Pre-Boot Authentication

- Set up a password that will be required at boot to decrypt and access the operating system.

Step 4: Rescue Disk Creation

- VeraCrypt will prompt you to create a Rescue Disk. Save it as an ISO file (copy the iso to a cloud account) and burn it to a CD/DVD or save it to a USB drive.

Step 5: Encryption Options

- Select the encryption and hash algorithms as described above.

Step 6: Encryption Test

- VeraCrypt will perform a pre-encryption test, which involves rebooting your system to verify that the bootloader and pre-boot authentication work correctly.

Step 7: Begin Encryption

- Once the test passes, the actual encryption process will start.

After Encryption

1. **Mount Encrypted Drives:**
    - Open VeraCrypt, select the encrypted drive and click **Mount**.
    - Enter your password (and keyfile if used) to access the drive.
2. **Access and Manage:**
    - Encrypted drives appear as regular drives in the system once mounted.
    - Use VeraCrypt to change passwords, add keyfiles, or dismount the drive when not in use.
3. **Secure Your Password and Keyfiles:**
    - Store your password and any keyfiles in a secure location, as losing them may result in permanent data loss.

Tips

- Keep the Rescue Disk in a safe place. It is critical for data recovery if the VeraCrypt bootloader is damaged.
- Regularly back up your encrypted data.
- If encrypting an external drive, ensure compatibility with other systems by installing VeraCrypt on them.

File Level Encryption: Open Source Encrypted Archives

File Level Encryption: Using 7 Zip

Prerequisites

1. **Download and Install 7-Zip:**
   - Visit the 7-Zip official website: https://www.7-zip.org/
   - Download and install the version suitable for your operating system.
2. **Ensure Strong Encryption Requirements:**
   - 7-Zip supports AES-256 encryption, which is highly secure.
   - Prepare a strong password for encrypting the archive.

Steps to Create an Encrypted Archive

1. Open 7-Zip

- Launch the **7-Zip File Manager** from the Start Menu or Desktop.

2. Select Files or Folders

- Navigate to the location of the files or folders you want to encrypt.
- Select the files or folders by clicking on them (hold Ctrl or Shift for multiple selections).

3. Add Files to an Archive

- With the files/folders selected:
  - Click **Add** in the toolbar or right-click and choose **7-Zip > Add to Archive**.

4. Configure Archive Settings

- In the **Add to Archive** window:
  - **Archive Format:** Choose **7z** for maximum compression and encryption options.

- **Compression Level:** Select your preferred level (e.g., **Normal** or **Ultra** for better compression but slower speed).
- **Encryption Section:**
    - Enter your password in the **Enter Password** and **Reenter Password** fields.
    - Check the box for **Encrypt file names** (important for complete protection, including hiding the list of files in the archive).
- Optional:
    - **Split to volumes:** If you need to create multiple smaller parts of the archive (e.g., for email or storage on limited-size devices).

5. Create the Encrypted Archive

- Click **OK** to begin the process.
- 7-Zip will compress and encrypt the files into the archive with the specified settings.

Testing and Using the Encrypted Archive

1. **Open the Encrypted Archive:**
    - Double-click the .7z file to open it with 7-Zip.
    - You'll be prompted to enter the password.
2. **Verify Encryption:**
    - Ensure that all files require a password to open.
    - If you enabled **Encrypt file names**, the archive's contents will not be visible without the password.
3. **Extract Files from the Archive:**
    - Right-click the archive, choose **7-Zip > Extract Here** (or similar), and enter the password when prompted.

Tips for Secure Encryption

1. **Use a Strong Password:**
   - Combine uppercase, lowercase, numbers, and symbols in your password.
2. **Store the Archive Securely:**
   - Save the encrypted archive on a secure drive or cloud storage.
3. **Backup the Password:**
   - Losing the password will make the encrypted archive inaccessible. File Level Encryption: Using WinRAR

Prerequisites

1. **Download and Install WinRAR:**
   - Visit the WinRAR official website: https://www.win-rar.com/
   - Download and install the appropriate version for your operating system.
2. **Strong Password:**
   - Have a strong password ready. It should include uppercase, lowercase, numbers, and special characters.

Steps to Create an Encrypted Archive

1. Open WinRAR

- Launch **WinRAR** from the Start Menu or Desktop shortcut.

2. Select Files or Folders

- Navigate to the location of the files or folders you want to encrypt.
- Select the files or folders by clicking on them (use Ctrl or Shift for multiple selections).

3. Add to Archive

- Right-click the selected files or folders.
- Choose **Add to Archive** from the context menu.

4. Configure Archive Settings

- In the **Archive name and parameters** window:
    - **Archive Name:** Set the name and location for your archive.
    - **Archive Format:** Choose **RAR** or **RAR4** (recommended for compatibility) or **ZIP** for cross-platform use.
    - **Compression Method:** Choose a compression level (e.g., Normal, Good, Best).

5. Set Encryption

- In the same window:
    - Click the **Set Password** button (near the bottom-right corner).
    - In the **Set Password** window:
        - Enter your password in the **Enter Password** and **Reenter Password** fields.
        - Check the box for **Encrypt file names** (important to hide the names and structure of the files in the archive).
    - Click **OK** to confirm.

6. Finalize the Archive

- Click **OK** in the **Archive name and parameters** window to start creating the archive.
- WinRAR will compress and encrypt the files. This may take some time, depending on the file size and compression level.

Testing and Using the Encrypted Archive

1. **Open the Encrypted Archive:**
   - Double-click the .rar or .zip file.
   - You'll be prompted to enter the password before accessing the contents.
2. **Verify Encryption:**
   - Ensure that the file names and contents are inaccessible without the password.
3. **Extract Files from the Archive:**
   - Right-click the encrypted archive.
   - Choose **Extract Here** or **Extract to [Folder]**.
   - Enter the password when prompted.

Best Practices for Secure Encryption

1. **Strong Passwords:** Use a strong and unique password to ensure security.
2. **Store Password Securely:** Losing the password will render the archive inaccessible.
3. **Encrypt File Names:** Always check **Encrypt file names** to ensure even the file list is protected.
4. **Backup:** Keep a secure backup of the archive to avoid accidental data loss.

Encrypting ONLINE Traffic: Data In Transit (In Flight)

For the majority of people, securing data in transit means encrypting browser communications. Today, the majority of people access email in the browser. Although some still use an email client such as Outlook, Mail, Thunderbird, etc. We speak a great deal about securing browsers and using tools like VPNs in Chapter 7.

HTTPS Only Mode

The simplest way to verify your browser is using an encrypted connection is to make sure it is connecting using HTTPS://. The S in https:// stands for Secure Socket Layer. It means that your browser is using a secure socket (encrypted) to connect and communicate with a website. Typically, that website will have a padlock icon preceding https:// in your browser window.

HTTPS Everywhere: https://www.eff.org/https-everywhere is a browser extension that can be installed so that your browser will only communicate with https:// enabled sites. However, at the time of this writing, most browsers have native support for an https:// only mode. You just have to turn it on.

For Chrome browsers, go to Settings > Security and Privacy > Security, scroll to the bottom, and then toggle to "Always use secure connections."

For Firefox desktop, go to Settings > Privacy & Security, scroll to the bottom, and then select Enable **HTTPS**-Only Mode.

For Edge, go to edge://flags/#edge-automatic-https and enable Automatic HTTPS. Then, hit the "restart" button. Or, visit edge://settings/privacy, scroll down, and turn on "Automatically switch to more secure connections with Automatic HTTPS."

For Safari, make sure you are using Safari 15. HTTPS is upgraded by default without any settings changes needed.

A second simple procedure is to always open a private browsing session when accessing the internet. It keeps your session from being tracked and reduces the chances of being targeted with unsolicited advertising and spyware.

Use a Secure Browser or Proxy Server

The TOR Browser

TOR is an acronym for "The Onion Router," referencing its layered encryption system that protects users' data and identity. It is a browser that you can download and install for free.

Primary Purposes of the Tor Browser

1. Enhancing Anonymity

Tor anonymizes your internet activity by encrypting your data and routing it through a network of volunteer-operated servers (or relays). Each relay only knows the previous and next server in the chain, not the full route or the content of the data, making it extremely difficult to trace the origin or destination of the traffic.

2. Bypassing Censorship

In regions where governments or ISPs block access to certain websites or services, Tor can help users bypass such restrictions. It allows access to the **dark web** and other parts of the internet that are otherwise inaccessible.

3. Protecting Privacy

Tor hides users' IP addresses, preventing websites, advertisers, or trackers from identifying them. This is useful for avoiding targeted advertising, surveillance, or data collection.

4. Securing Communications

Tor encrypts user data multiple times, ensuring privacy and security, especially over insecure networks like public Wi-Fi.

5. Enabling Whistleblowing and Journalism

Activists, journalists, and whistleblowers often use Tor to communicate securely and avoid detection by oppressive regimes or surveillance.

6. Research and Sensitive Work

Tor is used by researchers, legal professionals, and others who need to access information discreetly without revealing their identity or location.

Limitations of the Tor Browser

1. **Performance**

   Routing traffic through multiple relays slows down connection speeds.

2. **Not Entirely Anonymous**

    While Tor hides the user's IP, it cannot protect against malware, phishing, or user errors that reveal their identity. If users log into accounts or provide personal information, their anonymity is compromised.

3. **Exit Node Vulnerability**

    Data leaving the exit node is not encrypted unless the website uses HTTPS, potentially exposing data to the exit node operator.

4. **Blocked by Some Services**

    Certain websites and services may block Tor traffic, suspecting it as malicious or unauthorized.

Using Proxy Servers

A **proxy server** is an intermediary server that sits between a client (like a user's computer or device) and a destination server (like a website or application). It acts as a gateway that requests data on behalf of the client, relaying the data back to the client once it has been retrieved from the destination. Proxy servers serve multiple purposes, from improving network security to enhancing privacy, optimizing internet performance, and even circumventing geographic restrictions.

Accessing a **public proxy server** involves configuring your device or web browser to route your internet traffic through the proxy server, which then acts as an intermediary between your device and the internet. Public proxy servers are typically free and widely available, but they come with certain risks and limitations, such as slower speeds, potential privacy issues, and lack of encryption. Here's a step-by-step guide on how to access a public proxy server.

Primary Purposes of a Proxy Server

1. Improving Security

Masking the Client's IP Address:

A proxy server hides the real IP address of the client, replacing it with its own IP address.

This helps protect the identity and location of the client while interacting with the internet.

Traffic Filtering:

Proxy servers can filter incoming and outgoing traffic, blocking malicious content such as malware, ransomware, and harmful websites, thereby acting as a security gateway between users and the internet.

Access Control:

Organizations often use proxy servers to control access to the internet. They can block access to certain websites or content based on security policies, such as allowing or restricting employee access to specific online resources.

2. Privacy and Anonymity

Anonymizing Internet Activity:

A proxy server can be used to conceal the user's browsing activities, making it harder for websites, advertisers, and other entities to track the user's online behavior.

Bypassing Censorship:

In regions where internet censorship is implemented, proxy servers can help users access blocked websites by masking their location and routing traffic through a different region.

Avoiding Surveillance:

Proxy servers are used to avoid government or third-party surveillance, helping users maintain anonymity in certain high-risk situations (e.g., political activists or journalists in oppressive regions).

3. Bypassing Geo-Restrictions

Accessing Region-Locked Content:

Many online services (e.g., Netflix, BBC iPlayer) restrict content based on the geographic location of the user. A proxy server can make it appear as though the user is browsing from a different country, enabling access to region-restricted content.

Evading Government Censorship:

In countries with strict internet censorship (e.g., China's Great Firewall), proxies are used to bypass restrictions and gain access to blocked websites or platforms (e.g., Google, Facebook).

4. Improving Network Performance

Caching Content:

Proxy servers can cache frequently requested web content, such as images, videos, and web pages. When a user requests the same content, the proxy serves the cached version, reducing load times and saving bandwidth.

Load Balancing:

Proxies can distribute requests across multiple servers, balancing the load and preventing any one server from being overwhelmed. This improves performance, especially for websites with high traffic.

Reducing Bandwidth Usage:

By caching data and compressing traffic, proxy servers can reduce the overall bandwidth consumption of a network, improving the speed and efficiency of the internet connection.

5. Content Filtering and Monitoring

Parental Controls:

Proxy servers can be used to block certain types of content, such as adult websites or social media platforms, making them useful for parental control in home networks.

Enterprise Use for Content Monitoring:

Businesses can use proxy servers to monitor and control employee internet usage, blocking access to distracting websites or preventing access to potentially harmful content.

6. Accessing Internal Network Resources (Intranet)

Remote Access to Intranet:

A proxy server can allow remote employees or clients to securely access internal network resources (intranet sites, files, applications) by acting as a secure gateway.

7. Traffic Encryption

SSL/TLS Encryption for Secure Browsing:

Some proxy servers are capable of encrypting traffic using SSL/TLS, providing secure browsing even on public networks. This is particularly beneficial in safeguarding sensitive data, such as login credentials or financial information, from eavesdropping.

Steps to Access a Public Proxy Server

1. Find a Public Proxy Server

Search Online for Public Proxy Lists: Many websites provide lists of free public proxy servers. Some popular proxy listing sites include:

- Free Proxy List: https://www.freeproxylists.net/
- ProxyScrape: https://www.proxyscrape.com/
- HideMy.name Proxy List

Check Proxy Information: These sites will usually provide details such as:

- **IP address** of the proxy server
- **Port number**
- **Country/location**
- **Anonymity level** (Transparent, Anonymous, Elite)

2. Choose a Proxy Server

Select a proxy server based on the location (if you want to bypass geographic restrictions) and the type of anonymity it provides. **Elite Proxies** offer the highest level of anonymity, while **transparent proxies** may expose your IP address. ***Note*** that free proxies can be unreliable, and some may not work well with certain websites or services.

3. Configure Your Web Browser to Use the Proxy Server

- You can configure the proxy server either globally (for all internet traffic) or for specific applications like your web browser.

For Google Chrome (Windows, macOS, or Linux):

1. **Open Chrome Settings**:
   - Click the three dots in the top-right corner of Chrome and go to **Settings**.
2. **Open Advanced Settings**:
   - Scroll down and click **Advanced**.
3. **Open Proxy Settings**:
   - Under **System**, click on **Open your computer's proxy settings**.
4. **Configure Proxy Server (Windows)**:
   - In the **Internet Properties** window, go to the **Connections** tab and click **LAN settings**.
   - Check the box for **Use a proxy server for your LAN**.
   - Enter the **IP address** and **port number** of the public proxy server you want to use.
   - Click **OK** to save the settings.
5. **Configure Proxy Server (macOS)**:
   - In the **Network** preferences, select the network connection (e.g., Wi-Fi or

Ethernet), then click **Advanced**.

- Go to the **Proxies** tab and enter the IP address and port number in the **Web Proxy (HTTP)** section.
- Click **OK** to apply the changes.

For Mozilla Firefox (Windows, macOS, or Linux):

1. **Open Firefox Settings**:
   - Click the three horizontal lines (menu) in the top-right corner and select **Settings**.
2. **Configure Network Settings**:
   - Scroll down to the **Network Settings** section and click on **Settings**.
3. **Manual Proxy Configuration**:
   - Select **Manual proxy configuration**.
   - Enter the **proxy IP address** and **port number** in the corresponding fields.
   - If the proxy is for **HTTP** traffic, enter the same proxy settings for **SSL** or **FTP** if necessary.
4. **Save Settings**:
   - Click **OK** to save and apply the proxy settings.

4. Verify Proxy Connection

- After configuring the proxy, check if your connection is working by visiting websites like **WhatIsMyIP.com** or **IPLeak.net** to see if your public IP address is masked by the proxy server.
- If the proxy is set up correctly, the websites will display the proxy server's IP address, not your real IP.

Risks and Considerations of Using Public Proxy Servers

1. **Privacy and Security Risks**:

   Public proxies, especially free ones, may log your browsing activity or inject advertisements into the pages you visit. Be cautious when accessing sensitive information (e.g., logging into accounts or making transactions) through a public proxy. Public proxies may not encrypt your data, so sensitive information (e.g., passwords or personal data) could be intercepted.

2. **Slow Speed**:

   Public proxies are often overloaded with users, leading to slower browsing speeds. Additionally, proxy servers may throttle speeds or experience downtime.

3. **Lack of Reliability**:

   Public proxies can go offline unexpectedly or become unreliable. Since these proxies are often provided by volunteers, they may be poorly maintained or insecure.

4. **Access Issues**:

   Some websites or services actively block known proxy IP addresses. This may prevent you from accessing certain content when using public proxies.

Using a public proxy server is an easy way to anonymize your browsing, bypass geo-restrictions, and improve privacy. However, it comes with potential risks like privacy concerns, slower speeds, and security vulnerabilities. To ensure maximum privacy and security, consider using a paid VPN service or a private proxy instead.

Using a VPN

VPN software is not just for corporate users; it can be used by a normal user when connecting from unsafe public networks or when they want to access censored content anonymously.

The best advice to all people using VPNs is to download and install the OpenVPN client software. Take the time to learn to use this free, open-source VPN client. The OpenVPN client can be configured to connect to the server of most (if not all) major VPN service retailers.

The OpenVPN Community Downloads page can be found here:

https://openvpn.net/community-downloads/

There is an OpenVPN client installation for Windows, MacOS, and Linux distributions. In this section, I will be running through the client installation in Windows. On the OpenVPN downloads page, select and download the software installer for your version of Windows. Typically named something like:

Windows 64-bit MSI installer OpenVPN-2.6.12-1001-amd64.msi

Run the installer as the administrator. Accept all the installation defaults and agree to the license agreement. During this installation, a TAP driver will be installed. Once the installation completes, click Finish.

Configuring the OpenVPN Client

Every server that you will connect to with OpenVPN will have a unique configuration file. The configuration file must be downloaded for each server and imported into the OpenVPN before it can be used to connect to a server. Each configuration file contains the server information and connection settings.

In most cases, this means copying the files to the C:\Program Files\OpenVPN\config directory. Another way to do this is to open the OpenVPN client and import the config file via the GUI:

Right-click the icon for the OpenVPN GUI and click Run as administrator.

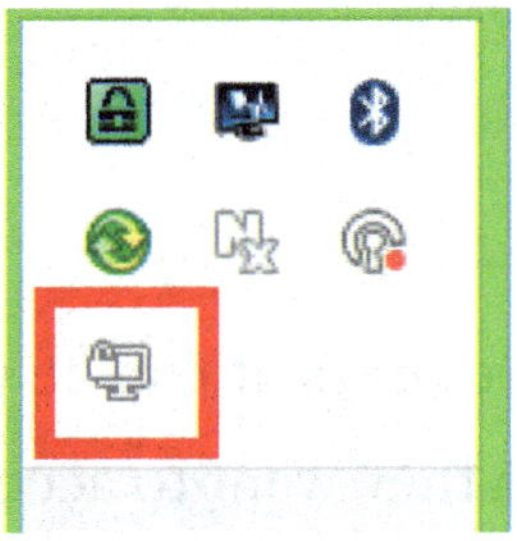

The application will start, and this icon will be displayed in your taskbar tray.

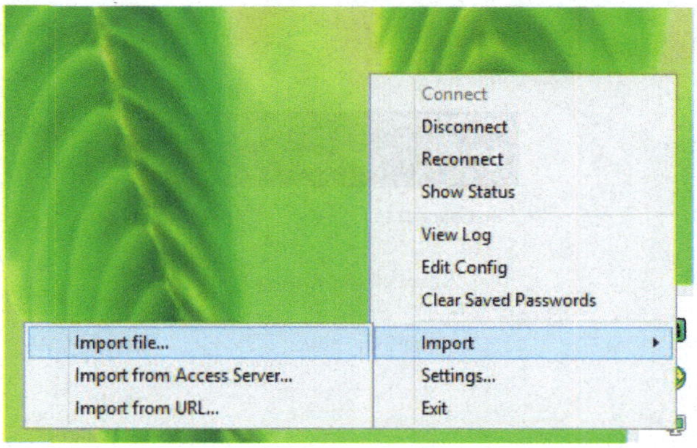

Right-click the icon in the tray and select Import from the menu.

Next, Click on import file.

Browse your local file system and import the server configuration file.

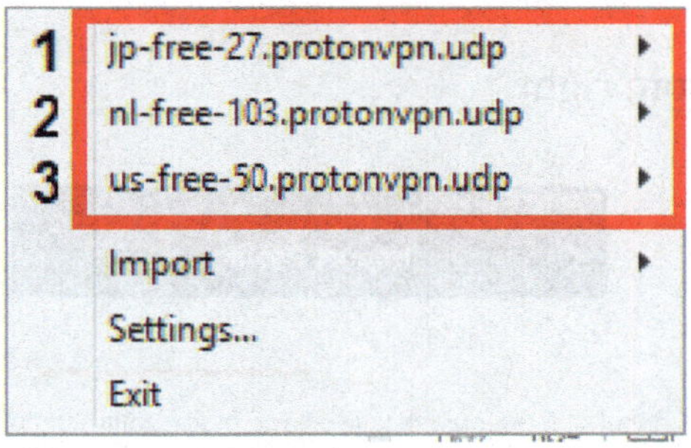

As you import each configuration file, it will be listed as a connection option.

In the image above, I have imported 3 proton VPN configuration files

The second OpenVPN client is called OpenVPN Connect. I describe the same process for importing profiles into that application below. The OpenVPN GUI is generally the most supported client. If you run into a situation where it does not work, you can try the OpenVPN Connect application.

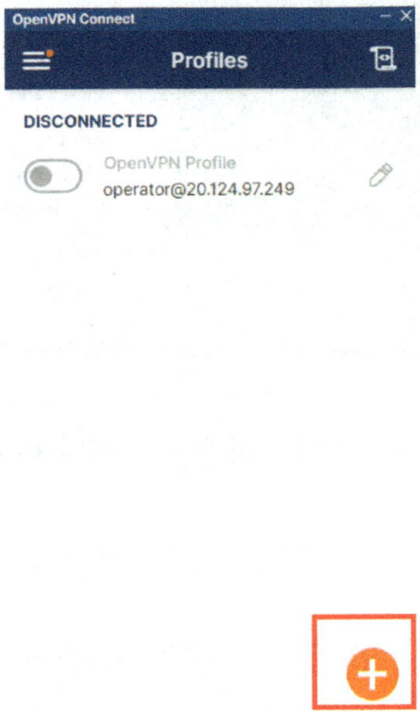

Click the + button in the bottom right.

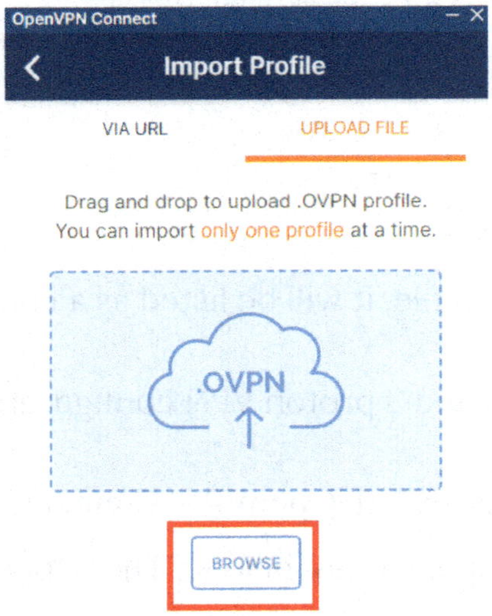

In the Import Profile window, select the Upload File.

Click the browse button.

Upload any downloaded server configuration files on the local computer.

Log into your account for the VPN service provider you have chosen to test. We tested ProtonVPN and Hide.me platforms for these examples. Mainly because they are examples of two different ways to configure a VPN connection in Windows. ProtonVPN using the OpenVPN client and Hide.me using the VPN client built into the Windows operating system.

Downloading ProtonVPN Server Configuration Files

Log into your ProtonVPN account. If you don't have an account, create one.

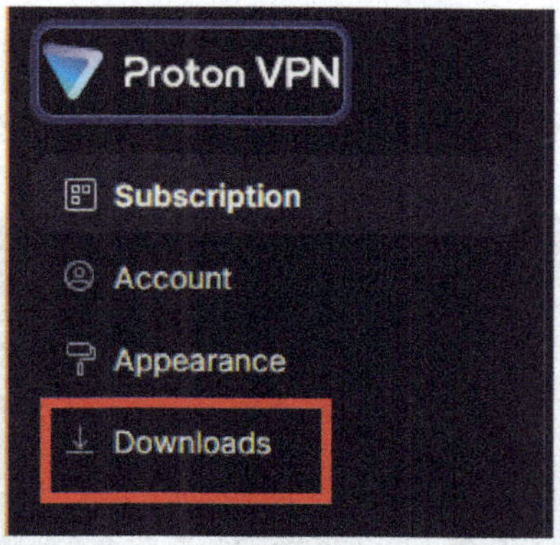

Click the Downloads link in the main menu.

On the downloads page, scroll down to the OpenVPN configuration files section.

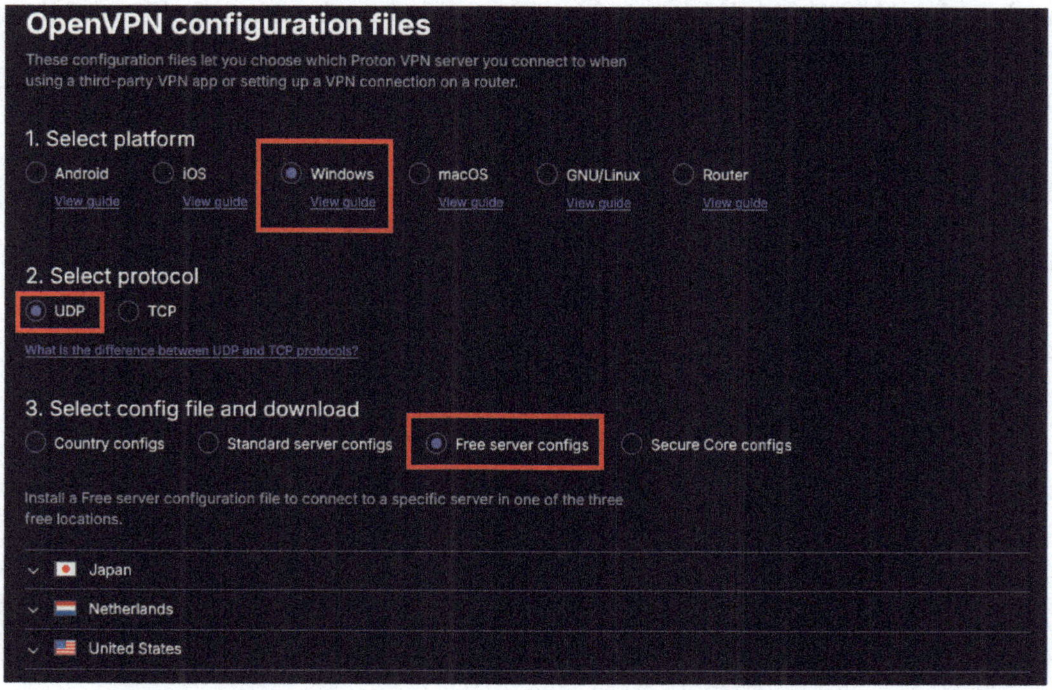

1. We selected Windows for our platform. You can see multiple platforms are supported.

2. The default protocol selected is UDP. It is the faster protocol.

3. We selected Free server configs to download

ProtonVPN offers free and paid accounts. We tested with a free account, and you can, too. Until you decide which platform suits your needs, it is best to test with a free account. If the free account meets your requirements, keep using it until you feel comfortable with upgrading to a paid account.

ProtonVPN offers free servers in 3 countries: Japan, the Netherlands, and the US. There are no geographical restrictions, you can connect to these free servers from any country.

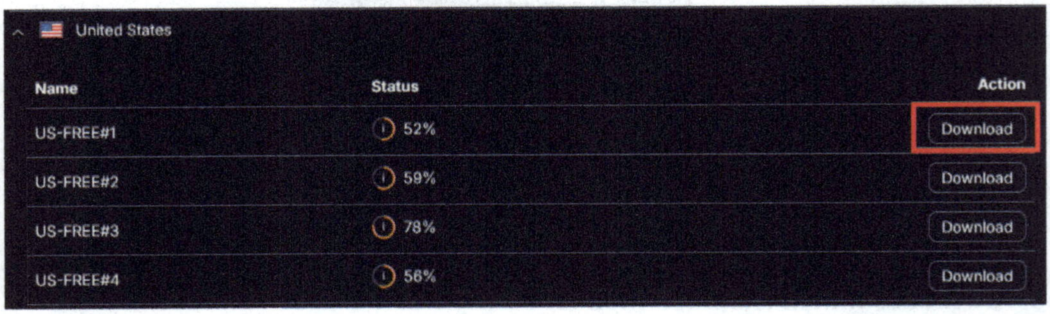

Expand the list of United States Free servers.

Click the download button in the Action column to download the config files for that server.

Simply import the file using the OpenVPN GUI as described in the previous section: Configuring the OpenVPN Client. The OpenVPN client connects to the server using IKEV2.

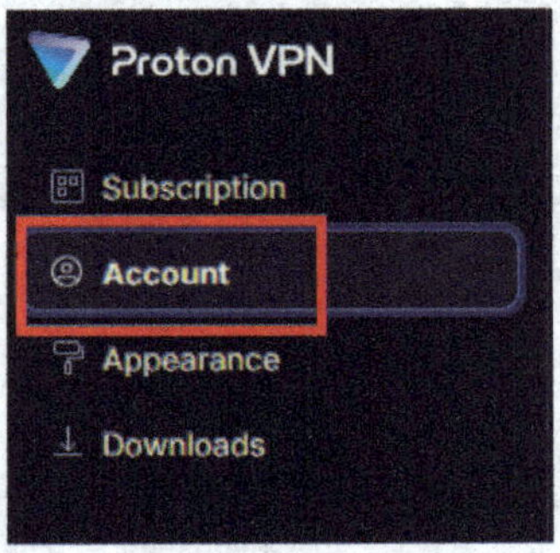

Return to the ProtonVPN main menu and click the Account link.

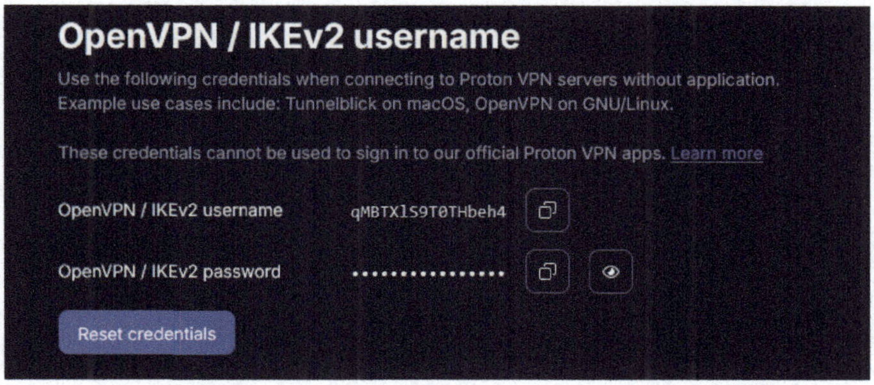

On the Account page, scroll down to the OpenVPN / IKEv2 username section: copy the username and password from this section. You will require them to connect when using the OpenVPN client. Instructions to configure the OpenVPN client for other VPN services:

NordVPN https://support.nordvpn.com/hc/en-us/articles/19749554331793-How-to-set-up-a-manual-connection-on-Windows-using-OpenVPN

CyberGhost https://support.cyberghostvpn.com/hc/en-us/articles/214109325-How-to-Set-Up-OpenVPN-client-on-Windows-10

Configuring the Windows Native VPN client

You can set up native VPN connections from within the Windows operating system.

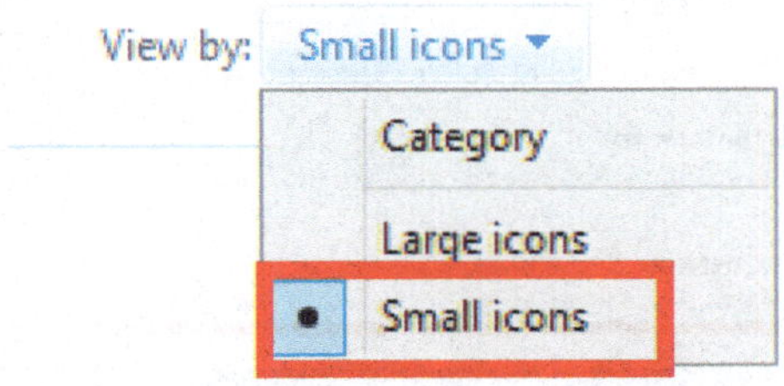

Open Control Panel and select View small icons.

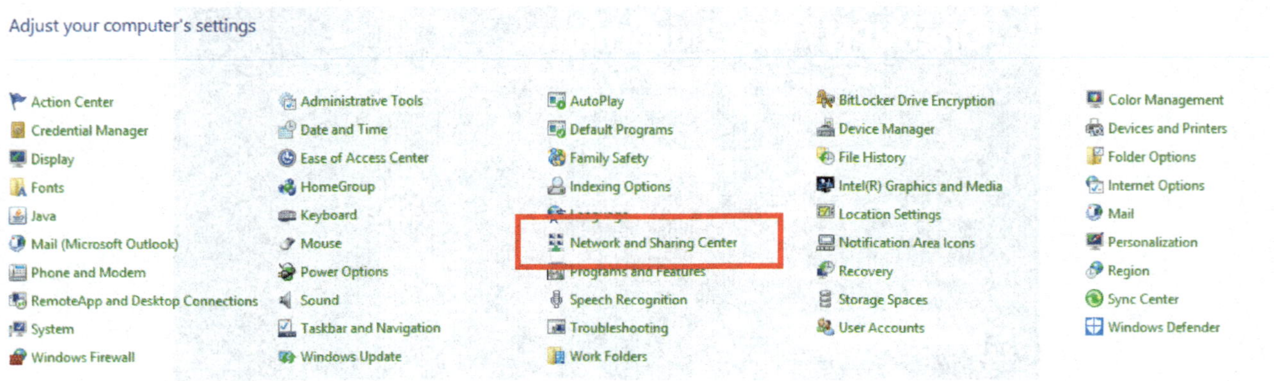

Click the Network and Sharing Center icon.

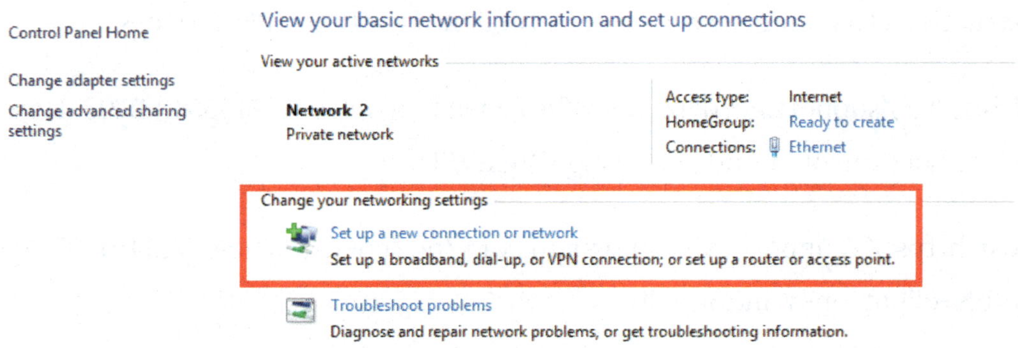

Click the Set up a new connection or network link.

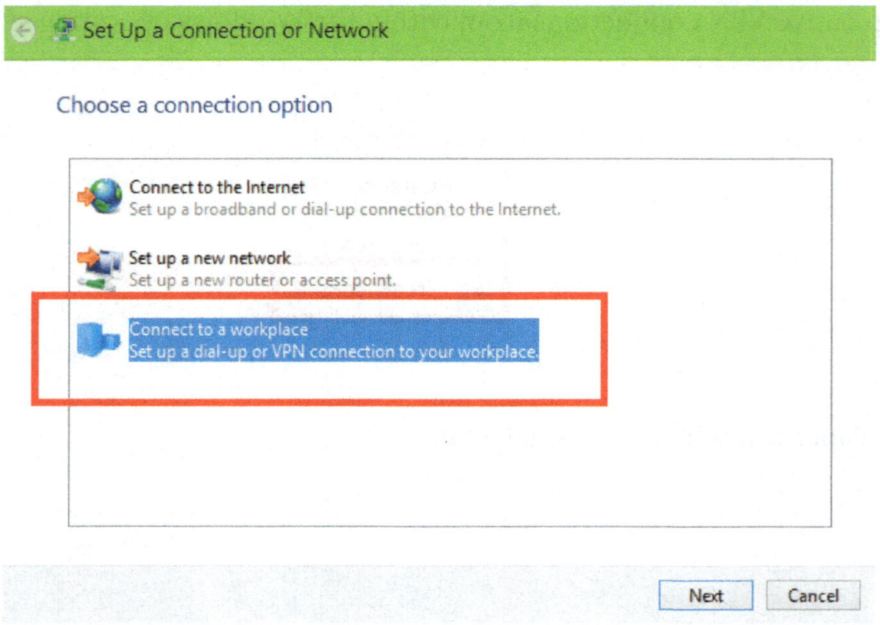

Choose to Set Up a VPN connection and click next.

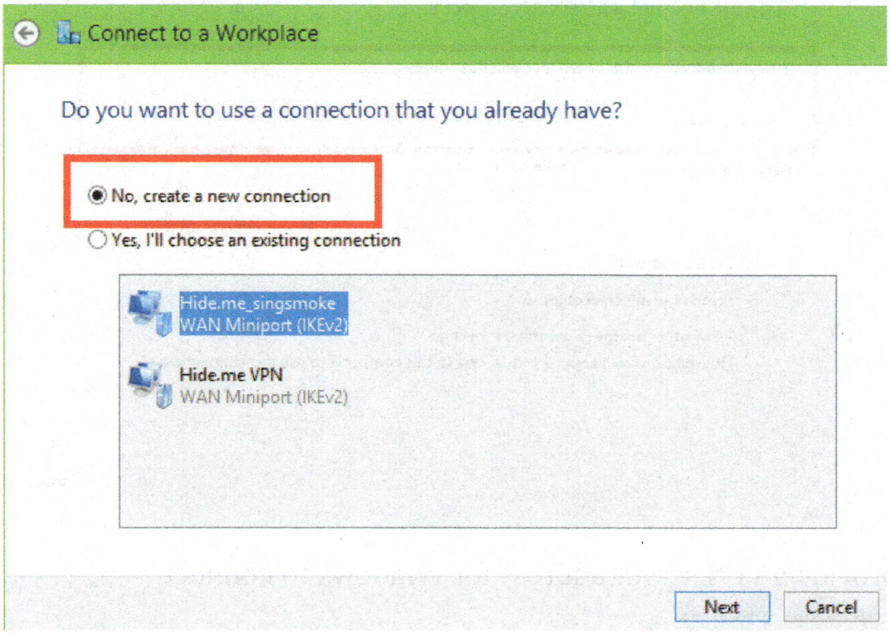

Select Create a New Connection and click Next.

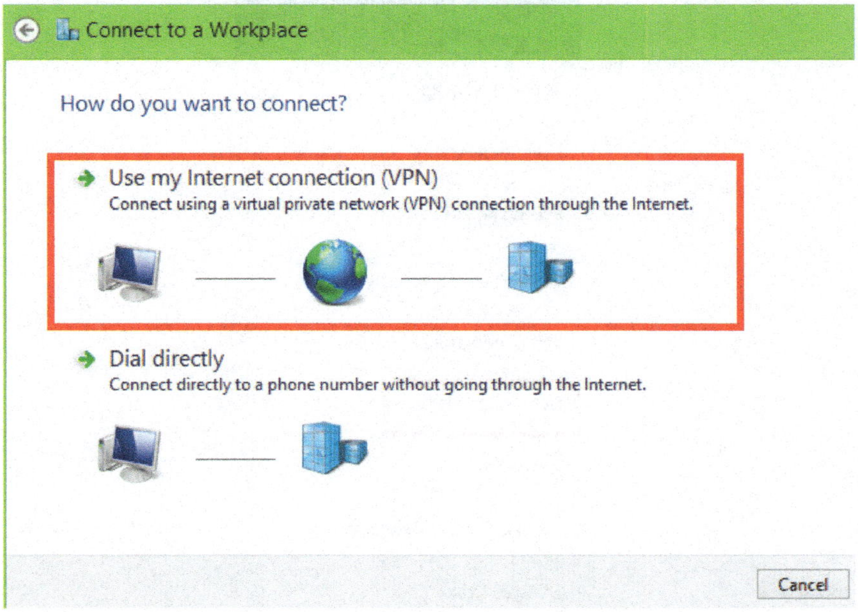

Select Use my Internet connection.

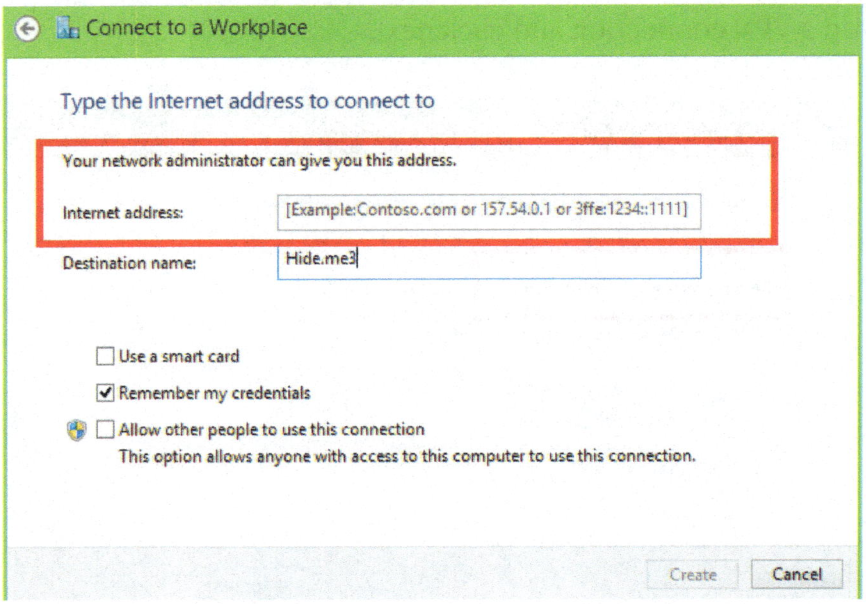

You need to provide a VPN server address for Windows to connect.

This information is provided by the VPN service provider. In this example, we will use a Hide.me free server address. First, I will log into my account if you do not have one, then create one.

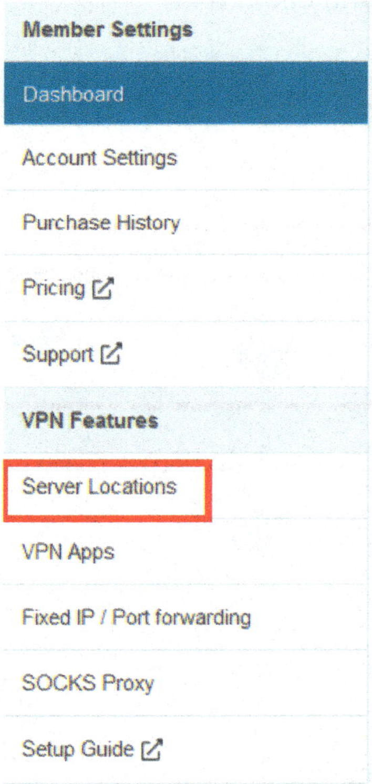

Click server locations on the main menu.

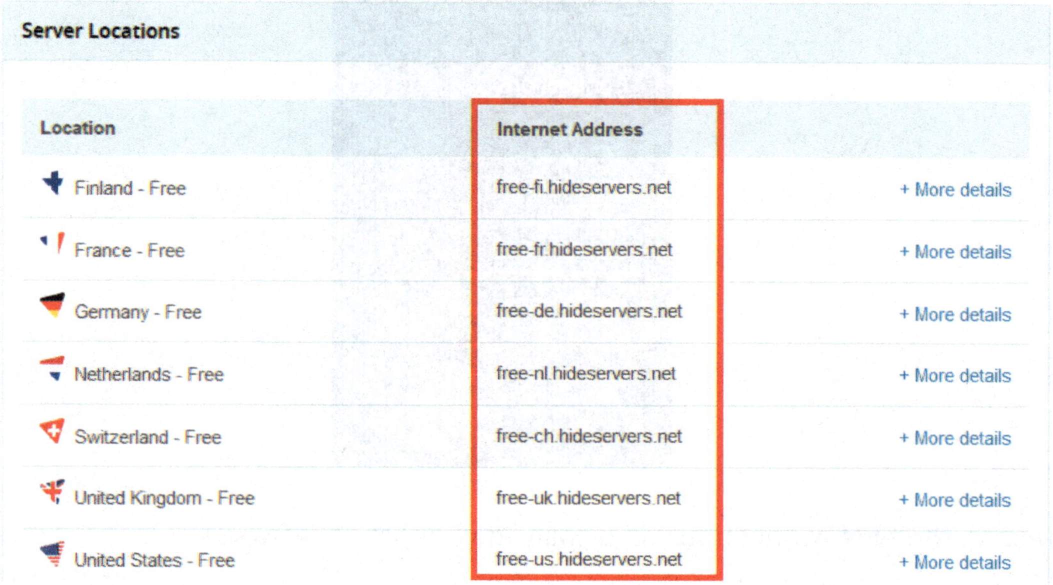

On the server location page, the server addresses will be listed in the Internet Address column. Free Servers will be at the top of the list. In my example, I will use the free Switzerland server: free-ch.hideservers.net.

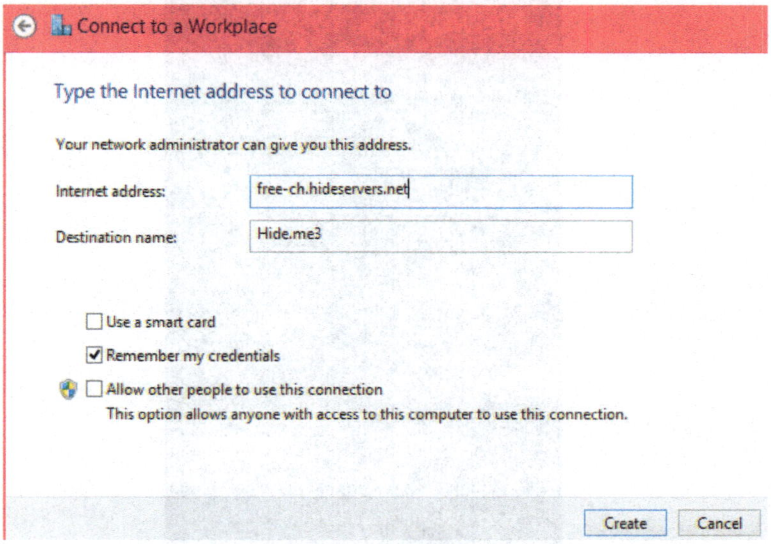

Enter the server address in the Windows client and click Create.

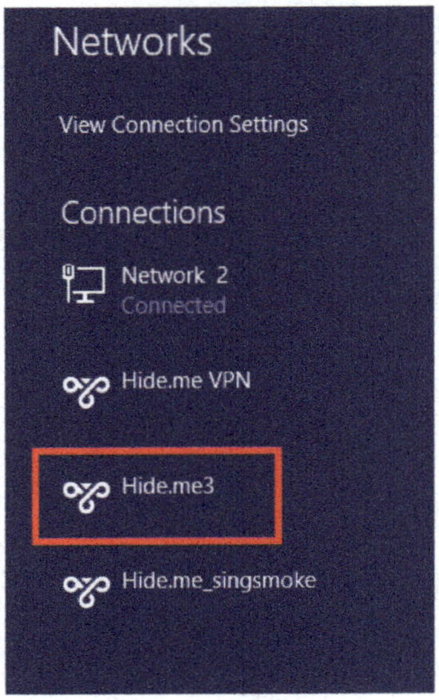

Once created, the VPN connection will display in your list of networks.

To display the network list, click the network icon on your taskbar.

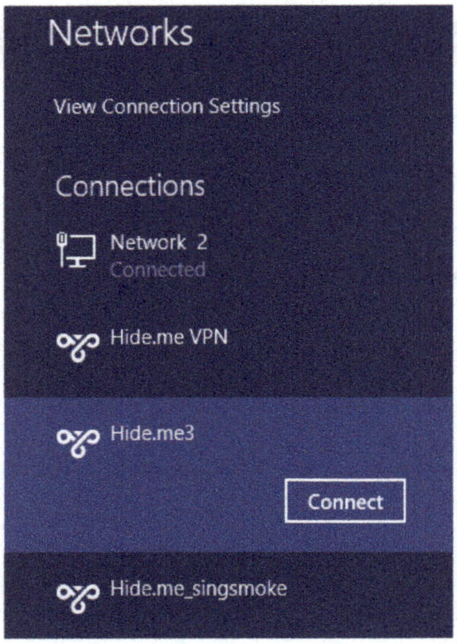

Select the newly created network and click connect.

You will be prompted to enter a username and password. Enter the username and password for your Hide.me account and click OK to connect to the VPN server.

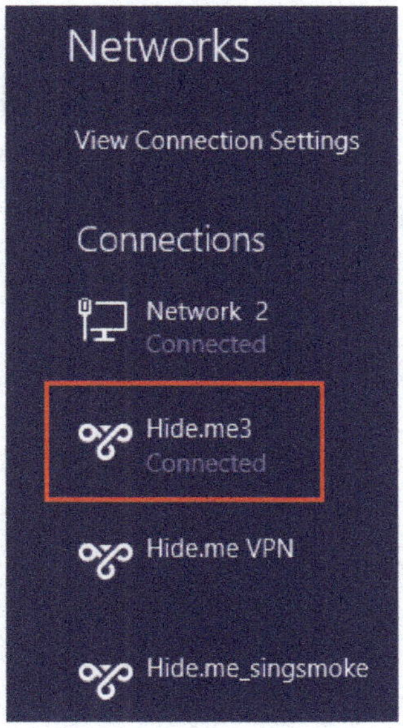

The status of the new network will change to connected

There are 2 tests to validate your VPN is working. Go to https://ipchicken.com to get your current external IP address. It will be displayed as below:

Go to https://iplocation.net. Plug in the IP address to get its geographic location. The server in our example should say that we are in Switzerland, and it does:

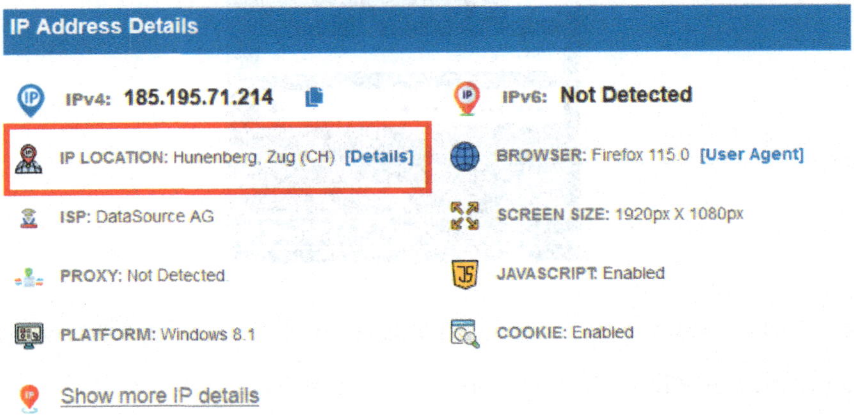

This test can be used to validate whether any VPN is configured and working correctly.

Finally, we suggest creating free accounts with multiple VPN vendors to test their OpenVPN server config files and VPN server internet addresses in a Windows client:

https://hide.me

https://protonvpn.com

https://cyberghostvpn.com

https://nordvpn.com

Experimenting with free accounts will let you know which service works best for you before upgrading to a paid account.

Chapter 5: Password Management

After the burglary, Clarice felt more vulnerable than ever. Though she had blocked her bank card and deactivated her phone, she realized that her online accounts might be at risk, too, and it was time to take action.

One evening, as she checked her bank account, a chilling thought struck her: What if someone had gotten into my accounts using my old passwords? For years, she had used the same simple passwords for many accounts. She hadn't thought much about it before, but now the fear of the thief accessing her money or personal information was very real.

The next morning, Clarice decided it was time for a change. She needed to create stronger passwords for all of her accounts. Simple ones like "Clarice123" were no longer safe. She spent the day updating the passwords for her most important accounts–banking and email. Each password was now long, with a mix of uppercase and lowercase letters, numbers, and symbols–far more difficult for anyone to guess.

But soon, Clarice faced a new challenge. How would she remember all of these complicated passwords? She had so many accounts, and each one had a different password. The thought of forgetting one and being locked out made her anxious.

Clarice knew she needed to make password rotation a part of her routine. It wasn't enough to just create strong passwords; she also needed to change them regularly to keep her accounts secure. Passwords shouldn't remain static for too long, as constant updates help reduce the risk of unauthorized access.

To manage the growing complexity of her security, Clarice also set up ***two-factor authentication (2FA)*** *for all her accounts that offered it. This added an extra layer of security, ensuring that even if someone guessed her password, they would still need a second piece of information–like a code sent to her phone–to access her account.*

With her new passwords and two-factor authentication in place, Clarice felt a sense of relief. She was taking control of her online security and reducing the risk of future threats.

We all need to be careful about keeping our online accounts safe. Using strong, unique passwords and adding extra security is really important nowadays. Let's explore some best practices for creating and managing secure passwords:

Creating a Strong Passwords

1. **Length Matters**

   Aim for a password that is at least 12 characters long. Longer is better.

2. **Use a Mix of Characters**

   Use uppercase and lowercase letters, numbers, and special characters in your password.

3. **Avoid Common Words and Phrases**

   Avoid using easily guessable information such as names, birthdays, common words, or phrases.

4. **Don't Use Dictionary Words**

   Avoid using words found in dictionaries. Create a passphrase or use a combination of unrelated words.

5. **Create Passphrases**

   Consider using a passphrase—a series of random words or a sentence. Passphrases are often easier to remember and are more secure than passwords.

6. **Avoid Personal Information**

   Do not include personal information like your name, username, or any part of your email address in your password.

7. **Use Unpredictable Combinations**

   Mix letters, numbers, and special characters unpredictably. Avoid common patterns like "12345" or "password."

8. **Avoid Reusing Passwords**

   Use a unique password for each of your accounts. Reusing passwords increases risk.

9. **Update Regularly**

   Rotate your passwords. Change them. Update them.

10. **Use a Password Manager**

    Use a password manager. Password managers can create and remember strong, unique passwords for each account.

11. **Two-Factor Authentication (2FA, MFA)**

    Enable two-factor (Multi-Factor) authentication whenever possible. If your password is compromised, there is another layer of security.

12. **Test Your Password**

    Use online tools or services provided by reputable security organizations to check the strength of your password. These tools can help you identify and rectify weak passwords.

Adopting these best practices can significantly enhance your cybersecurity. But it's not just about creating strong passwords—managing them effectively is equally important. This is where two-factor (multi-factor) authentication and password managers come into play.

Implementing Two-Factor (Multi-Factor) Authentication

Two-factor authentication (2FA) is one of the most effective ways to secure your accounts. It requires not just a password but also a second form of verification, making it much harder for attackers to gain access. The second factor required to authenticate is something:

- That You Know - such as a Passphrase
- That You Are - biometrics: fingerprint, retinal scan
- That You Have - code from an authenticator app

Enhance Security

2FA, also called MFA (multi-factor authentication), provides an additional layer of protection beyond just a password. Even if a password is compromised, the attacker would still need a second form of authentication to access the account.

Defend Password Guessing & Password Reuse

With traditional passwords, attackers may use various methods to guess or crack passwords. 2FA greatly reduces the chances of unauthorized access by requiring a second authentication step. When users reuse passwords across multiple accounts, attackers can use compromised credentials from one site to gain access to others. With 2FA, a second authentication factor is required even if a password is stolen.

Secure Sensitive Transactions

For sensitive transactions, such as financial transactions or changes to account settings, 2FA ensures that only authorized users can make changes. Using a VPN for banking transactions is highly recommended. Phishing attacks often trick users into providing their login credentials on fake websites, but with 2FA, the attacker cannot proceed without the second factor. In a man-in-the-middle attack, an attacker intercepts communication between two parties. 2FA helps protect against such attacks because even if your password is intercepted, the attacker lacks the second authentication factor.

Mobile App Authenticators

Many 2FA methods, such as mobile app authenticators or hardware tokens, are more secure than SMS, which is vulnerable to SIM swapping. These tools generate one-time codes and better protect your accounts. Whenever possible, choose app-based authenticators or hardware tokens over SMS for stronger security.

Password Management Tools

Managing multiple complex passwords can be overwhelming, but password managers simplify this task. These tools not only store your passwords securely but also generate strong, unique passwords for each account, making it easier to maintain good security habits. Some benefits of using a password manager include:

1. Generate strong, complex, and unique passwords for each of your accounts.
2. Store and organize all your passwords in one secure location.
3. Use advanced encryption techniques to secure your password vault.
4. Eliminates the need to remember multiple complex passwords.
5. Support for biometric authentication methods, such as fingerprint or face recognition.

Autofill Feature Protects Against Phishing & Keyloggers

Password managers automatically fill in usernames and passwords for you. This saves time and reduces errors. They prevent phishing attacks because they can detect fake or malicious sites. They protect against keyloggers that capture keystrokes when typing passwords.

Secure Storage, Synchronization & Updates

Password managers allow you to securely store other sensitive information, such as credit card details, secure notes, and personal information. Many password managers offer synchronization across multiple devices. It ensures your passwords are accessible and up-to-date on multiple devices. Changing passwords regularly is a recommended security practice. Password managers help you generate and update passwords with minimal effort.

Stronger Security & Recovery Options

Password managers include features like password strength analysis, encouraging users to create stronger and more secure passwords. They provide the ability to securely share passwords with trusted individuals or team members without revealing the actual password. If you forget your master password, they provide secure recovery options so you can regain access to your accounts.

By combining strong password generation, secure storage, and convenient access across devices, password managers contribute significantly to the overall improvement of cybersecurity hygiene and protection against various online threats. Keeping it simple also works. Make sure your passwords are unique, long, and stored safely. If you have them in a notebook written on paper, that works just as well because it is off the network and unhackable. Low-tech solutions are extremely effective for security.

Leading Password Managers

Here's a comparison of some of the leading password managers, focusing on their features and pricing as of September 2024.

1. **Zoho Vault**

   Features:

- Unlimited passwords, notes, and storage
- Unlimited devices
- Save and autofill passwords
- Passwordless login (unlock vault with Zoho OneAuth, Windows Hello, etc.)
- Password generator
- Security dashboard

- Data backup
- Offline access
- Mobile apps
- Browser Extensions (Chrome, Firefox, Edge, Safari, Vivaldi, and Brave)
- Audit trails
- Zoho OneAuth - MFA
- Integration with Zoho apps - Mail, Desk, Projects, Flow

Pricing:

Starting at $1 per user per month

2. **Bitwarden**

Features:

- Password storage and generation
- Autofill for passwords and forms
- Secure notes and file storage
- Two-step login and multi-factor authentication (MFA)
- Password sharing and organization with folders
- Open-source code for transparency
- Self-hosting option for advanced users

Pricing:

- Free Plan: Basic password management and generation.

- Premium Plan: $3.33/month, includes advanced features.
- Family Plan: $5.00/month (up to 6 members), includes Premium features.
- Business Plan: Starts at $5.00/user/month with enterprise features.

3. **LastPass**
   Features:

- Password generation and storage
- Autofill for passwords and forms
- Secure notes and document storage
- Password sharing with others
- Dark web monitoring
- One-touch login with biometrics
- Multi-factor authentication (MFA) support
- Emergency access

Pricing:

- Free Plan: Basic password management, autofill, and password generator.
- Premium Plan: $4.99/month, with advanced features: dark web monitoring, etc.
- Family Plan: $6.99/month (up to 6 members), Premium features.
- Business Plan: Starts at $6.00/user/month, with enterprise features.

4. **1Password**
   Features:

- Password storage and generation
- Autofill for passwords and credit cards
- Secure notes, documents, and vaults
- Travel Mode to hide sensitive data while traveling
- Watchtower for security updates and vulnerability alerts
- Integration with multiple devices and platforms
- Organization and team management features
- Multi-factor authentication (MFA)

Pricing:

- Personal Plan: $2.99/month, all features for one user.
- Family Plan: $4.99/month (up to 5 members), Personal features.
- Team Plan: $3.99/user/month, with team management and advanced sharing features.
- Business Plan: $7.99/user/month, includes enterprise features.

5. **Dashlane**
   Features:

- Password storage and generation
- Autofill for passwords, forms, and payment information
- Secure file storage and VPN for browsing securely
- Dark web monitoring and security alerts
- Password health reports and breach alerts

- Emergency access
- Multi-factor authentication (MFA)

Pricing:

- Free Plan: Basic password storage and generation.
- Premium Plan: $5.99/month, includes advanced features: VPN.
- Family Plan: $8.99/month (up to 6 members), Premium features.
- Business Plan: Starts at $6.00/user/month, business features and tools.

6. **Keeper**
   Features:

- Password storage and generation
- Autofill for passwords and forms
- Secure file storage and dark web monitoring
- Breach monitoring and password security analysis
- Secure messaging and encrypted photo storage
- Multi-factor authentication (MFA)
- Emergency access

Pricing:

- Free Plan: Basic password management and storage.
- Premium Plan: $3.75/month, includes dark web monitoring.

- Family Plan: $7.50/month (up to 5 members), includes Premium features.
- Business Plan: Starts at $4.50/user/month, with advanced security features.

So, *which one is the best?*

Zoho provides an excellent free plan with extensive features, and its paid plans are competitively priced for those seeking more advanced options. **Bitwarden is notable for its open-source model and low pricing**, making it an attractive choice for cost-conscious users who value transparency. **Dashlane sets itself apart with unique features**, such as a VPN included in its Premium plan, which may justify its higher cost for some users. **Keeper offers strong security features and competitive pricing**, which is especially appealing for families and businesses. Each password manager has its strengths, so the best choice will depend on your specific needs and budget.

Chapter 6: Social Media Security

Idris sat at his desk, the soft light of his computer screen casting a glow on his face. Social media had become a big part of his life, a way to share thoughts, moments, and memories with friends. But with college applications coming up, a worrying thought started to cross his mind.

He had heard about students whose old posts were found and misunderstood, causing embarrassment or even rejection from their dream colleges. His social media profiles felt like a public journal, open for anyone to read. Some posts that seemed harmless at the time could now be seen in a negative light.

As he scrolled through his profile, Idris realized how much of his life was out there for anyone to see. Photos with friends, casual updates, shared articles—all pieces of who he was. He knew it was time to take control, to separate what he shared with close friends and what he kept private from the public. Privacy settings, which he had never paid much attention to, now seemed very important.

Idris knew he needed to act. He started by making his posts more private, only sharing them with close friends and family. His public profile became more guarded, a version of his life that he was okay with the world seeing. He changed his password to something stronger, turned on multi-factor authentication, and checked the security settings on all his accounts. Step by step, he began to feel safer, like he was taking back control.

This shift in perspective is important for everyone, especially in an era where social media has become an integral part of our lives. The average person spends 2 hours per day scrolling through some form of social media content, often without realizing the risks associated with oversharing. While platforms provide opportunities for connection, they also expose us to potential threats—from misuse of our personal information to social engineering attacks.

General Tips for All Platforms

Enable Multi-Factor Authentication (MFA)

Why: Even if someone gets your password, MFA adds an extra layer of protection.

How: Enable MFA on platforms that support it (e.g., Google Authenticator, SMS codes, or Authy). Most major social media platforms, like Facebook, Instagram, and Twitter, support MFA.

Use Strong Unique Passwords

Why: Password reuse is risky. If a password is compromised on one platform, it can give access to others.

How: Use a password manager (like 1Password or Bitwarden) to generate and store strong passwords. Ensure each social media account has its own unique password.

Limit Third-Party Apps Access

Why: Some third-party apps and websites may have access to your social media accounts, and not all are trustworthy.

How: Revoke any unnecessary or suspicious apps that have access to your account. On Facebook, go to Settings > Apps and Websites and remove unneeded apps.

Monitor Account Activity

Why: Unexpected login attempts or unfamiliar activity may indicate an attempt to compromise your account.

How: Enable notifications for logins from unrecognized devices or locations. Some platforms like Instagram and Facebook notify you if they detect suspicious login activity.

Limit Sharing Personal Information

Why: Sharing too much personal information can expose you to identity theft or security threats.

How: Think before posting sensitive information like your address, phone number, travel plans, or financial details.

Be Cautious with Links and Attachments

Verify the legitimacy of links before clicking on them.

Educate Yourself

Why: To stay informed and defend against phishing scams circulating on social platforms.

How: Pay attention to security notifications and alerts from the social media platforms themselves. Follow security experts and subscribe to their newsletters.

Privacy Settings on Social Platforms

Protecting yourself from abuse is the most important aspect of social media security. By limiting what you share, you provide less of an attack surface. What do I mean by this? Oversharing on the internet with people you have never met does not always end well. Keep in mind that you may be accidentally sharing information that can help someone identify where you live or the passwords you use. Any personal details you share on social media build a profile about your life. This information can be used to send targeted advertisements or customize a spear-phishing attack.

Your children and elderly parents must understand that when a post is made on social media, the following information is shared by default:

- Time of the post
- Your location when you made the post
- The post links to your profile
- Personal details such as contact information, birthday, or gender
- Links to others with whom you've connected
- Links to the friends and people you have tagged
- Pictures that identify you and the people in your life
- Pictures and videos that identify your location.

Configuring privacy settings on social media platforms controls the visibility of your personal information and ensures a safer online experience. While the steps may vary slightly depending on the platform, here's a general guide on how to configure privacy settings on popular social media platforms:

FaceBook

Settings & Privacy

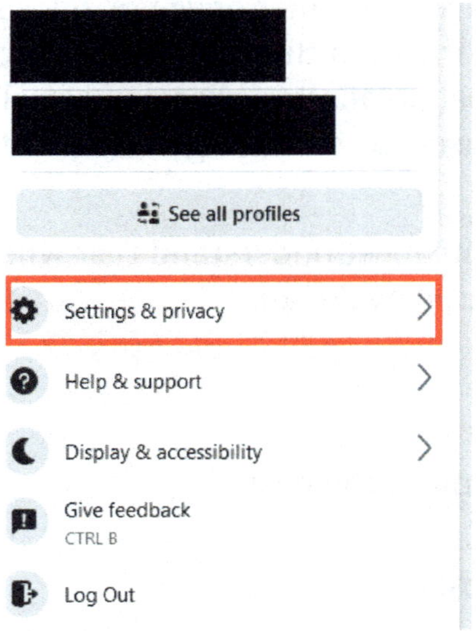

Click on the down arrow in the top right corner, select "Settings & Privacy". You arrive on the Settings and Privacy page. The main menu provides options for you to adjust your account's privacy and security settings. We will go down the menu exploring the sections that matter in greater detail.

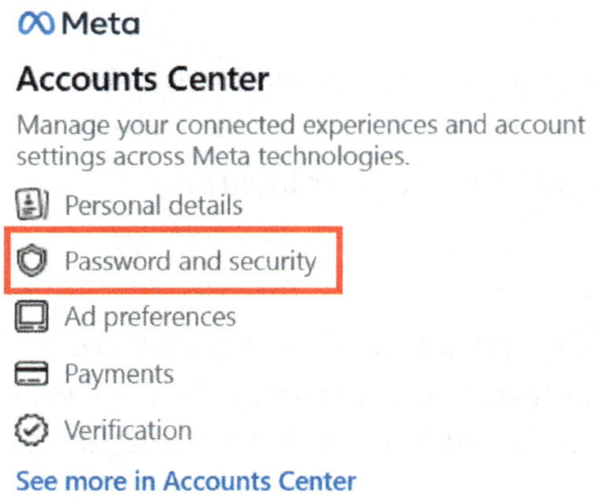

The first submenu you will see on the settings and privacy page is the Meta Accounts Center. Click on the password and security section link. It will redirect you to the Meta Accounts Center page, where you can properly secure your password.

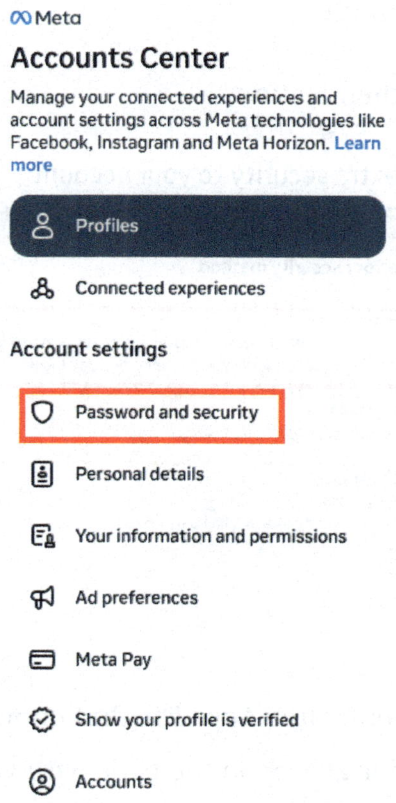

Select Password and Security on this menu.

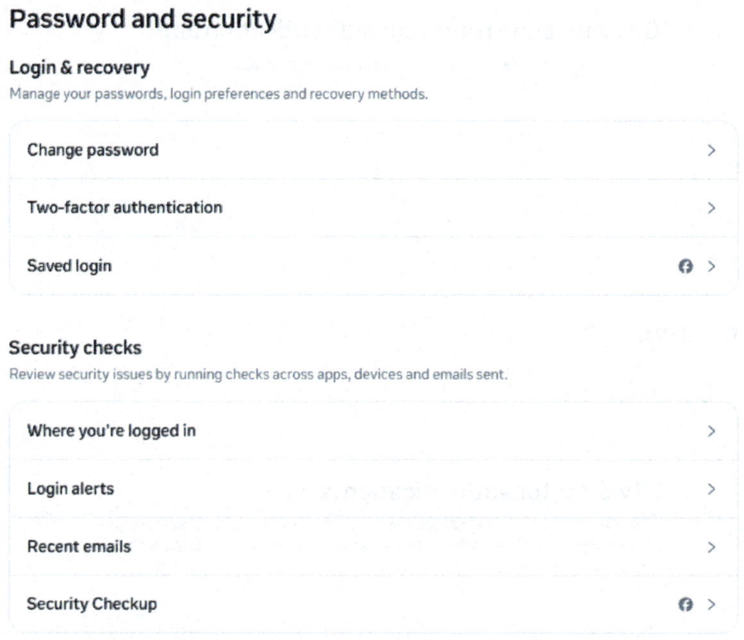

There are 3 important steps you can take right now to make your account more secure.

1. Update your password. Choose a unique complex password for your account that is 16 characters or more in length.
2. Turn on Two-factor authentication.

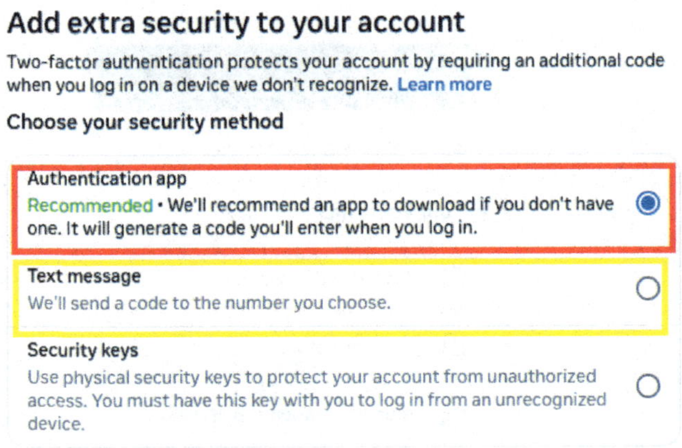

We recommend using an authenticator App. The 2nd choice is to send a text to your phone. Instructions to set up the app for 2FA. Scan the code with your authenticator app.

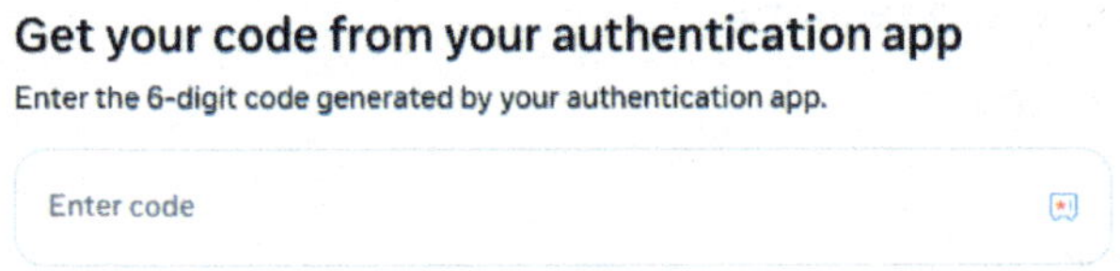

Enter the code in your app.

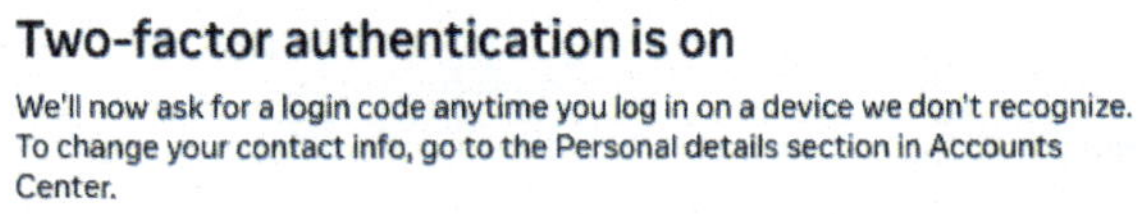

If you see this message, you were successful.

3. Run a Security Checkup on your account. You will see the option to do this at the bottom of the password and security page.

The Security Check Up is part of the Privacy Checkup suite of tools that we review in the following section.

Tools and Resources

The second important section of this menu is Tools and Resources. Under which, we have the Privacy Checkup. Using the tools provided here is the fastest and simplest way to increase your account's overall security.

Privacy Checkup

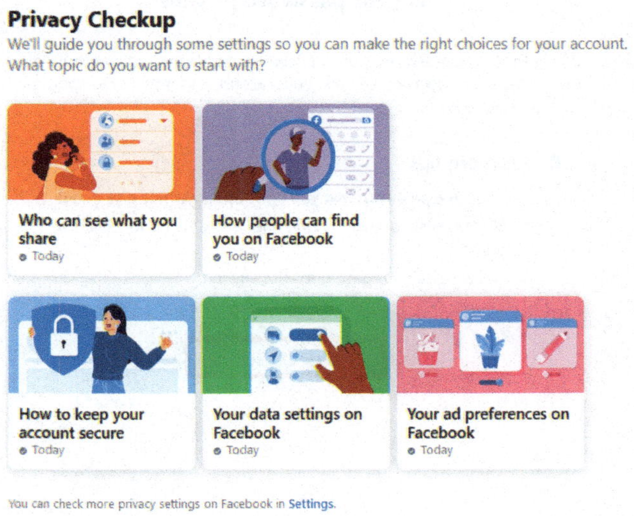

Under Tools and Resources, the first menu option is the Privacy Checkup. Privacy Checkup is a quick and easy way to secure your account settings without taking a deep dive. Each of the images on this page is a wizard that will help you secure a section of your account. The wizards guide you through setting your account and data access permissions. The Security Check-Up is represented by the "How to keep your account secure" icon.

When you click this image, the wizard will open a new window that instructs you to use a unique password for your Facebook account. If the current password is in use for any other cloud or social media account, it advises you to change it so that it is unique. That is only one example of how these wizards work. Select one and follow the instructions.

In our example, we use the Security Checkup.

Click this logo, then click Continue.

The first screen asks that you change your password, so it is complex and unique.

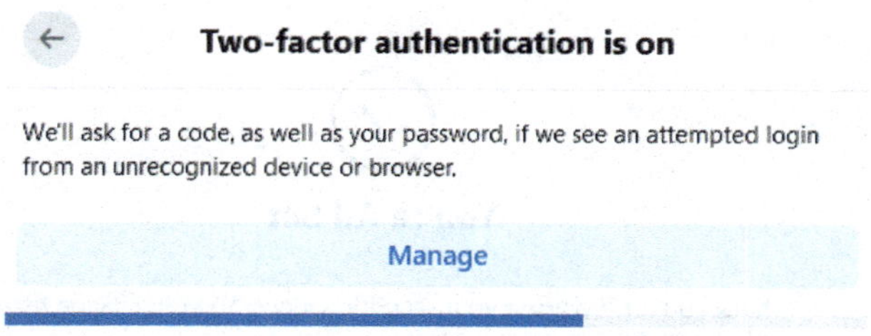

The next screen checks for 2FA. In our case, it is on. If yours is off, turn it on.

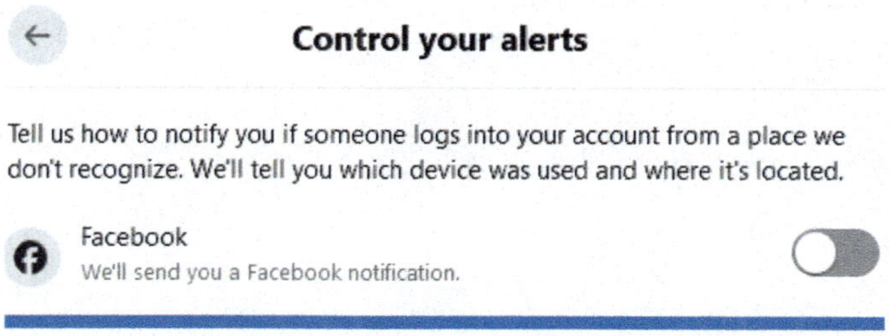

How do you want to be contacted if Facebook suspects a breach?

Provide an email address where you can receive notifications. Turn on In-app and email notifications.

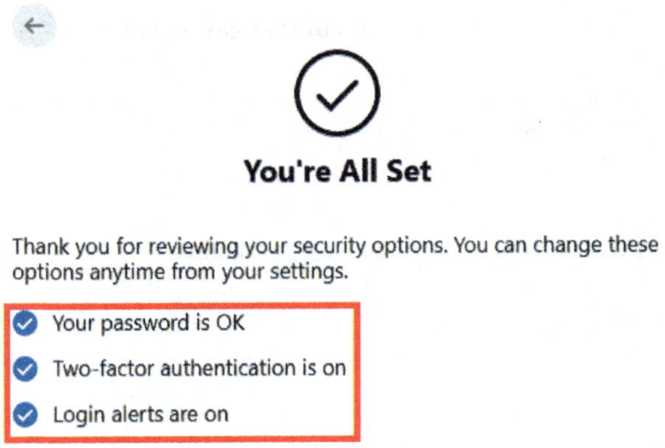

You want your report card to look like this.

Supervision

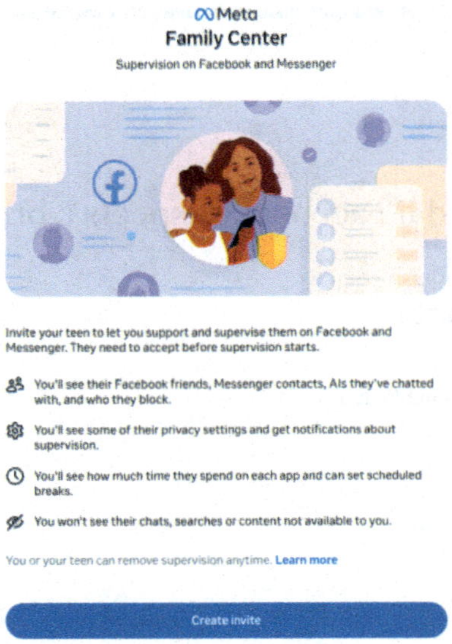

If you are a parent or guardian of minor children, supervision is important. Clicking this link will take you to the Family Center. Here, you can arrange to monitor your child's account. Send the invite to their email address. When they accept the invitation, you can begin monitoring the account. Obviously, you will create your child's email address and accept the invitation on their behalf (just sayin').

Audience Settings

The final option in this section is the Default Audience Settings gear icon. This brings up the window below that displays three options.

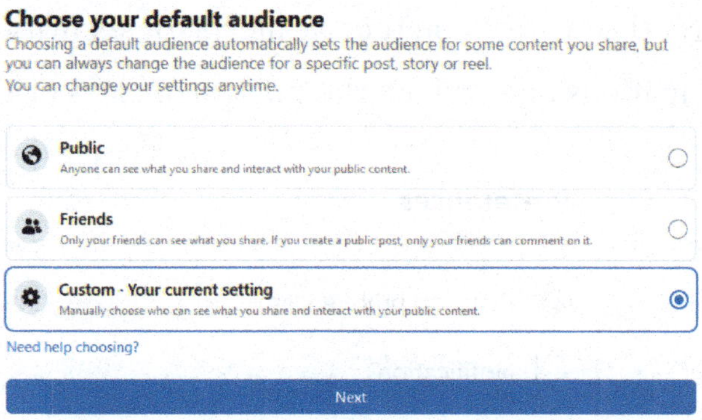

Typically, you would select Custom and then Next. In the following screen, you can set viewing permissions for viewing your posts to a level which makes you comfortable. Click Next.

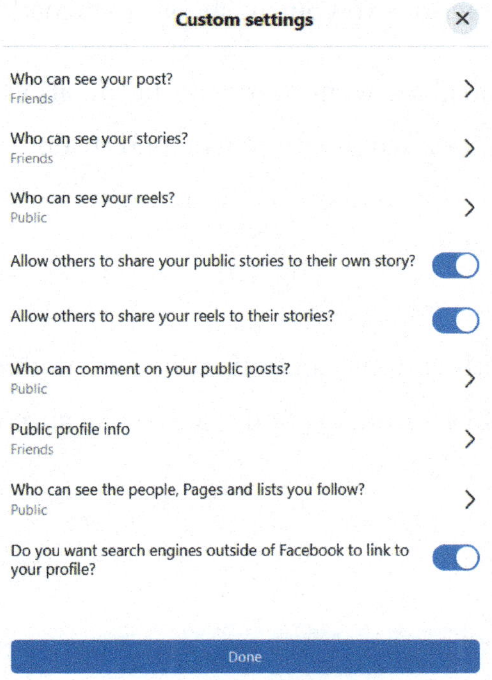

On the next screen, you can see the permissions setting for posts and stories. Reels are set to public, which essentially means anybody. By clicking each setting, you can restrict access to what the public can view. You can also limit your exposure by restricting external search engines from linking to your profile.

Preferences

Setting notifications correctly ensures you receive alerts for security-related events. Make sure that you get critical notifications and reduce the noise from less critical messages.

Reactions: Turn off seeing reactions to your posts or posts made by others

Notifications: Choose how and if you want to receive notifications. There are many notifications available for birthday reminders, when you get tagged, friend requests, calendar events, etc. The truth is you can turn most of them off. They are noisy.

In the "Where you receive notifications" section, make sure under Email that your primary email address is correct. In the SMS section, expand it and make sure it is set like the image below:

Audience and Visibility

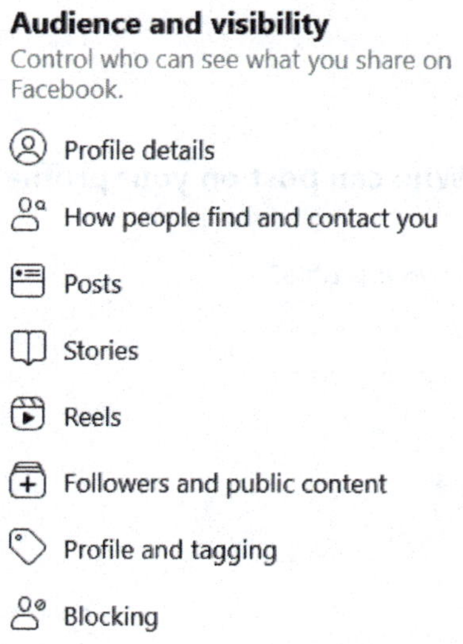

Profile Details link takes you to your profile page, where you can update your profile information.

The **How people find and contact you** page lets you choose who can send you friend requests and see your friends list. We recommend you instruct Facebook not to suggest you at all under any circumstances.

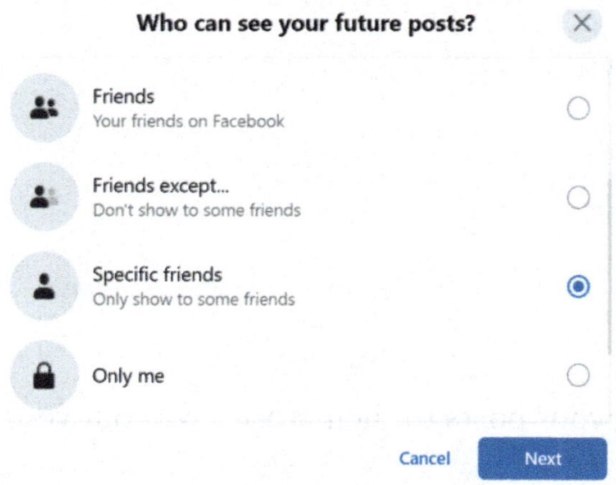

Posts page allows you to limit who can see what you post. It is a good idea to limit this to Specific Friends or Only me. You can make these same choices when sharing your stories and reels.

The **Followers and Public content** page lets you control who can follow you, who can see who you are following, who can comment on your posts. Set this option at your comfort level.

Profile and Tagging

Set this to Only me.

You can automatically hide undesirable comments made on your posts by creating a list of keywords that will be hidden if detected. It is better to just be mindful of your public posts.

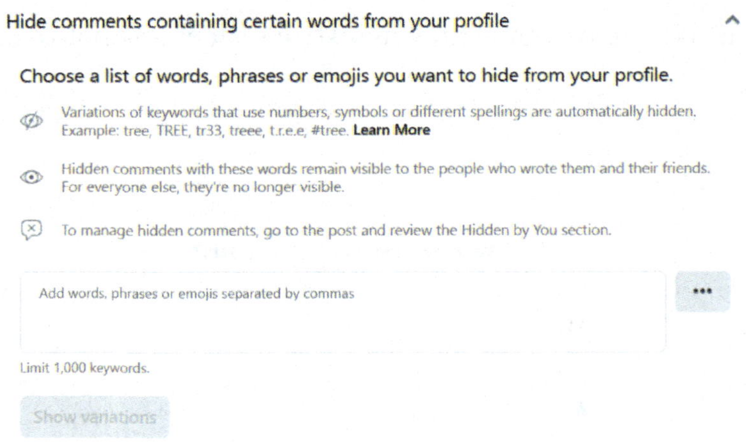

Block others from sharing your posts to their stories without your permission.

Set who can see your future posts that you are tagged in to Friends or Specific Friends.

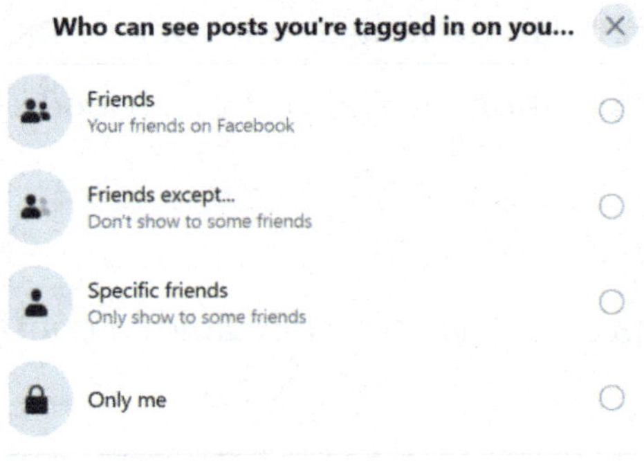

Allow only Friends to see when you are tagged...

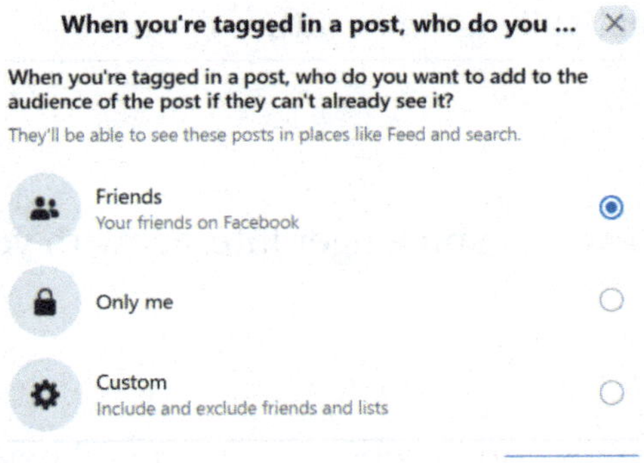

Turn on the feature to review tags added to your posts before they appear online.

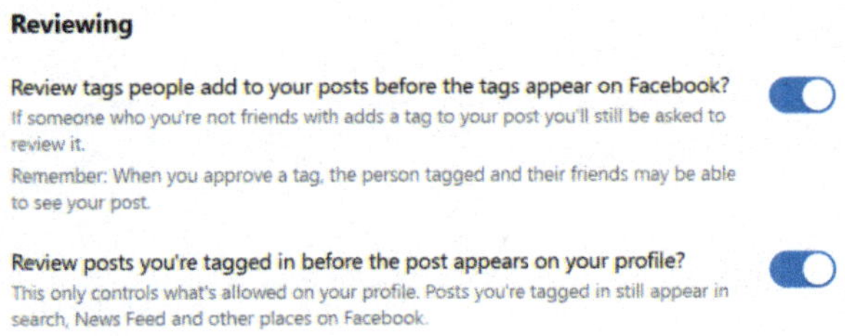

Blocking Management Page

Restricted List

When you add someone's profile to your Restricted list, they won't see posts that you share only to Friends. Only Public posts.

Block users

Once you block someone, they can no longer see your posts, timeline, tag you, invite you to events or groups, start a conversation, or add you as a friend.

Block messages

When you block a Facebook profile, they won't be able to contact you in Messenger either.

Block app invites

Block app invites to automatically ignore future app requests from that person's profile.

Block event invites

Blocking event invites automatically ignores future events

Block Pages

Once you block a page, that page can no longer interact with your posts

Payments Section

Unless you are running a business on Facebook, you should have no entries in this section.

The Your Activity Section

Activity Log

Every single action that you take on the FB platform is recorded. What you were doing and when you did it. We have provided a snippet of a sample Account Activity Log below:

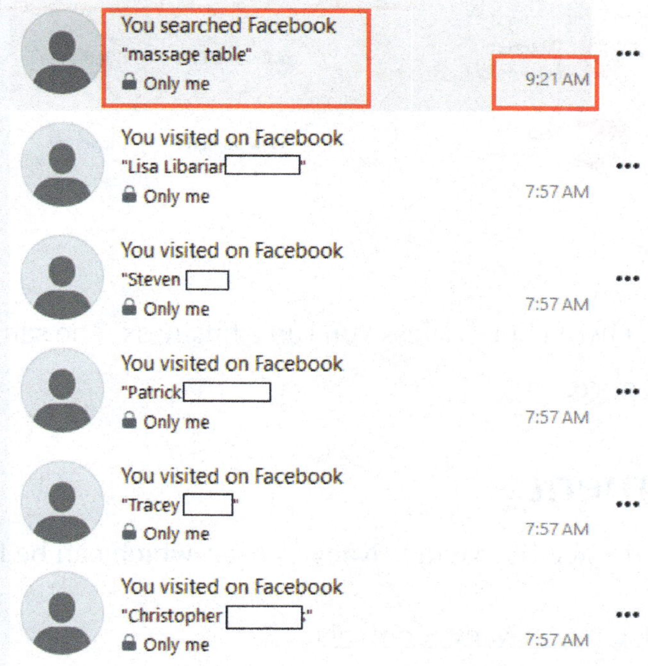

We encourage you to visit this section. It provides a glimpse of the mountain of data being collected by Meta on an hourly basis. In the Your Activity Section, there are 10 sub-sections if you include the Trash and Archive sections. Each section has multiple data points being collected regarding your activities. Every click you make is being tracked, recorded, and used to build a profile of your habits for monetization, marketing, and influence.

Apps and Websites

This page displays apps and websites you've logged into with Facebook or connected to your

Facebook account. Removed expired apps and anything you do not recognize.

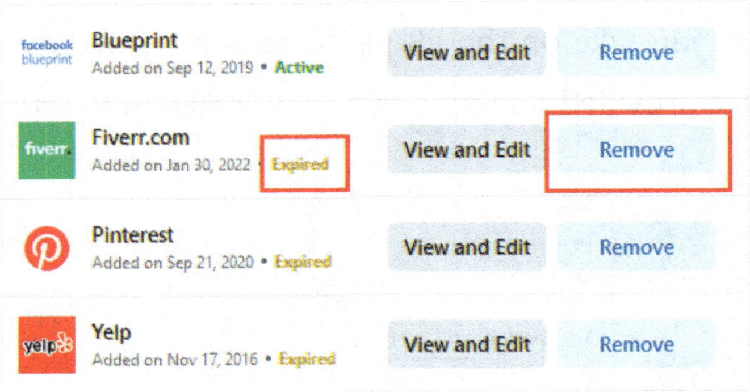

Business Integrations

There should be nothing listed here unless you run a business. The same rules apply here as for the Apps and Websites page.

Data Management

At this time, we will introduce the Meta Privacy Center, which can be found here:

https://www.facebook.com/privacy/controls

The Meta Privacy Center is a subset of the larger Terms and Policies section of the site. We encouraged you to review the entire section. However, for the sake of brevity and security, we are focusing on the settings section of the Meta Privacy Center.

It has 4 major areas:

1. Accounts Details
2. Audience Settings
3. Ad Preferences
4. Your Information and Permissions

We will be placing our emphasis on section 4. Managing your information. The other 3 topics were covered in previous sections.

The best place to manage your information is in the Accounts Center. The link in the Meta

Privacy Center will take you to the Accounts Center. Selecting Your Information and Permissions on the main menu displays this page:

Your Information and Permissions

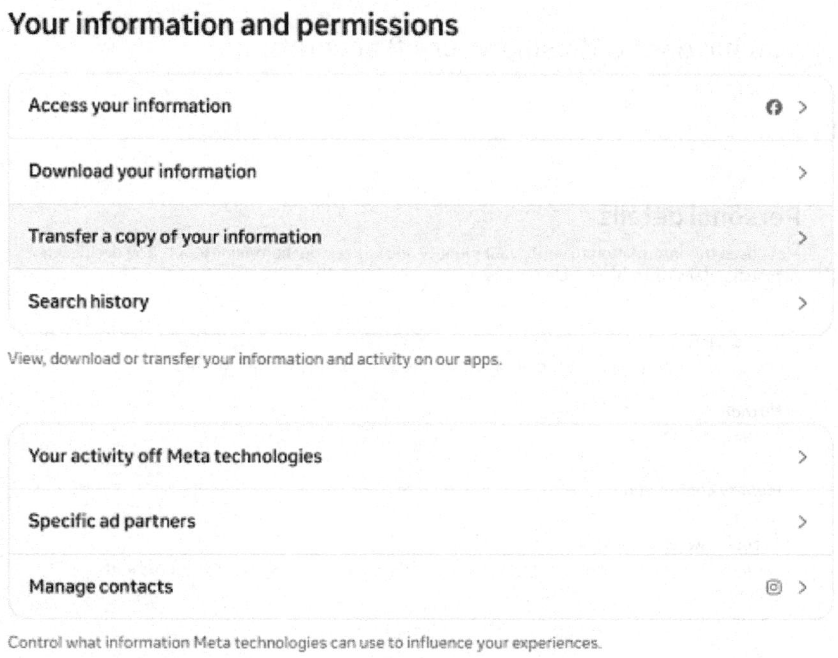

Access your information

Takes you to a vast section of the site very similar to the Your Activity section, which has already been covered. It is another window through which you can view your:

Logged Activity

Personal Information

Connections

Security

Apps and Websites

Download your information

You can download your FB information to make a backup, transfer it, or save it prior to deleting your account.

Search History

Displays your recent search history.

Your activity off Meta technologies

List of Apps/Sites you have visited using your FB account.

Personal Details

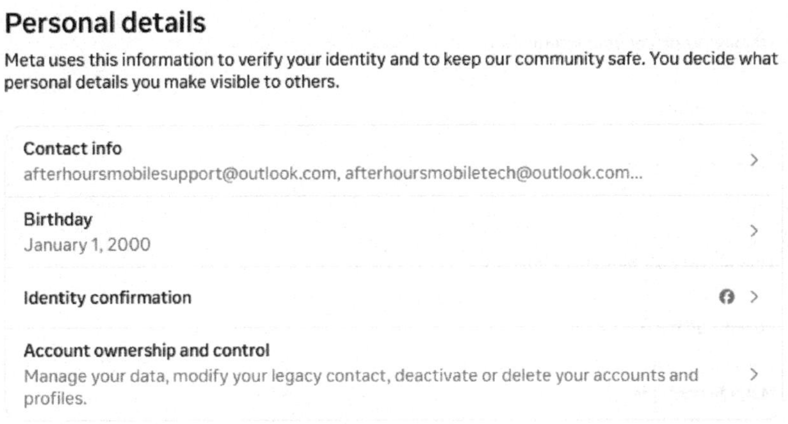

In this section, you can:

- Update your contact information
- Share your birthday (not recommended)
- Confirm your identity
- Account ownership and control allow you to instruct Facebook what to do with your account if you are deceased. You can also cancel and delete your account from here.

Account Ownership and Control

This may seem morbid, but it is important. It instructs FB what to do with your account in the event of your death. Transfer control to a particular person or entity or delete it.

You can find more information about securing FaceBook. Log in to access the help and support center:

Privacy and Settings: https://www.facebook.com/settings/

Privacy Checkup: https://www.facebook.com/privacy/checkup/?source=settings

Meta Accounts Center: https://accountscenter.facebook.com

Meta Family Center: https://familycenter.facebook.com/dashboard/?entrypoint=settings

Account Notifications: https://www.facebook.com/settings/?tab=notifications

Blocking Unwanted Interactions: https://www.facebook.com/settings/?tab=blocking

Apps and Websites: https://www.facebook.com/settings/?tab=applications

Data Management: https://www.facebook.com/help/contact/1638046109617856

Terms and Policies: https://www.facebook.com/policies_center

These help pages can be accessed without logging into a FB account:

https://www.facebook.com/help

https://www.facebook.com/help/213802165366955

https://www.facebook.com/help/325807937506242

https://www.facebook.com/help/messenger-app/193677450678703

https://www.esafety.gov.au/key-issues/esafety-guide/facebook

We did a deep dive into the Facebook Security and Privacy settings. We will not be covering the remaining platforms with the same level of detail. Facebook is owned by Meta. Meta owns **Messenger, Instagram,** and **WhatsApp**. Many of the settings found in the Meta Account Center can be applied to these other Meta platforms.

We want you to take away a universal theme. Re-read General Tips for All Platforms. Use it as a guide as you review privacy settings on other platforms. Each platform will have different menus and tools. The goal is to adjust the settings to minimize your exposure to risks by making maximum use of the security tools provided on the platform.

Instagram

As stated, Instagram is owned by Meta, the parent company of Facebook. Many of the settings in the Meta Account Center will be applicable to Instagram.

Account Privacy

Go to your profile and tap the three horizontal lines in the top right corner.

Select "Settings" >> "Privacy." Adjust settings like "Account Privacy," which controls who can see your posts and stories.

Story Controls

In the Privacy settings, find "Story" controls to manage who can reply to your stories and who can see your stories.

Comments and Messages

Customize settings for comments and messages, including who can comment on your posts and who can send you direct messages.

You can find more information about securing Instagram here:

https://help.instagram.com/196883487377501

https://help.instagram.com/811572406418223

https://help.instagram.com/116024195217477

https://help.instagram.com/448523408565555

https://www.esafety.gov.au/key-issues/esafety-guide/instagram

X (Formerly Twitter)

Tweet Privacy

Click on your profile picture and select "Settings and Privacy." >> "Privacy and safety" tab. Adjust settings like "Protect your Tweets" to make your tweets private.

Who Can Tag You

In the same "Privacy and safety" tab, go to "Photo tagging" to manage who can tag you in photos.

Safety and Email Preferences

Explore additional privacy and safety settings, including muted accounts, blocked accounts, and email preferences.

You can find more information about securing Twitter here:

https://help.twitter.com/en/safety-and-security/x-privacy-settings

https://www.esafety.gov.au/key-issues/esafety-guide/instagram

LinkedIn

We can secure our LinkedIn personal accounts in a few steps.

Enable Two-Factor Authentication (2FA)

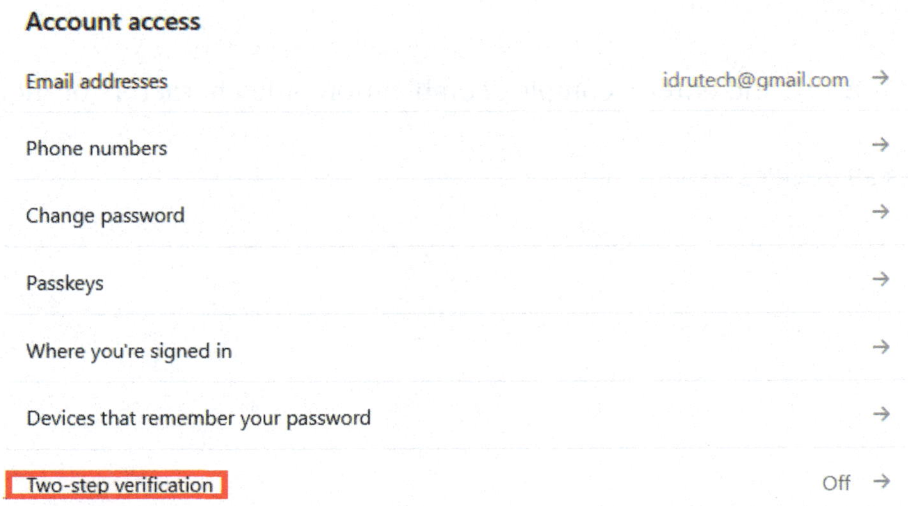

Click your profile icon at the top right and select Settings & Privacy

Click the Sign in & Security link in the main menu

Click Two-Step Verification on the Account Access page that appears on the left

Set a Strong Password

Click your profile icon at the top right and select Settings & Privacy

Click the Sign in & Security link in the main menu

Click the Change Password option

Update your password and enter a complex combination of 16 characters or more.

Check requires all devices to sign in

Review Account Access

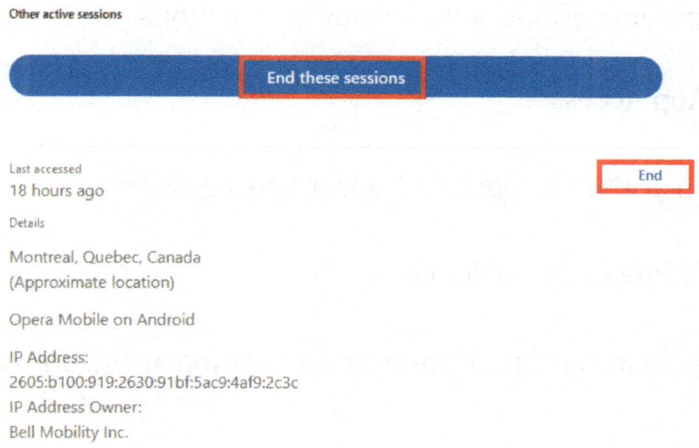

Click your profile icon at the top right and select Settings & Privacy

Click the Sign in & Security link in the main menu

Click the Where you are signed in option

End all inactive sessions

Control Profile Visibility

Click on your profile picture and select "Settings & Privacy."

Go to the "Visibility" tab to control who can see your activity and connections.

Adjust settings related to who can see your connections and who can follow you.

Restrict visibility of your email and phone number.

The page has 2 parts. Section 1 is Visibility of your profile & network, and Section 2 is Visibility of your LinkedIn activity. There are numerous settings on this page. Review this page carefully and select the most appropriate settings for your case.

Manage Your Connections and Network

Log in and click "My Network" on the menu at the top of the page.

Click the down arrow to expand "Manage My Network."

Click Connections

Regularly review your connections. Remove any connections you don't recognize or trust.

Manage Third-party App Access

Click your profile icon at the top right and select Settings & Privacy

Click the Data Privacy link in the main menu

Click Permitted Services in the Other Applications section at the bottom of the page.

Manage Data Access

Click your profile icon at the top right and select Settings & Privacy

Click the Data Privacy link in the main menu

Configure settings related to how LinkedIn uses your data

On this page, you can opt out of sharing data with 3rd parties

You can find more information about securing LinkedIn here:

https://www.linkedin.com/help/linkedin/answer/a1338877/understanding-your-privacy-settings? lang=en

https://www.linkedin.com/help/linkedin/answer/a1337839

Snapchat

Privacy Settings

Tap on your Bitmoji or profile icon in the top left corner. Go to "Settings" and then "Privacy."

Adjust settings like "Who Can..." for Story viewing, contact requests, and more.

Location Sharing

Review and manage location-sharing settings for Snaps and Map features.

You can find more information about securing SnapChat here:

https://help.snapchat.com/hc/en-us/sections/5690164367636-Privacy-Settings

https://www.esafety.gov.au/key-issues/esafety-guide/snapchat

Limiting Personal Information Exposure

Here are practical tips to reduce your digital footprint and limit information sharing:

Regularly Adjust Social Media Settings & Passwords

Regularly review and customize privacy settings on your social media accounts. Control who can see your posts, personal information, and friend lists. Use strong, unique passwords for each online account. Regularly update your passwords and consider using a password manager for added security.

Minimize Personal Details, Use Nicknames & Delete Unused Accounts

Avoid oversharing personal details on social media profiles. Minimize the inclusion of sensitive information such as your address, phone number, or detailed workplace information. Consider using pseudonyms or nicknames instead of your full name on certain platforms. This can help prevent the easy identification of your online presence. Regularly audit and clean up your online accounts. Delete inactive accounts.

Online vs. Real Friends

Only accept friend or connection requests from people you know and trust. Avoid sharing overly personal or revealing photos online. Be mindful of the potential implications of sharing images, especially those that may disclose your location or daily activities. Be cautious about connecting with people you have no contact with offline.

Limit Public Wi-Fi & Restrict Mobile Apps

Adjust privacy settings on mobile apps to restrict access to your location, contacts, and other sensitive information. Periodically review and adjust the permissions granted to apps on your devices. Remove unnecessary permissions to limit the access apps have to your personal information. Only grant permissions that are necessary for the app's functionality. Never access sensitive accounts or conduct financial transactions when connected to public Wi-Fi networks. Use a Virtual Private Network (VPN) for added security.

Opt-Out & Use Disposable Emails

Consider using disposable or secondary email addresses for online registrations and services that do not require your primary email. Check websites for privacy policies and opt-out options for data collection. Some websites allow users to opt out of certain types of data tracking.

Educate Yourself About Privacy Tools

Familiarize yourself with privacy tools and technologies that enhance online privacy, such as encrypted messaging apps and privacy-focused search engines. Keep certain profiles or accounts private if possible. For example, limit the visibility of professional profiles on job-seeking platforms. Avoid participating in online quizzes or surveys that request personal information. Such activities can be used to gather data for targeted advertising or phishing.

Google Yourself

Regularly conduct online searches for your name to see what information is publicly available. If you find inaccurate or sensitive information, take steps to address it. By implementing these practices, you can significantly reduce the exposure of your personal information online and maintain greater control over your privacy.

Staying vigilant and regularly reviewing your online presence helps protect your digital identity.

Recognizing Social Engineering Attacks

Recognizing social engineering attacks protects you from being manipulated into revealing sensitive information or giving unauthorized access to resources. The tactic relies heavily on exploiting human psychology rather than advanced technical tools to gain initial network access.

The social engineering game is about hacking a human. Yes, if you can be deceived into giving up your own critical data, then you have been compromised. It starts with you. The truth is you can only be compromised if you agree to be deceived. As we mentioned at the beginning, "cyber security is a mindset that requires you to be present, aware, vigilant..."

By now, you are familiar with several forms of social engineering, such as phishing, scam emails, and social media scraping. We will now add additional communication channels where social engineering attacks can occur.

- Vishing (via phone) occurs when you receive a call from "tech support" asking you to update your password. Always verify that support calls are from an approved service.
- Smishing (via text) happens when you receive a text claiming you've inherited a fortune, but to secure it, you need to send $3000 and some personal details.
- Pretexting (my personal favorite) is an old-school con job. The attacker contacts you using a fake identity, creating an urgent scenario to trick you into divulging sensitive information, such as your social security number.

Social engineering attacks involve psychological manipulation rather than technical exploits. Here are common signs to help you recognize a social engineering attack:

Urgency & Emotional Manipulation

Attackers may create a sense of urgency or fear to pressure you into immediate action. Often using emotional manipulation, such as appeals to sympathy, urgency, or flattery. Be cautious of language that aims to exploit your emotions and trust, and always verify the legitimacy of such requests.

Unusual Requests & Unusual Behavior

Be cautious of unexpected requests for sensitive information, such as passwords, Social Security numbers, or financial details. Legitimate entities usually do not request such information via unsolicited communication. If the communication tone or style differs significantly from the sender's usual behavior, it could be a sign of a social engineering attempt. Attackers may mimic the writing style of known contacts. If a friend or colleague makes an unusual request for sensitive information or financial assistance, verify the request through a separate and trusted communication method.

Email Spoofing & Impersonation

Check email addresses carefully for slight misspellings, extra characters, or domain name variations. Attackers often use email spoofing to make it appear as if the email is from a legitimate source. Be wary of messages or calls claiming to be from authority figures, government agencies, or law enforcement. Verify their identity independently through official channels. Be skeptical of unexpected calls from individuals claiming to be technical support or IT personnel. Legitimate organizations usually do not make unsolicited technical support calls.

Too Good to Be True Offers

Be skeptical of emails or messages offering incredible deals, prizes, or opportunities that seem too good to be true. Social engineers often use enticing offers that require a small fee to manipulate individuals. Social engineers often request payment through gift cards or wire transfers. Be cautious if someone asks for these forms of payment, especially if it seems urgent.

Phishing Emails

Pay attention to unsolicited emails with suspicious links or attachments. Hover over links to preview the actual URL before clicking. Be cautious if the email encourages you to download files or click on links. Look for inconsistencies in the information provided. Social engineers may not have accurate details about you or the organization they claim to represent. Be wary of unexpected contact attempts, especially if they come through channels you don't typically use for communication. Independently verify the information presented to you, especially if it involves sensitive or personal details. Contact the supposed sender through official offline channels to confirm requests.

Baiting and Quizzes

Social engineering attacks may involve tricking users into visiting malicious websites. Be cautious of online quizzes or surveys that request personal information. These can be used to gather data for targeted attacks. These websites may contain redirects or pop-ups. If something feels off or too good to be true, trust your instincts and take the time to verify the legitimacy of each communication.

Monitor Your Accounts

Regularly monitor your accounts for unusual activities. Set up alerts for any changes to your account information or login activity.

Being vigilant and skeptical can go a long way in preventing social engineering attacks. If in doubt, verify information independently through trusted channels and avoid taking immediate actions based on unsolicited requests. Awareness and healthy skepticism play key roles in recognizing and mitigating social engineering risks.

Chapter 7: Email Security

Margaret and Hannibal sat side by side on the living room couch, both bent over their smartphones, squinting at the screens. Ever since Evan and Clarice convinced them to get smartphones a few months ago, they'd been learning the ropes of the digital world. Today, they were tackling something that had been confusing them for a while: emails.

Margaret stared at an email claiming she had won a "huge cash prize" and needed to click a link to claim it. "Hannibal, look at this," she said, holding her phone closer to him. "Do you think it's real? Should I click it?"

Hannibal glanced at his own phone, where a similar email popped up, this one warning him of a problem with his bank account. "I got one too... but it doesn't feel right," he muttered, scratching his head. "But what if it's something serious? They're saying my account could be locked."

They both sat in silence, unsure of what to do next. The emails looked important, but something felt off. They were new to this digital world and were curious, but they weren't sure what to trust. Down the hall, they could hear Idris and Aditsan playing on their devices, effortlessly navigating technology. Margaret sighed. "Maybe we should wait for Evan to help us. Or ask one of the kids."

Hannibal nodded in agreement but still hovered his finger over the email, tempted to figure it out on his own. "Better safe than sorry," he said, setting his phone down for now.

As Margaret and Hannibal continue to learn about their smartphones and email, they, like many others, are at risk of falling for scams. This situation highlights the importance of recognizing the signs of email fraud, especially when new to technology. In this chapter, we will explore how to spot email scams and protect ourselves from phishing attempts.

Spotting Email Scams

Recognizing email scams is crucial for protecting yourself online, especially when navigating this digital space for the first time, like Margaret and Hannibal. As we delve into email security, you'll find that scammers often use emails to trick people into sharing private information or sending money. These scams come in a variety of forms, but they usually have a few key warning signs that, with practice, you can learn to spot.

This chapter will walk you through more detailed strategies for spotting and avoiding these scams. Like Margaret and Hannibal, many people are learning to navigate these risks, and with a little knowledge, you can protect yourself and stay safe online.

Securing Your Email Account

Enable 2-Factor Authentication

Gmail

Log into your account: https://myaccount.google.com

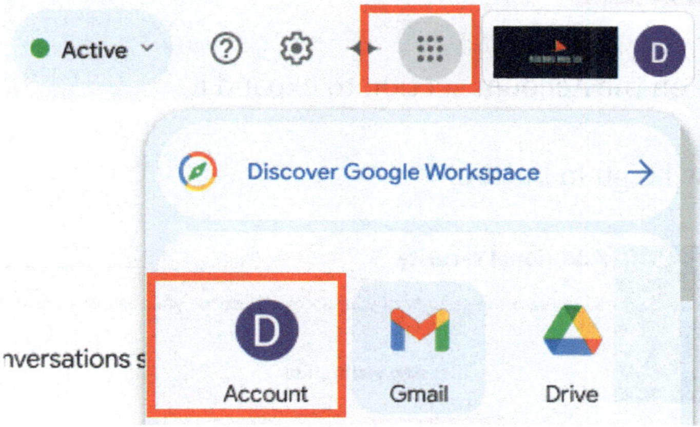

Click on the dots shaped in a square

Click the Account icon in the menu

Click the Security link on your Account's main menu

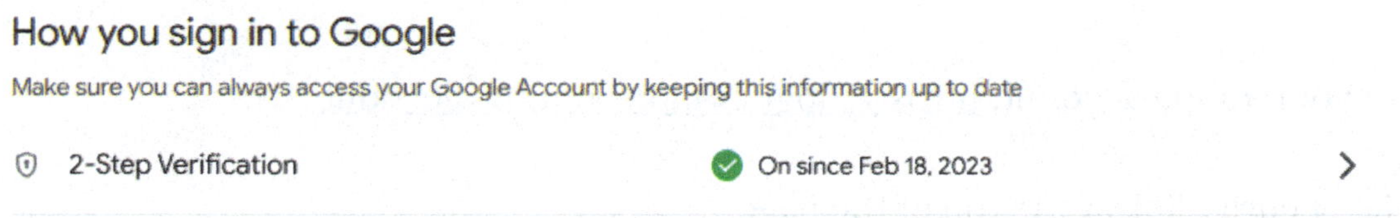

In the How You Sign Into Google Section of the page

Click 2-Step Verification

We recommend using an Authenticator App

Outlook

Log into your Microsoft account: https://account.microsoft.com

Click the Security link in the main menu.

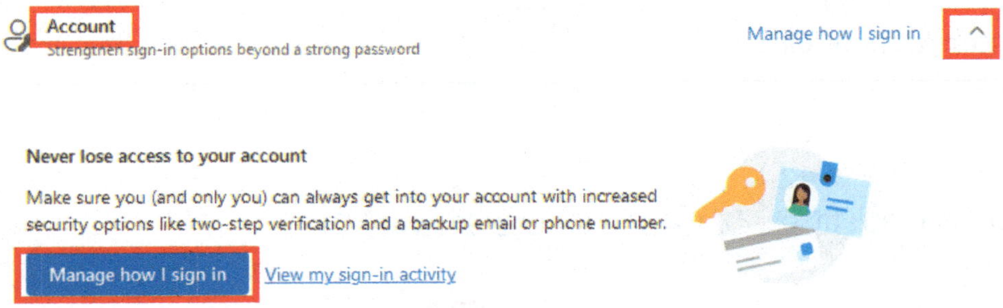

Click the down arrow on the Account section to expand it.

Click the Manage How I Sign In button.

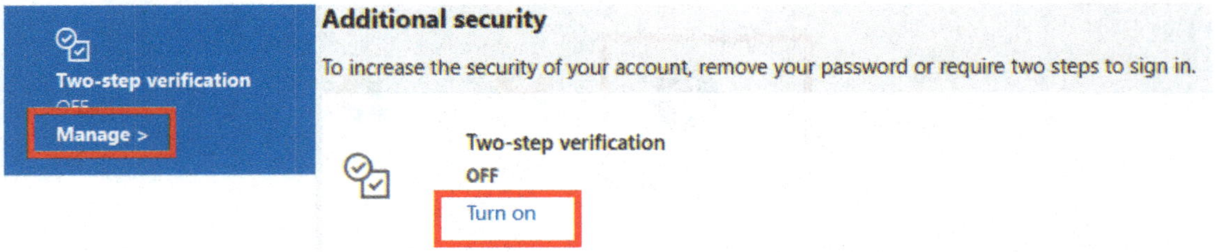

Click the manage link under 2-Step Verification in the main banner.

Or Click the "Turn on" link under 2-Step Verification under Additional Security.

Yahoo

Login to your Yahoo account: https://login.yahoo.com/myaccount

Click the Security link at the top of the page.

Click the enable 2-step verification link.

We recommend using an authenticator app.

Set Up a Strong and Unique Password

Gmail

Log into your account: https://myaccount.google.com

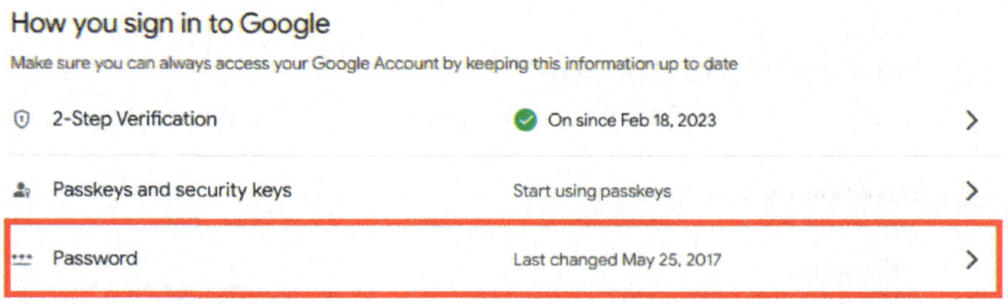

Click the Password link on your Google Account Security page.

Update the password to be a complex, unique, and 16-character.

Outlook

Log into your Microsoft account: https://account.microsoft.com

Click the Security link in the main menu

Click the down arrow on the Account section to expand it

Click the Manage How I Sign In button

Click the arrow next to Enter Password to expand

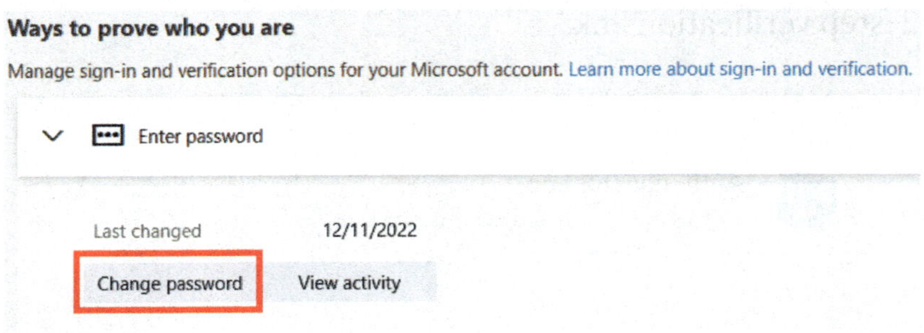

Click the Change Password button to update your password

Yahoo

Login to your Yahoo account: https://login.yahoo.com/myaccount

Click the Security link at the top of the page

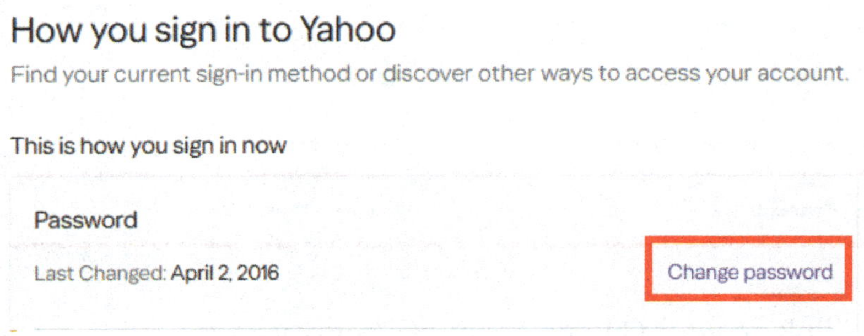

Click Change Password link in the How to Sign in to Yahoo section

Review Account Activity

Gmail

Log into your Google account

Click the Security link on your Account's main menu

Click on "Recent security events"

Click on "Your devices" to see where your account has been accessed from.

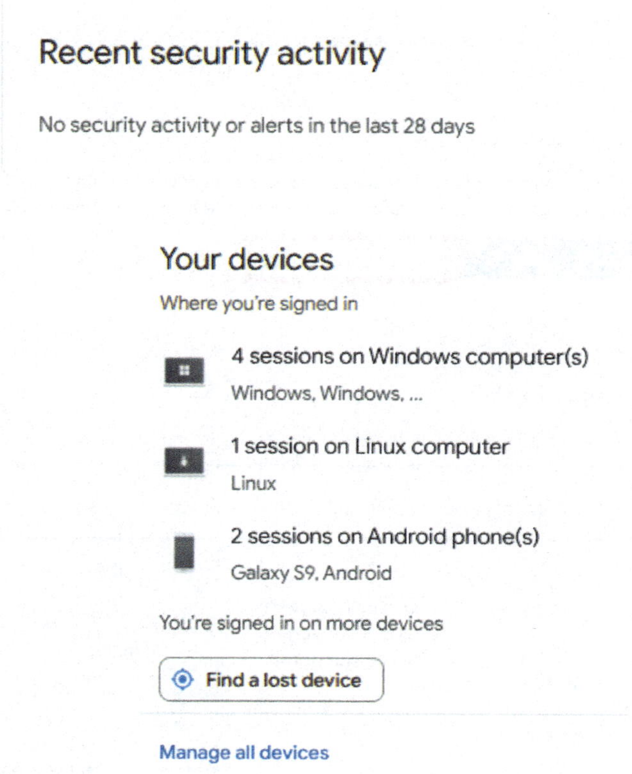

Outlook

Log into your Microsoft account: https://account.microsoft.com

Click the Security link in the main menu

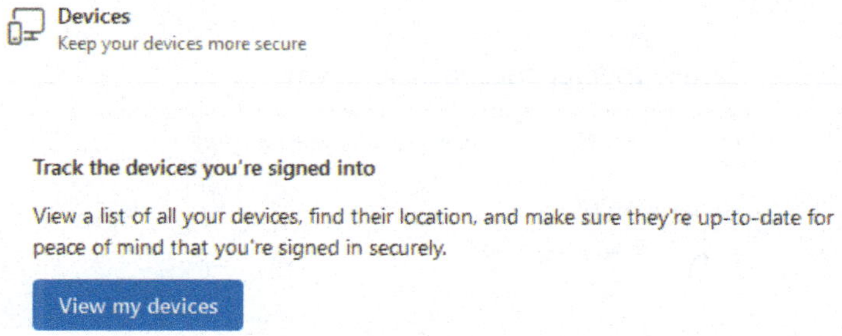

At the bottom of this page, you can view connected devices

Click the down arrow on the Account section to expand it

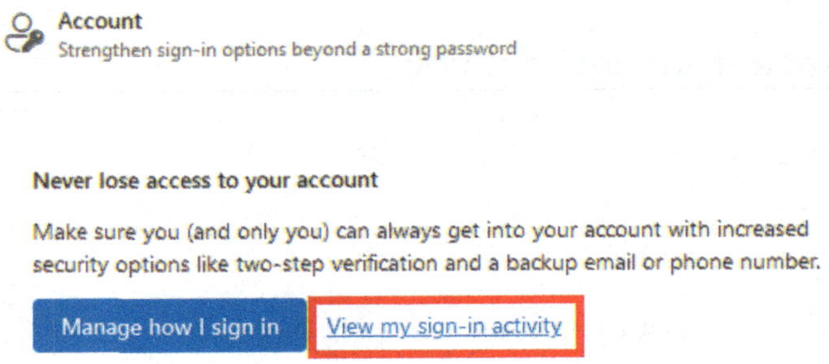

Click the View My Sign-in Activity Link

View recent account activity

Yahoo

Login to your Yahoo account: https://login.yahoo.com/myaccount

Click the Recent Activity link at the top of the page

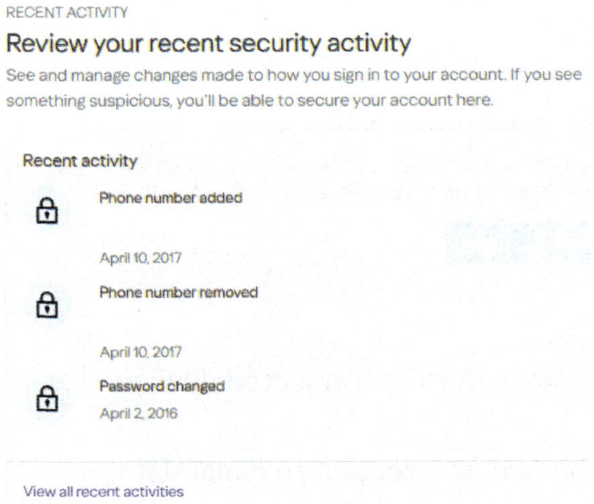

On this page, you can see recent activity and connected devices

Set Up Account Recovery

Gmail

On the Security page in the Account Recovery section

Set a recovery email address

Set up a backup phone number for 2-step verification (MFA)

Outlook

Log into your Microsoft account: https://account.microsoft.com

Click the Security link in the main menu

Click the Manage How I Sign-in button

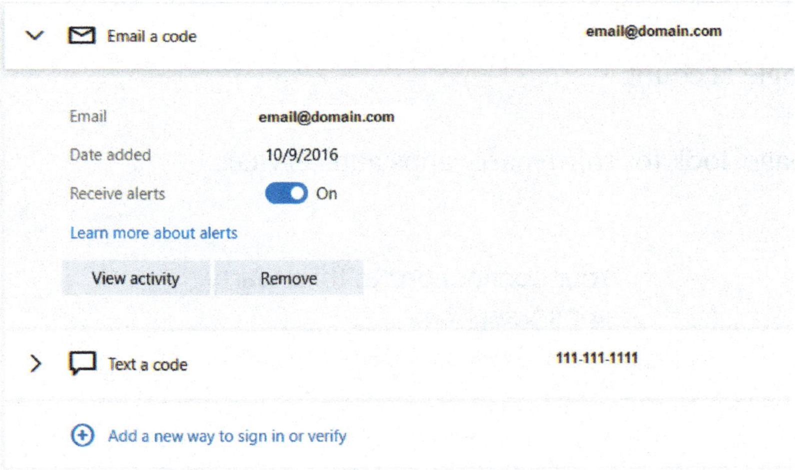

Add a recovery email address and phone number

Yahoo

Login to your Yahoo account: https://login.yahoo.com/myaccount

Click the Security link at the top of the page

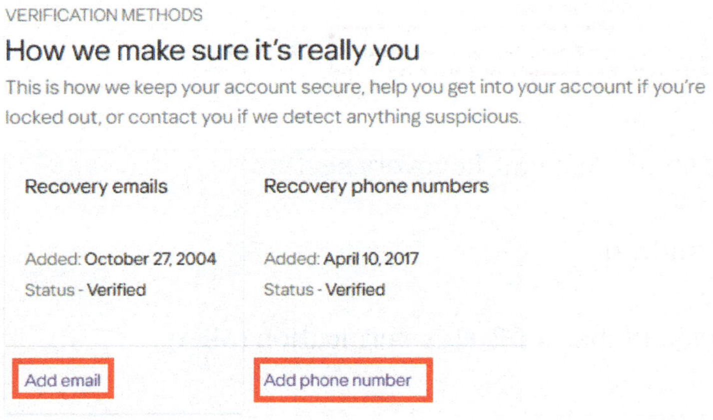

Add a recovery email address and phone number

Review Third-Party Account Access

Gmail

Log into your Google account

On the Security page, look for third-party apps and services

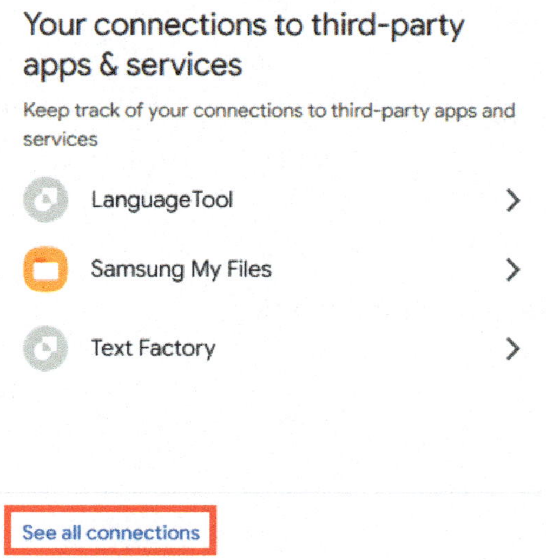

Click the "See all connection link"

Verify the apps you have allowed access

Outlook

Log into your Microsoft account: https://account.microsoft.com

Click the Privacy link in the main menu

Scroll down to App Acces

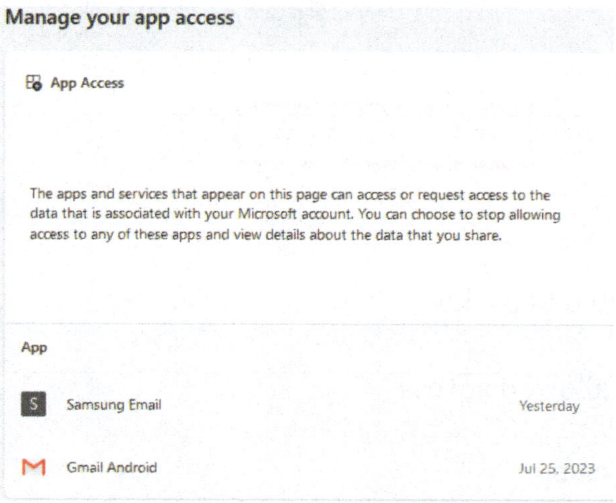

Verify the apps you have allowed access

Yahoo

Login to your Yahoo account: https://login.yahoo.com/myaccount

Click the Recent Activity link at the top of the page

Scroll down to the connected apps section

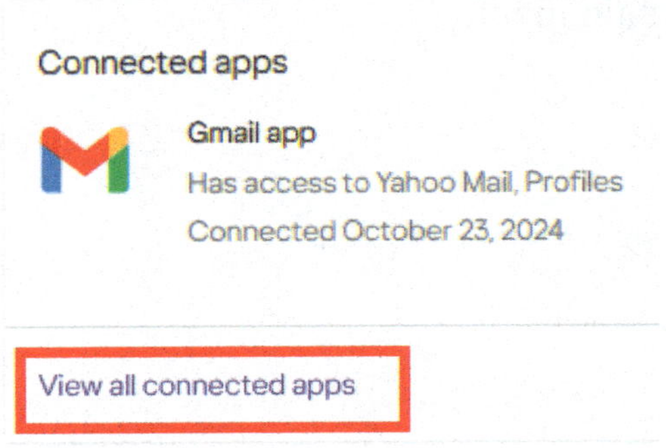

Click the View all connected apps link

Verify the apps you have allowed access

Key Indicators of Email Scams

Grammar Mistakes & Generic Greetings

Watch out for spelling or grammar mistakes in emails, as scammers often lack the professionalism of legitimate organizations. Scam emails often use generic greetings like "Dear User" or "Dear Customer" instead of addressing you by name. Legitimate organizations typically personalize their communications. Scam emails often create a sense of urgency, threatening consequences if you don't take immediate action. Be skeptical of emails that claim your account will be suspended, or you must urgently verify information.

Check the Sender's Email Address

Check the sender's email address. Scammers may use email addresses that resemble legitimate ones but have subtle misspellings or variations. Also, check the email headers to see if the sender's information has been spoofed. Scammers may manipulate the "From" address to appear legitimate. Scammers often impersonate well-known organizations or government agencies. Verify the legitimacy of the email by contacting the organization through official channels. Legitimate emails from companies often include a professional email signature. Scam emails may lack this or have an inconsistent signature.

Also, check for email authentication features like DKIM (DomainKeys Identified Mail) and SPF (Sender Policy Framework) to verify the email's legitimacy (Advanced).

How to Check Email Headers

Outlook Desktop

1. Double-click an email message to open it outside of the Reading Pane.

2. Click File > Properties.

3. Header information appears in the Internet headers box.

   Tip: You can highlight the information in that box, press Ctrl+C to copy, and paste it into Notepad or Word to see the entire header at once.

Outlook Webmail

1. Open the suspicious email message

2. Click the three dots ... at the top right-hand side of the window

3. Select View message details in the menu that appears

4. The message details will appear in a new window

   sTip: You can highlight the information in that box, press Ctrl+C to copy, and paste it into Notepad or Word to see the entire header.

Apple Mail

1. Go to the Mail app on your Mac.

2. Choose View > Message > All Headers.

3. To view fewer header fields again, choose View > Message > Default Headers.

Gmail

4. From a browser, open Gmail.

5. Open the email you want to check the headers for.

   Next to Reply ↰, click More ⋮ > Show original.

6. In a new window, the full header shows.

7. Click Copy to clipboard.

Verify Suspicious Requests and Unusual Behavior

Be cautious if the email's tone or style deviates from what you expect from the sender. This could indicate a scam. Be skeptical of emails offering incredible deals, prizes, or opportunities that seem too good to be true. Scammers use enticing offers to lure victims. If an email requests money, gift cards, or sensitive information urgently, verify it with the sender using a trusted communication method. Scammers may target you using information from data breaches, crafting phishing emails that seem authentic. Hover over any links in the email to preview the actual URL and determine its destination.

Avoiding Malicious Attachments

Do Not Open Unsolicited Attachments or Links

Avoid clicking on attachments or links from unknown or unexpected sources, as these may contain malware. Hover your mouse over any links in the email (including those in the body or the signature) to preview its destination. Make sure the link points to a legitimate domain and matches the domain of the sender.

Use Email Security Features & Enable 2FA

Enable and use email security features your email provider provides, such as antivirus, attachment scanners, spam filters, and sender authentication. Implement 2FA on your email accounts. Even if someone steals your credentials, this adds another layer of protection.

Update Software & Stay Informed

Keep your email client and operating system up to date. Software updates often include security patches that protect against vulnerabilities. Stay informed about common email phishing tactics. Educate yourself and your colleagues on recognizing and avoiding malicious email attachments. Be cautious of attachments with uncommon or executable file types. If you receive a password-protected attachment unexpectedly, verify the sender's identity before opening it. If you receive a suspicious email with a malicious attachment, report it to your ISP (Internet Service Provider) or email provider. This helps improve security measures for everyone.

Scan Attachments with Antivirus & Enable Preview Mode

Use reliable antivirus software to scan attachments before opening them, ensuring they're safe. If you receive an email with an unexpected attachment, refrain from opening it immediately. Verify the legitimacy of the email with the sender through a separate communication method.

Report suspected scam emails to your email provider. This helps improve their filters and protects others from falling victim to the same scams. Disable automatic image and content loading in your email client's preview mode. This prevents potentially harmful content from loading automatically.

How to Disable Automatic Image and Content Loading

Outlook

1. On the File tab, choose Options > Trust Center
2. Under Microsoft Outlook Trust Center, click Trust Center Settings.
3. Check the Don't download pictures automatically in HTML e-mail messages or RSS items check box.

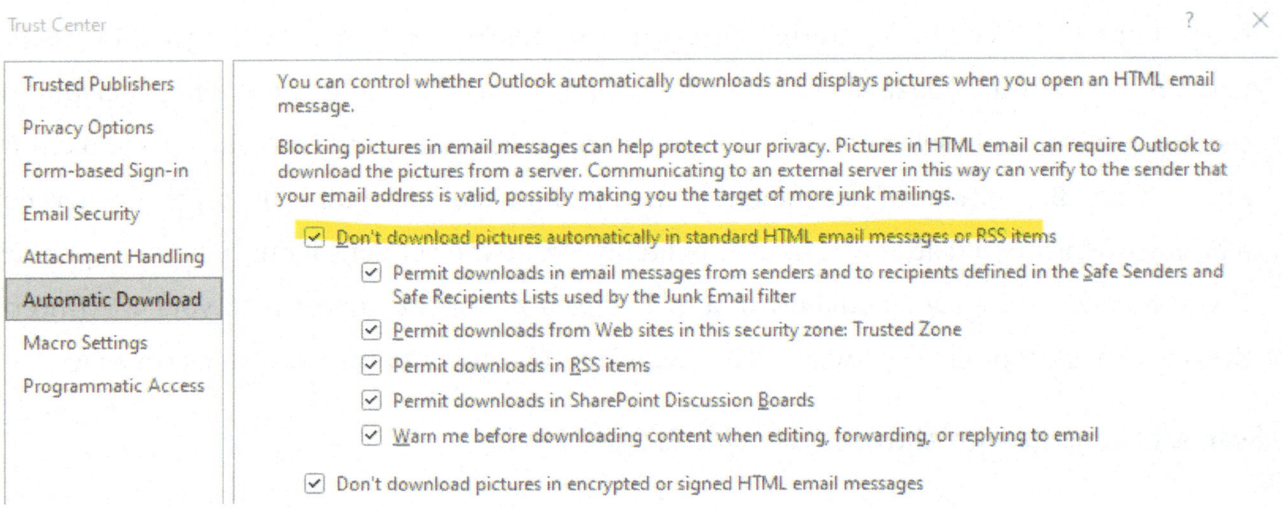

Apple Mail

1. Mail > Preferences > Viewing
2. Uncheck box marked > Load Remote Content in Messages

Gmail

1. Click the Settings Gear in the top right corner
2. Click the See All Settings link
3. Click the General Tab
4. Select the radio button marked > Ask Before Displaying External Images

Yahoo Mail

1. Settings > More Settings > Viewing email
2. Under Show images, Select the radio button marked “Ask before showing external images

Safe Email Practices

Safe email practices help us maintain online security and protect our personal information from threats like phishing, malware, and unauthorized access. Here are some recommended safe email practices:

Do not Click Objects in Unsolicited Emails

Avoid clicking links or attachments in unsolicited emails or messages. Do not open or download attachments in unsolicited emails or messages. Criminals use links and attachments to redirect users to malicious websites.

Rotate Strong Passwords

Create strong and unique passwords for your email accounts. Avoid using easily guessable information, and use a combination of letters, numbers, and symbols. Change your passwords regularly. Use a unique password for each of your accounts.

Encrypted Email Services

Consider using email services that offer end-to-end encryption for your messages. This ensures that even if intercepted, your emails remain private. Regularly review your email account activity for any unauthorized access or suspicious logins. Many email providers offer activity logs or alerts. Consider having separate email accounts for different purposes. For example, use one for personal communication and another for online registrations or subscriptions. Avoid accessing sensitive information or logging into your email accounts when connected to public Wi-Fi networks. Use a virtual private network (VPN) for added security.

Backup Important Messages

Regularly back up important emails to ensure you have a copy in case of accidental deletion or account compromise.

Incorporating these email practices enhances security. It will reduce the risk of falling victim to email-related threats. Stay vigilant and be cautious with your email interactions.

Chapter 8: Safe Browsing Habits

Aditsan loved the internet. He could spend hours playing games or looking up fun facts about animals and space. It felt like a never-ending world full of excitement and new things to discover. One day, he told his parents about a new friend he made online while gaming. "He's so cool!" Aditsan said. "We play together all the time."

His parents exchanged a glance. His dad gently asked, "Have you ever met this friend in person?"

Aditsan shook his head. "No, but we chat all the time. He seems really nice."

His mom smiled, but there was concern in her eyes. "Aditsan, we need to talk about something important. Not everyone online is who they say they are."

"What do you mean?"

His dad explained, "Sometimes people pretend to be someone they're not. They might act friendly, but they could have bad intentions. Just because you're talking to them in a game or on the internet doesn't mean they're really a friend."

His mom added, "That's why we need you to be careful. If you've never met someone in real life, it's hard to know if they're telling the truth about who they are. We don't want you to get hurt."

Aditsan felt a bit uneasy, realizing he hadn't thought about that before. He had always assumed everyone online was just like him—interested in fun and games. His parents told him about something called "catfishing," where people lie about who they are and how there are also bullies online. "It's not to scare you," his dad said. "We just want you to enjoy the internet safely."

After their talk, Aditsan understood why his parents were concerned. He promised to be more careful, and from then on, he always talked to them about his online experiences. He still loved playing games and browsing the web, but he felt better knowing how to stay safe.

Aditsan's experience is a reminder of how easy it is to overlook the potential dangers online. Understanding how to browse safely, recognize threats, and avoid risky interactions is important, especially when it comes to protecting personal information.

How to Recognize & Avoid Phishing Attacks

Recognizing phishing attacks is critical for online security. A phishing message is an email or text that appears to be from a legitimate source but is actually sent by a threat actor with malicious intent. Firstly, all organizations have their own email domain, so before opening an email, ensure the domain matches the sender's. For example, if the sender's address reads paypal@notice-access-273.com we can guarantee that it is not an email from Paypal. Even Google never sends a message to its customers from a support@gmail.com account.

Legitimate companies never request sensitive information via email...they know that email is not secure. Suppose an email is full of grammatical errors and questionable composition that should be an immediate red flag. Legitimate companies send well-composed, vetted messages before being sent to their customer base. A legitimate request will rarely force us to act hastily or under duress. If the email is an emergency or the message is written in a tone that causes anxiety, remember that scare tactics are a common phishing strategy.

Finally, if you receive an offer via email that sounds too good to be true...it probably is. Do your due diligence and check every email address and domain aspect. Never click a link in any email, especially one containing an offer that seems unbelievable.

Here are some tips to help you minimize the risk of falling victim to phishing attacks.

Use a Reputable Password Manager

Consider using a password manager to generate and store complex passwords securely. This helps reduce the risk of falling victim to phishing attacks that target password credentials. Examples include:

- Zoho Vault
- BitWarden

Regularly Check Financial Statements

Regularly review your bank and credit card statements for unauthorized or suspicious transactions. Report any discrepancies to your financial institution immediately.

Be Cautious on Social Media

Be mindful of the information you share on social media. Avoid sharing personal details that could be used in phishing attacks. Report phishing emails to your email provider or organization's IT department. This helps prevent others from falling victim to the same attacks.

Stay Informed

Stay informed about the latest phishing techniques and scams. Cybercriminals continually adapt their tactics, so staying updated is crucial. Phishing education is readily available and is being provided by reputable institutions:

https://www.cyber.gc.ca/en/guidance/dont-take-bait-recognize-and-avoid-phishing-attacks

https://www.cisa.gov/secure-our-world/teach-employees-avoid-phishing

https://www.microsoft.com/en-ca/security/business/threat-protection/attack-simulation-training

https://ironscales.com/guides/phishing-awareness-training/phishing-education-for-employees

https://www.knowbe4.com/

Adopting these practices can significantly reduce the risk of falling victim to phishing attacks and enhance your overall online security. Being vigilant and proactive in protecting your personal information is essential in the digital age.

How To Identify Suspicious Websites

Identifying suspicious websites is crucial for maintaining online security. Cybercriminals often create fake websites to trick users into providing sensitive information or downloading malware. Here are tips to help you identify suspicious websites.

Verify the Website's Reputation

If you are suspicious of a website, the first thing to do is a WHOIS lookup of the domain to see who owns it and when it was registered. You can do a WHOIS lookup at any site that sells domain names. The best site to find WHOIS information is:

https://who.is

The second thing is to check the domain's reputation. If you paste a domain name or URL into one of the sites below, they will return information about its reputation. The tools on these sites use an algorithm to provide a trust score.

Use online tools and services that provide website reputation scores. Some web browsers and security software also offer built-in tools to check the reputation of websites. I've included links to some reputation-checking sites below:

https://www.scamadviser.com

https://transparencyreport.google.com/safe-browsing/search?hl=en

https://www.virustotal.com/gui/home/url

https://global.sitesafety.trendmicro.com/

https://www.getsafeonline.org/checkawebsite/

https://www.urlvoid.com/

If the site checker returns a low trust score or unfavorable review regarding the site you are checking, it would be prudent to avoid future interactions.

Check the Website URL & Design

Examine the website's URL carefully. Look for misspellings, extra characters, or variations of legitimate domain names. Cybercriminals often create URLs that resemble well-known sites. Legitimate websites often have a professional design and layout. Be suspicious of websites with poor design, broken links, or inconsistent branding.

Look for "https//" and the Padlock Icon

Ensure the website uses a secure connection by checking for "https//" in the URL. Additionally, look for a padlock icon in the address bar . This indicates that the website encrypts data during transmission. Avoid interacting with pop-up windows on websites. Legitimate websites rarely use intrusive pop-ups.

Verify the Site's Contact Information & Purpose

Legitimate websites typically provide contact information, including a physical address and customer support details. If this information is missing or seems suspicious, exercise caution. Be cautious if the website's content or offerings seem too good to be true. Phishing websites often promise unrealistic deals or benefits to lure users.

Verify SSL Certificates

Check the website's SSL certificate by clicking on the padlock icon in the address bar. Ensure the certificate is valid and issued by a reputable Certificate Authority.

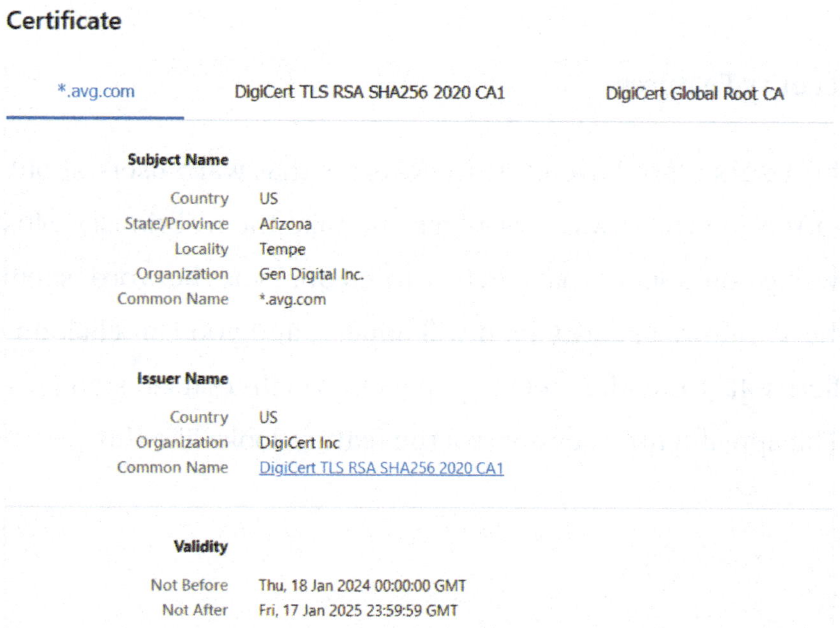

- The **Subject Name** section's common name must match the domain name in question.

- In the **Issuer** section, the organization listed should be a reputable certification authority.

- In the **Validity** section, the start and expiry dates should be valid.

Check for Trust Seals

Legitimate websites often display trust seals or logos from security organizations. Seals can be easily forged, so use additional verification methods. Trust seals should not be blindly trusted because, as mentioned, they can be forged. Verify with the Better Business Bureau or local Chamber of Commerce whenever possible.

Avoid Downloading Files from Untrusted Sites

Be cautious when downloading files from websites, especially if the source is unknown. Malicious websites may distribute malware through downloads. Check a site's reputation score prior to downloading. If the site's reputation score is a fail, do not download and seek an alternative.

Use Browser Security Features

Modern web browsers often have security features that warn users about potentially harmful websites. Pay attention to browser warnings and take them seriously. Most antivirus software has a safe browsing component that can be turned on. Type the word "security" in the Windows search box. The Windows security icon will appear, and you can click on it. Clicking the icon opens the Microsoft Defender security panel, which comes standard with all Windows installations. The app and browser control the feature looks like this:

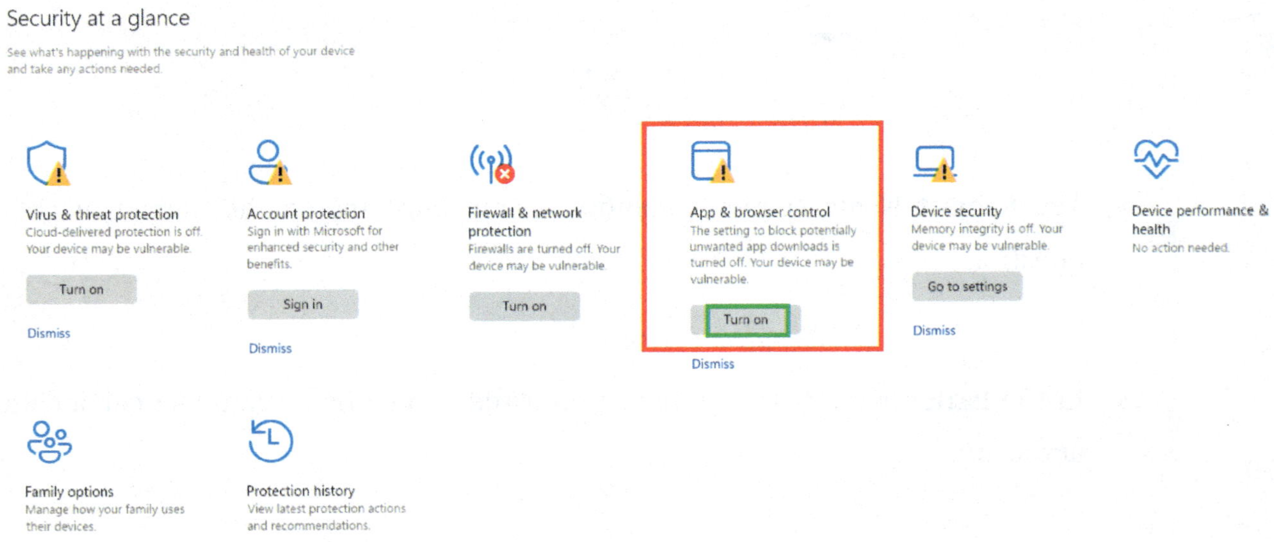

Verify Domain Age

Check the age of the website's domain using WHOIS lookup tools. New or recently registered domains may be more suspicious. Go to who.is in your web browser. Enter the domain name in the lookup tool.

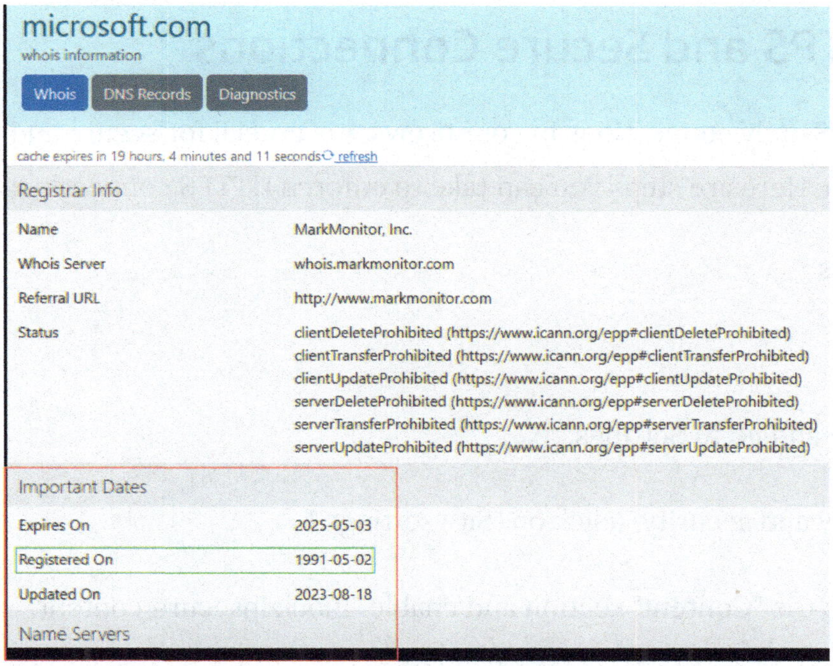

Verify Social Media Presence

Check if the website has an official and active presence on social media. Legitimate businesses often maintain social media profiles on LinkedIn, Facebook, etc. Legitimate websites typically have clear and comprehensive privacy policies. Be wary if a website lacks a privacy policy or if the policy seems unclear or suspicious.

Use Web Browser Extensions

Consider using browser extensions or tools that help identify and block malicious websites. These tools can provide an additional layer of protection. Remember that phishing attacks can take various forms, including emails, text messages, phone calls, or even messages on social media. Always exercise caution and verify the legitimacy of communications, especially when dealing with sensitive information or unexpected requests. If in doubt, contact the supposed sender through official channels before taking any action. Staying vigilant and using a combination of the above tips will help you identify and avoid suspicious websites, reducing the risk of falling victim to online scams or malware. Learn about phishing and educate others in your family or community. Training and awareness are effective tools for preventing phishing attacks.

Using HTTPS and Secure Connections

Ensuring HTTPS-only connections in your browser is crucial for secure and encrypted website communication. Here are steps you can take to enforce HTTPS connections:

Browser Settings

Google Chrome

Open Chrome and go to Settings.

Under "Privacy and security," click on "Site settings."

Scroll down to the "Content" section and enable "Block insecure content."

Mozilla Firefox

Open Firefox and go to Preferences. Navigate to the "Privacy & Security" section.

Scroll down to the "Security" section and check the box for "Block dangerous and deceptive content."

Use the "HTTPS Only" Mode

Some browsers have introduced a dedicated "HTTPS Only" mode. Enabling this mode ensures that the browser connects to websites over HTTPS whenever possible. Here's how to enable it in some popular browsers

Google Chrome

Enabled by default

Open Chrome and go to Settings.

Under "Privacy and security," click on "Security." Enable the "HTTPS only" mode.

Mozilla Firefox

Open Firefox and go to Preferences. Navigate to the "Privacy & Security" section.

Scroll down to the "HTTPS-Only Mode" and enable it.

Microsoft Edge

1. Open Microsoft Edge Settings

    - Launch Microsoft Edge
    - Click on the three-dot menu (...) in the top-right corner
    - Select Settings from the dropdown menu.

2. Navigate to Privacy, Search, and Services

    - In the left-hand sidebar, click on Privacy, search, and services.

3. Scroll to Security

    - Scroll down to the Security section.

4. Enable "Automatically switch to more secure connections with Automatic HTTPS."

    - Under the Security section,
    - you will see an option labeled "Automatically switch to more secure connections with Automatic HTTPS."
    - Turn on this option by toggling the switch to On.

5. Choose the HTTPS-Only Mode Setting. After enabling, you will see two options:

1. "Upgrade connections to HTTPS only when websites are likely to support it": This option is a more lenient approach where Edge will attempt to upgrade to HTTPS but will fall back to HTTP if the HTTPS version isn't available.

2. "Always switch from HTTP to HTTPS (connection errors might occur more often)": This is the stricter option that will always attempt to use HTTPS, even if it might cause connection errors on websites that don't support HTTPS.

    - Select the one that best suits your needs.

6. Restart Edge (if necessary)

Although not always required, it's a good practice to restart your browser to ensure that the settings take effect. Once this setting is enabled, Edge will try to use HTTPS for all connections, improving your browsing security.

HSTS (HTTP Strict Transport Security)

HSTS is a web security policy mechanism that helps protect websites against man-in-the-middle attacks such as protocol downgrade attacks and cookie hijacking. Most modern browsers support HSTS. Ensure that it is enabled by default, and you can check by typing 'chrome//net-internals/#hsts' in the Chrome address bar.

Configure Browser Security Settings

Review and configure your browser's security settings to prioritize HTTPS connections. Check for settings related to security, privacy, and content blocking. There are several quick steps you can take to make your browsing experience more secure. To start, block browser cookies, disable saved passwords, install strong antivirus software, use a VPN, disable autofill, and update your browser.

Bing

- Click the three dots in the top right-hand side of the browser window
- Click Settings

In the window that appears, turn on all the security features. For children and the elderly, you may opt for the Strict rather than Balanced option selected in the image.

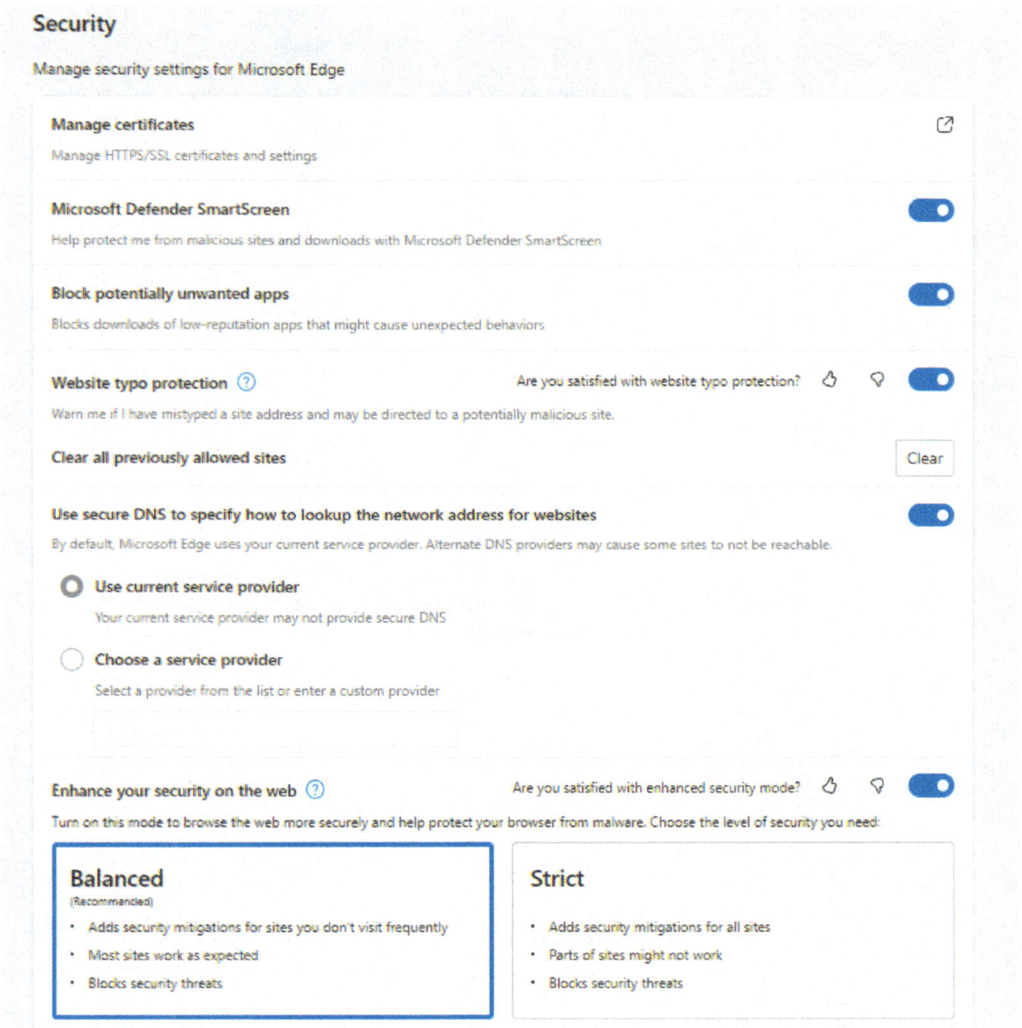

Chrome

- Click the three dots in the top right-hand side of the browser window
- Click Settings
- Click Privacy and Security in the main menu

- Select the Safe Browsing option
- In the Advanced section, turn on always secure connections and secure DNS

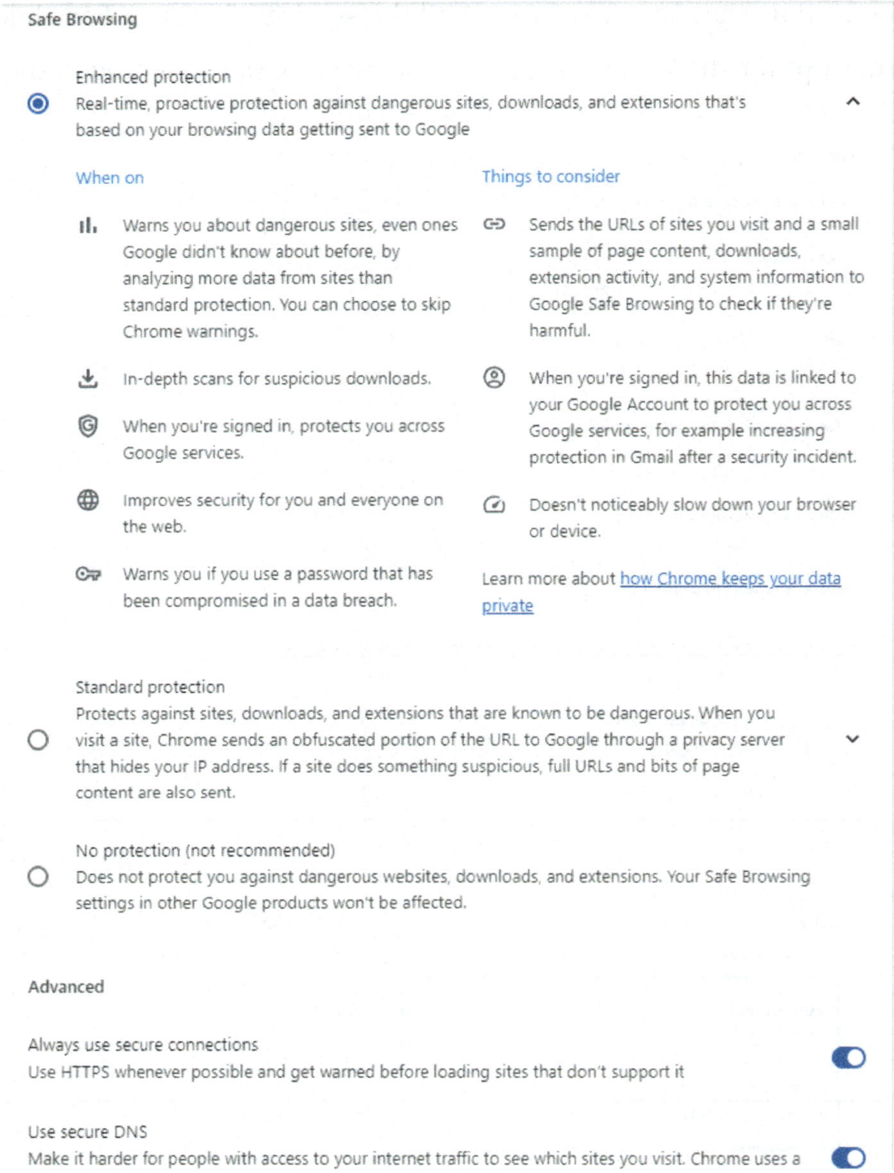

Firefox

- Click the three horizontal lines on the top right-hand side of the browser window.
- Click Setting in the menu that appears.

- Click Privacy and Security in the main menu.

- Select the radio button Strict option.

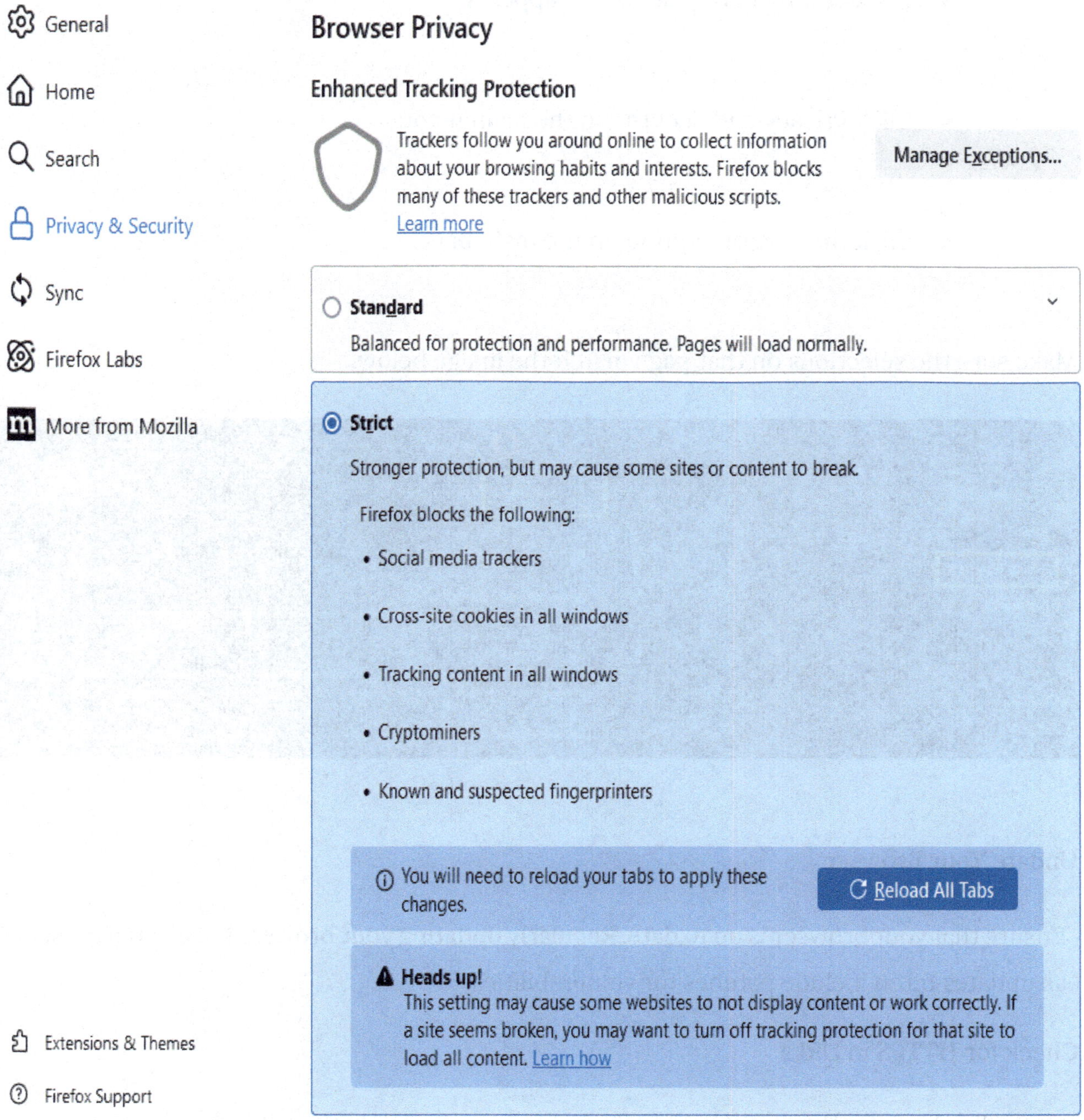

Opera

- Click the three horizontal lines in the top right-hand side of the browser window.
- Click Setting in the menu that appears.
- Click Privacy and Security in the main menu.
- Click the security option on the main page.

Make sure the selections on that page match the image below:

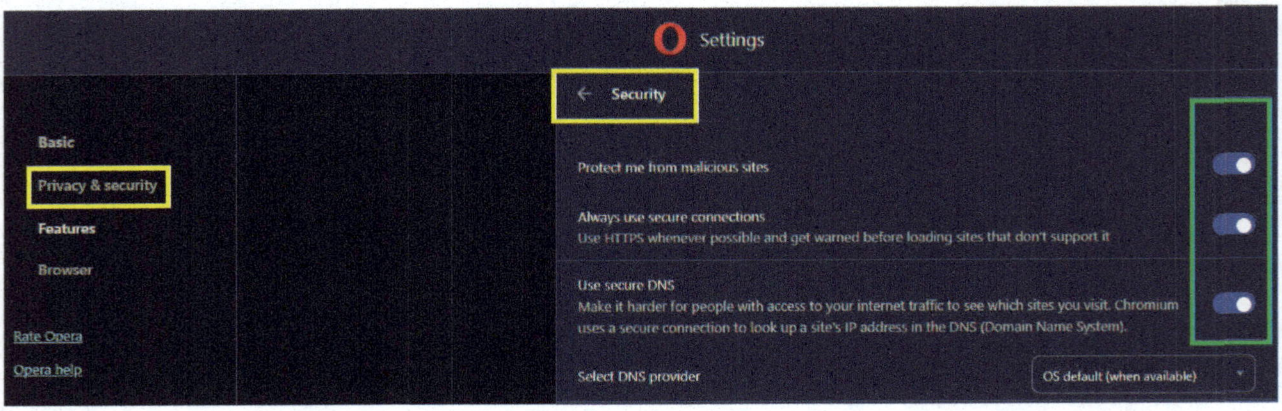

Update Your Browser

Ensure that your browser is up to date. Regularly updating your browser is essential for security, as updates often include patches for vulnerabilities.

Check for HTTPS in URLs

Manually check for "https//" in the URL before entering sensitive information. Be cautious if a website doesn't use HTTPS, especially for login pages or when submitting personal details.

Secure Browsers

Some browsers, such as Brave, focus on privacy and security by default. Consider using browsers that prioritize these features such as:

- Brave: https://brave.com/download/ - A secure alternative to Chrome
- DuckDuckGo: https://duckduckgo.com
- Tor: https://www.torproject.org/download/
- Mullvad: https://mullvad.net/en/
- Firefox: https://www.mozilla.org/en-US/firefox/new/
- Opera: https://opera.com

Honorable Mention

- Vivaldi: https://vivaldi.com
- Epic: https://epicbrowser.com
- Waterfox: https://www.waterfox.net
- Microsoft Edge: https://www.microsoft.com/en-us/edge/?form=MA13FJ

Use a Secure Connection (VPN)

This author recommends using a VPN application installed on the local computer, which protects all of the activity on your device, including browsing using any browser.

While not directly related to enforcing HTTPS, using a Virtual Private Network (VPN) can add an extra layer of security by encrypting your internet connection. It ensures that your data remains secure, even when connected to public Wi-Fi networks. You will be able to find a free VPN browser extension for every single browser. These can be found in the following places:

- Chrome Webstore
- Apple App Store
- Firefox Extension
- Microsoft Edge AddOns

Enforcing HTTPS connections protects your data while it is in flight and helps maintain online security. Following these steps and using secure browsing practices can minimize the risk of falling victim to various online threats.

Chapter 9: Home Network Security

Evan had always thought he was tech-savvy enough to handle setting up his home Wi-Fi. But recently, something had been bothering him. His network felt vulnerable, especially with so many devices connected—his kids' tablets, the smart TV, and even the fridge. He had heard stories about hackers accessing home networks through unsecured devices, which made him uneasy.

One afternoon at work, he decided to ask for advice while grabbing a coffee. He spotted Josh, a friend from the IT department, and approached him. "Hey Josh," Evan started, "I've been thinking a lot about my home network. We have all these smart devices connected, and I'm not sure I've done enough to keep it secure. Any chance you could help me set things up properly?"

Josh smiled. "You're not alone, man. A lot of people don't realize how exposed their home networks can be, especially with all the smart gadgets we use nowadays. But don't worry—there are some simple steps you can take to lock things down."

That evening, Josh came over with his laptop in hand. As they sat down by Evan's router, Josh explained everything straightforwardly. "First things first, we need to change your router's default username and password. Most people don't realize these factory settings are common knowledge, and attackers can easily find them online."

Evan nodded, following Josh's guidance as they logged into the router's control panel. "Let's change your Wi-Fi password while we're here," Josh continued. "Make sure it's strong, at least 16 characters, using a mix of letters, numbers, and symbols. Also, it's a good idea to change the default network name. Right now, your SSID broadcasts your router's brand, making it easier for hackers to figure out what kind of security they're dealing with."

As they worked, Evan felt a growing sense of relief. These small changes were making a big difference. But he had one more concern. "What about all these devices we have connected to my kids' tablets, the smart TV, even the fridge? Is there a way to make sure they're not a weak spot?"

Josh nodded. "Definitely. One of the best things you can do is create separate networks for your family's devices and your smart home gadgets. Most modern routers let you set up a guest network—use that for any visitors or devices like your TV and fridge. These smart devices don't have the same security as your phone or laptop, so keeping them on a different network protects your main one."

By the end of the evening, Evan had a completely restructured home network. It felt good knowing that his family's devices were safer and that he had taken steps to protect his personal information.

Securing Wi-Fi Networks

Securing your home Wi-Fi network doesn't have to be complicated. Like Evan, you don't need to be an expert, but making a few simple changes can make all the difference in protecting your network from unauthorized access, cyber threats, and privacy breaches. Let's walk through some of the key steps you can take to improve your home Wi-Fi security.

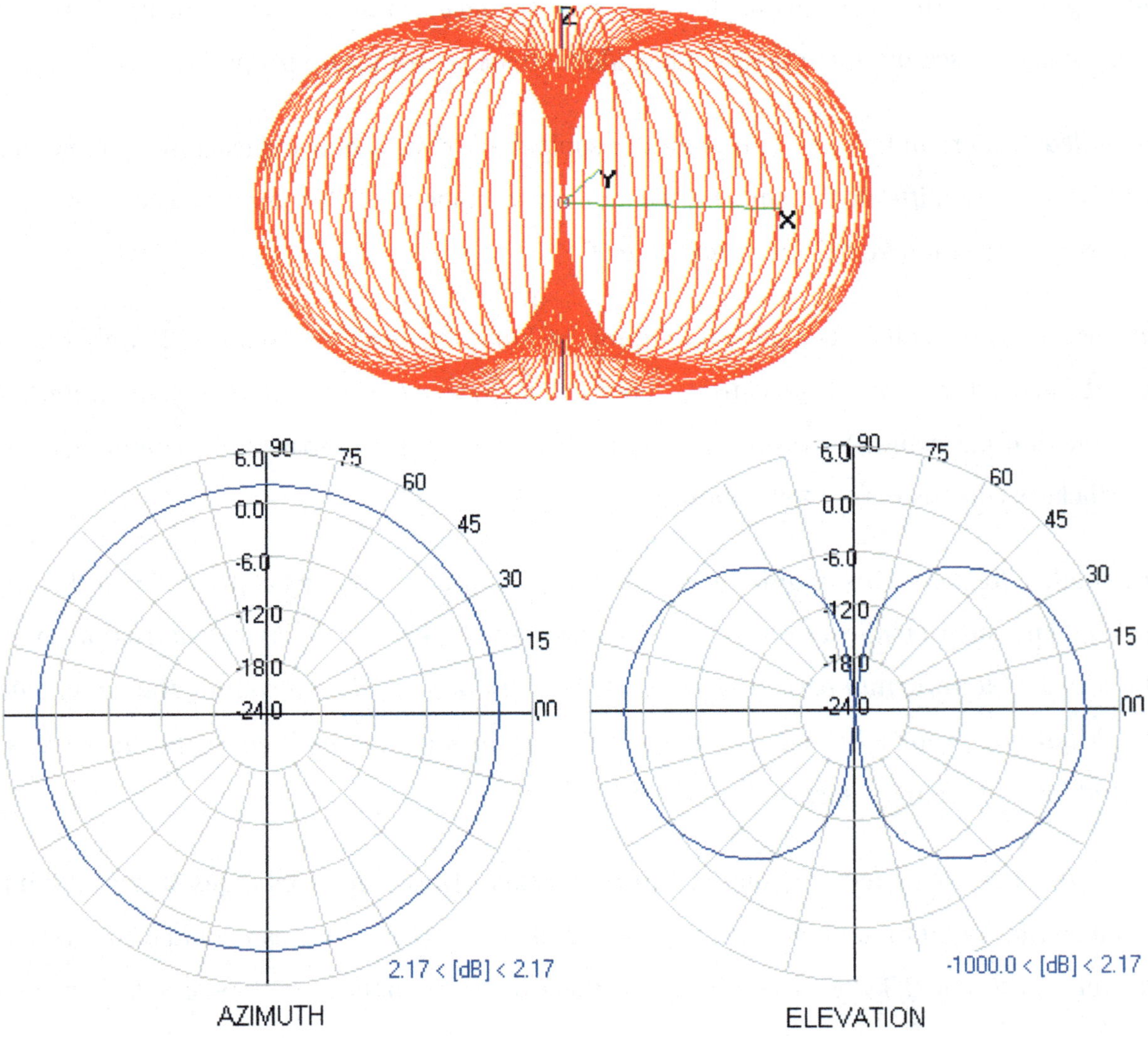

Figure 1: Wireless Network Signal Pattern

The red diagram in the figure shows that most home wireless networks radiate a 3-dimensional signal that is in the shape of a donut. The antenna is in the center of the donut on the z-axis.

Change Default Router Credentials

Change the default username and password for your router's administrative interface. Default credentials are often known to attackers, making it easier for them to gain unauthorized access. Typical steps to access your router and do this on a Windows network are:

- Open Windows Command Prompt
- Type in "ipconfig"
- Locate your default gateway in the output.

```
Wireless LAN adapter Wi-Fi:

   Connection-specific DNS Suffix  . : Home
   IPv4 Address. . . . . . . . . . . : 192.168.1.2
   Subnet Mask . . . . . . . . . . . : 255.255.255.0
   Default Gateway . . . . . . . . . : 192.168.1.1
```

- Type the IP Address of the default gateway into a browser (i.e., Chrome)
- Enter your router's login credentials.
- Open WiFi settings
- Change the default admin username.

To find the default gateway on a MAC device, open the terminal and type "route get default." On Linux devices, the same steps can be followed by opening a terminal and typing "ifconfig" or "ip route."

Enable Your Router's Firewall

Enable the built-in firewall on your router to filter incoming and outgoing traffic. This adds an extra layer of protection against potential cyber threats. Most home routers will have a menu that has 3 main sections:

- Basic Configuration
- Advanced configuration
- Logs

Generally, settings related to the router's firewall features will be in the Advanced Configuration >> Security or WAN (Wide Area Network) section of the menu. Here, you can also review and configure the firewall settings, including rules to block unwanted incoming traffic and allow only necessary.

Use a Strong Network Administrator Password

Set a strong password for accessing the router's administrative settings. This password is different from your Wi-Fi password and adds an extra layer of security. Set up 2FA admin access if your router supports it.

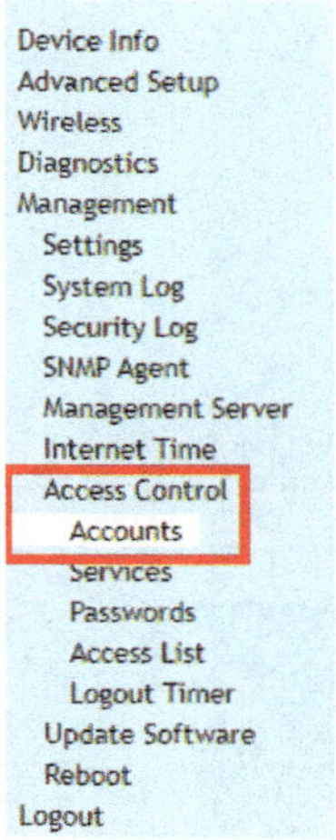

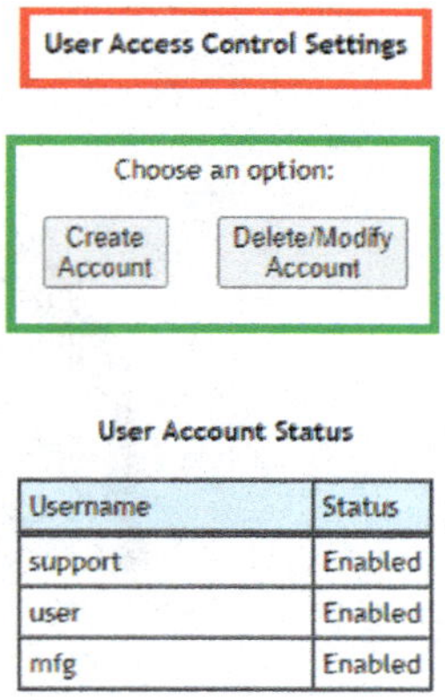

Regularly Update Router Login Credentials

Periodically update the login credentials for accessing the router's administrative settings. This helps prevent unauthorized access over time. Disable the default administrative user that came with the router and create a new administrative user with an obscure name.

Admin Username: Jasper

Password: U*@L;P"5my+rC-:{(cj39Y

Before disabling the default, the administrator logs out and logs in to test the new admin user that you created. Once the new user has been tested, disable the default admin that came with the router.

Physically Position Router Strategically

Place your router in a central location in your home to reduce the likelihood of signal leakage outside your premises. This minimizes the chances of unauthorized users connecting to your network. The router should be placed at a high elevation, away from external walls and windows.

Strong Wi-Fi Password & WPA2/3 Encryption

Set a strong and unique password for your Wi-Fi network. Combine upper and lowercase letters, numbers, and symbols to create a robust passphrase. Avoid using easily guessable information. Use the latest encryption standard available for Wi-Fi, such as WPA3. This ensures a more secure connection between your devices and the router. If WPA3 is not available, use WPA2 as a minimum.

Change Default SSID (Network Name)

Default SSID names tend to announce the make and model of your WiFi Router or Access Point (AP). Avoid giving away free information about your network hardware. Change the default network name (SSID) to something unique. Avoid using personal information that could be easily associated with you.

Turn Off SSID Broadcast

Disable SSID broadcast if your router allows it. This does not provide huge security benefits, but I believe that every little bit counts. If it's easy, do it. This prevents your Wi-Fi network's name from being visible to devices searching for available networks.

Minimize Vulnerabilities in Router Configuration

Change the default IP address range of your router to a less common one. This helps deter automated attacks that target routers with default settings. Additionally, disable any unnecessary features or services on your router that you're not using. This reduces the potential attack surface.

Update Router Firmware

Regularly check for and install firmware updates provided by the router manufacturer. These updates often include security patches and improvements. This can be done in the Router Management section of the menu. There will usually be an Update Software page, as depicted below.

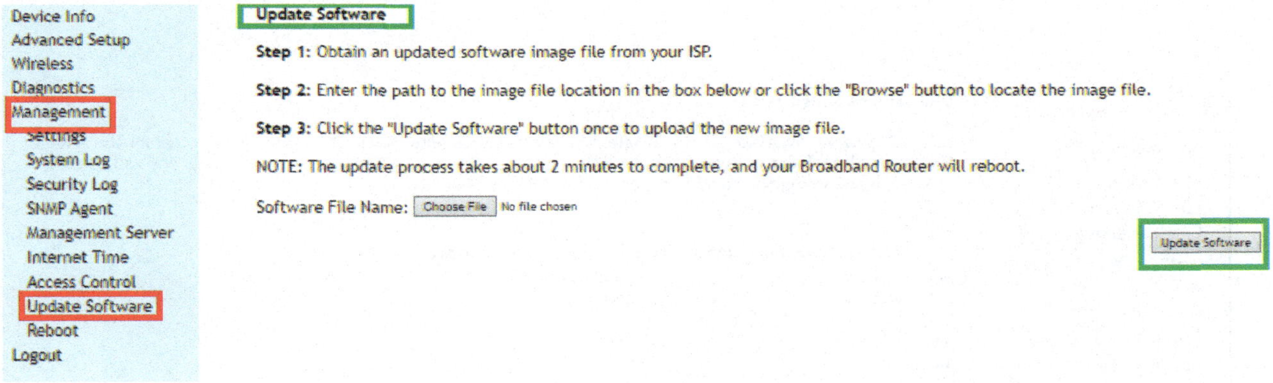

Monitor Connected Devices

Regularly check the list of connected devices on your router's admin interface. If you notice any unfamiliar devices, investigate and take appropriate action. You can do this on the DHCP-connected devices page in real-time:

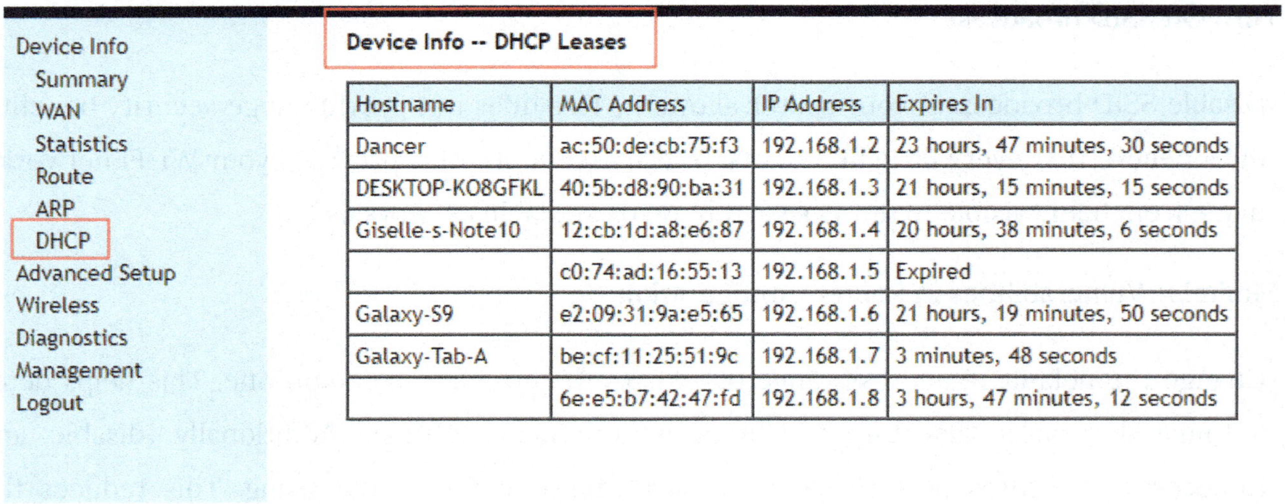

Secure DNS Settings

Ensure that your router is using secure DNS settings. You can manually configure DNS servers or use those provided by your Internet Service Provider (ISP). You can use your ISP DNS servers or choose to use static secure DNS servers offered by Cisco Umbrella (Formerly OpenDNS), Cloudflare, Comodo, etc. An example of secure DNS server IP addresses that can be used to configure the Static DNS settings are below.

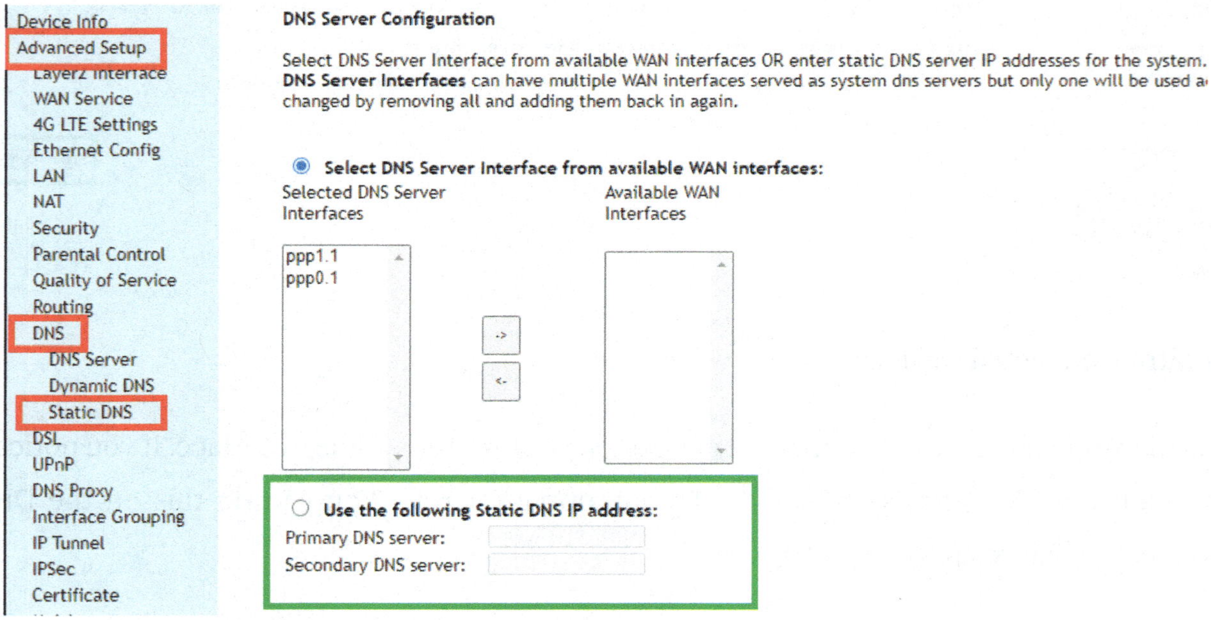

Comodo

https://help.comodo.com/topic-72-1-766-9103-.html

8.26.56.26

8.20.247.20

Cloudflare

https://developers.cloudflare.com/1.1.1.1/setup/

1.1.1.1

1.0.0.1

OpenDNS

https://www.opendns.com/setupguide/

208.67.222.222

208.67.220.220

Secure Remote Access

If you need remote access to your home network, use secure methods such as Virtual Private Network (VPN) connections. Avoid using insecure protocols like Remote Desktop Protocol (RDP) directly over the internet. Most people will not require this feature, so it should be disabled. Only allow your router to be accessed from the LAN (Local Area Network).

Separate Guest Network

If your router supports it, set up a separate guest network for visitors. This network should have a different password and no access to your primary network. This is an option for families that have a lot of visitors that they do not want on the family network. The main security reason for a guest network at home is to separate your IOT devices from the family LAN (Local Area Network).

Implement MAC Address Filtering

Use MAC address filtering to only allow specific devices to connect to your Wi-Fi network. This adds an extra layer of control over authorized devices. This level of security will physically lock down your network, only allowing devices on the Allow list to have access.

Change Default IP Address Range

Change the default IP address range of your router to a less common one. This helps deter automated attacks that target routers with default settings. This is a lot easier than it sounds.

- First, log into your WiFi Router.
- Click Settings from the main navigation menu
- Click Local Network settings
- There should be a link or button to edit the router settings
- Typical router address is 192.168.1.1, as in the image below
- Change the 3rd digit (known as the 3rd octet) to a number between 20 - 200
- Change the 3rd digit in the DHCP Server start IP address to match
- Save the settings

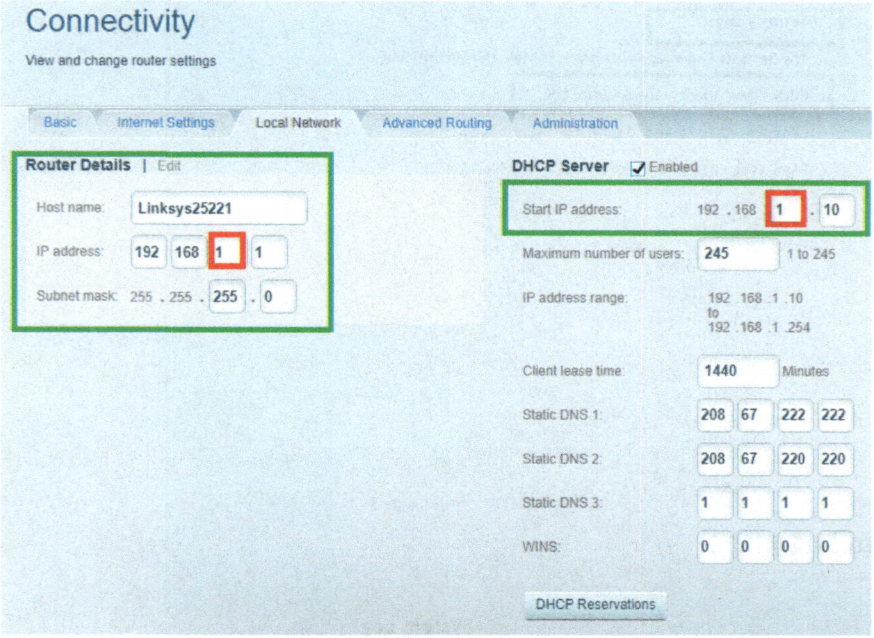

Secure Devices Connected to Wi-Fi

Ensure that devices connected to your Wi-Fi network have up-to-date security software. This includes antivirus and anti-malware protection if they are PCs, laptops, or handheld mobile devices. If they are IOT or network devices, ensure that the firmware is up to date. Keep the IOT and guest devices on a segregated network (more about this later). Stress the importance of Wi-Fi security and make sure everyone understands the risks of playing fast and loose on the WiFi network.

Turn on and Check Router Logs

Periodically review the router logs to identify any suspicious activity. Unusual log entries may indicate a security issue. When you log into your router, you will find logs in the management or troubleshooting section of the menu.

In the sample image below, the system and security logs for this router are in the management section.

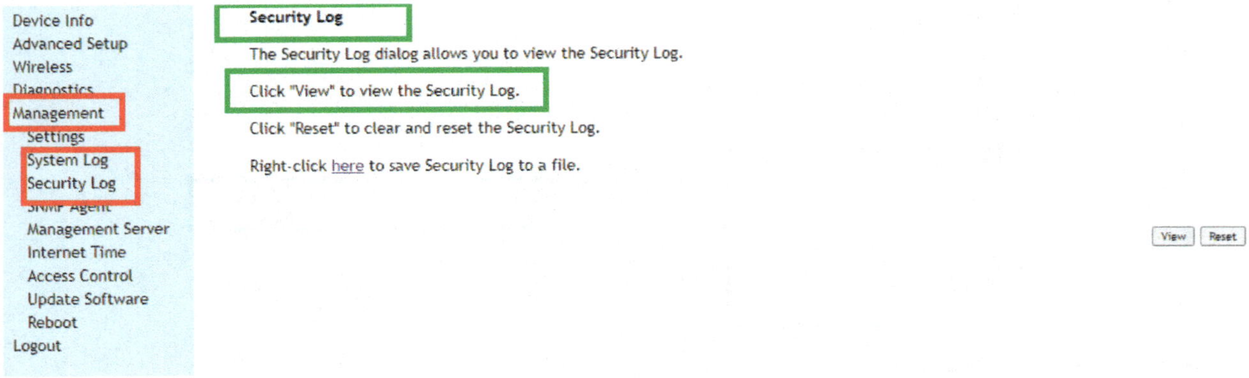

Sample System Log

System Log

Date/Time	Facility	Severity	Message
Jan 1 00:01:02	daemon	crit	syslog: PPP server detected.
Jan 1 00:01:02	daemon	crit	syslog: PPP session 271 established.
Jan 1 00:01:05	daemon	crit	syslog: PPP LCP UP.
Jan 1 00:01:05	daemon	crit	syslog: Received valid IP address from server. Connection UP.
Sep 22 11:02:18	daemon	err	syslog: CAH:Pha Tick delta 1727002868 > max 5
Sep 22 11:02:57	kern	crit	kernel: eth1 (Ext switch port: 1) (Logical Port: 9) Link UP 1000 mbps full duplex
Sep 22 11:02:57	kern	crit	kernel: eth2 (Ext switch port: 2) (Logical Port: 10) Link UP 1000 mbps full duplex
Sep 22 11:03:05	kern	crit	kernel: eth1 (Ext switch port: 1) (Logical Port: 9) Link DOWN.
Sep 22 11:03:05	kern	crit	kernel: eth2 (Ext switch port: 2) (Logical Port: 10) Link DOWN.
Sep 22 11:03:08	kern	crit	kernel: eth1 (Ext switch port: 1) (Logical Port: 9) Link UP 1000 mbps full duplex
Sep 22 11:03:08	kern	crit	kernel: eth2 (Ext switch port: 2) (Logical Port: 10) Link UP 1000 mbps full duplex
Sep 22 11:18:31	kern	crit	kernel: eth1 (Ext switch port: 1) (Logical Port: 9) Link DOWN.
Sep 22 11:18:32	kern	crit	kernel: eth2 (Ext switch port: 2) (Logical Port: 10) Link DOWN.
Sep 22 11:18:35	kern	crit	kernel: eth1 (Ext switch port: 1) (Logical Port: 9) Link UP 1000 mbps full duplex
Sep 22 11:18:36	kern	crit	kernel: eth2 (Ext switch port: 2) (Logical Port: 10) Link UP 1000 mbps full duplex
Sep 22 11:18:43	kern	crit	kernel: eth1 (Ext switch port: 1) (Logical Port: 9) Link DOWN.
Sep 22 11:18:43	kern	crit	kernel: eth2 (Ext switch port: 2) (Logical Port: 10) Link DOWN.
Sep 22 11:18:46	kern	crit	kernel: eth1 (Ext switch port: 1) (Logical Port: 9) Link UP 1000 mbps full duplex
Sep 22 11:18:46	kern	crit	kernel: eth2 (Ext switch port: 2) (Logical Port: 10) Link UP 1000 mbps full duplex
Sep 22 11:19:24	kern	crit	kernel: eth1 (Ext switch port: 1) (Logical Port: 9) Link DOWN.
Sep 22 11:19:24	kern	crit	kernel: eth2 (Ext switch port: 2) (Logical Port: 10) Link DOWN.
Sep 22 11:19:28	kern	crit	kernel: eth1 (Ext switch port: 1) (Logical Port: 9) Link UP 1000 mbps full duplex
Sep 22 11:19:28	kern	crit	kernel: eth2 (Ext switch port: 2) (Logical Port: 10) Link UP 1000 mbps full duplex
Sep 22 11:19:35	kern	crit	kernel: eth1 (Ext switch port: 1) (Logical Port: 9) Link DOWN.
Sep 22 11:19:35	kern	crit	kernel: eth2 (Ext switch port: 2) (Logical Port: 10) Link DOWN.
Sep 22 11:19:39	kern	crit	kernel: eth1 (Ext switch port: 1) (Logical Port: 9) Link UP 1000 mbps full duplex
Sep 22 11:19:39	kern	crit	kernel: eth2 (Ext switch port: 2) (Logical Port: 10) Link UP 1000 mbps full duplex

Refresh Close

Sample Security Log

Security Log

Message
2024-09-24T11:23:04+00:00 ID 3: Authorized login success::U admin:N HTTP:P 80:IP 192.168.1.3
2024-09-24T11:23:06+00:00 ID 3: Authorized login success::U admin:N HTTP:P 80:IP 192.168.1.3
2024-09-24T11:26:38+00:00 ID 3: Authorized login success::U admin:N SSHD:P 22:IP 192.168.1.3
2024-09-24T11:33:35+00:00 ID 3: Authorized login success::U admin:N HTTP:P 80:IP 192.168.1.3
2024-09-24T11:33:37+00:00 ID 3: Authorized login success::U admin:N HTTP:P 80:IP 192.168.1.3

Refresh Close

Separate Guest Network & Monitor Usage

Securing your home Wi-Fi guest network is important to protect your main network and personal devices while still providing internet access for visitors. Here are steps to secure your home Wi-Fi guest network. Many routers support the creation of a separate guest network. Set up a dedicated SSID and password specifically for guest use. This network should be isolated from your main network.

We enable Guest networks in the router's wireless settings. The figure that follows gives a generic example of how to enable a guest network. Most routers will have these features, but it may look different in your router interface. You will note in the figure that I have enabled the following features on the Guest network:

- Client Isolation
- Max No. of Clients

Client isolation or network isolation is an important security feature that segments the network. It blocks devices on your guest wifi network from communicating with computers on your home network.

Use Strong Guest Wi-Fi Password & WPA3 Encryption

Set a strong and unique password for the guest network. Ensure it is different from the password used for your main network. Use a combination of letters, numbers, and symbols. If your router supports it, use the latest encryption standard, such as WPA3, for the guest network. If not, use WPA2. Avoid using WEP, as it is less secure.

Create VLANs & Enable Network Isolation

If your router supports it, enable network isolation or client isolation for the guest network. This prevents devices connected to the guest network from communicating with each other. Configure the guest network to provide internet access only and restrict access to other devices on the network. If your router supports Virtual LANs (VLANs), configure a VLAN for the guest network. This provides network segmentation so that guests will not be able to access shared files or printers on your main network.

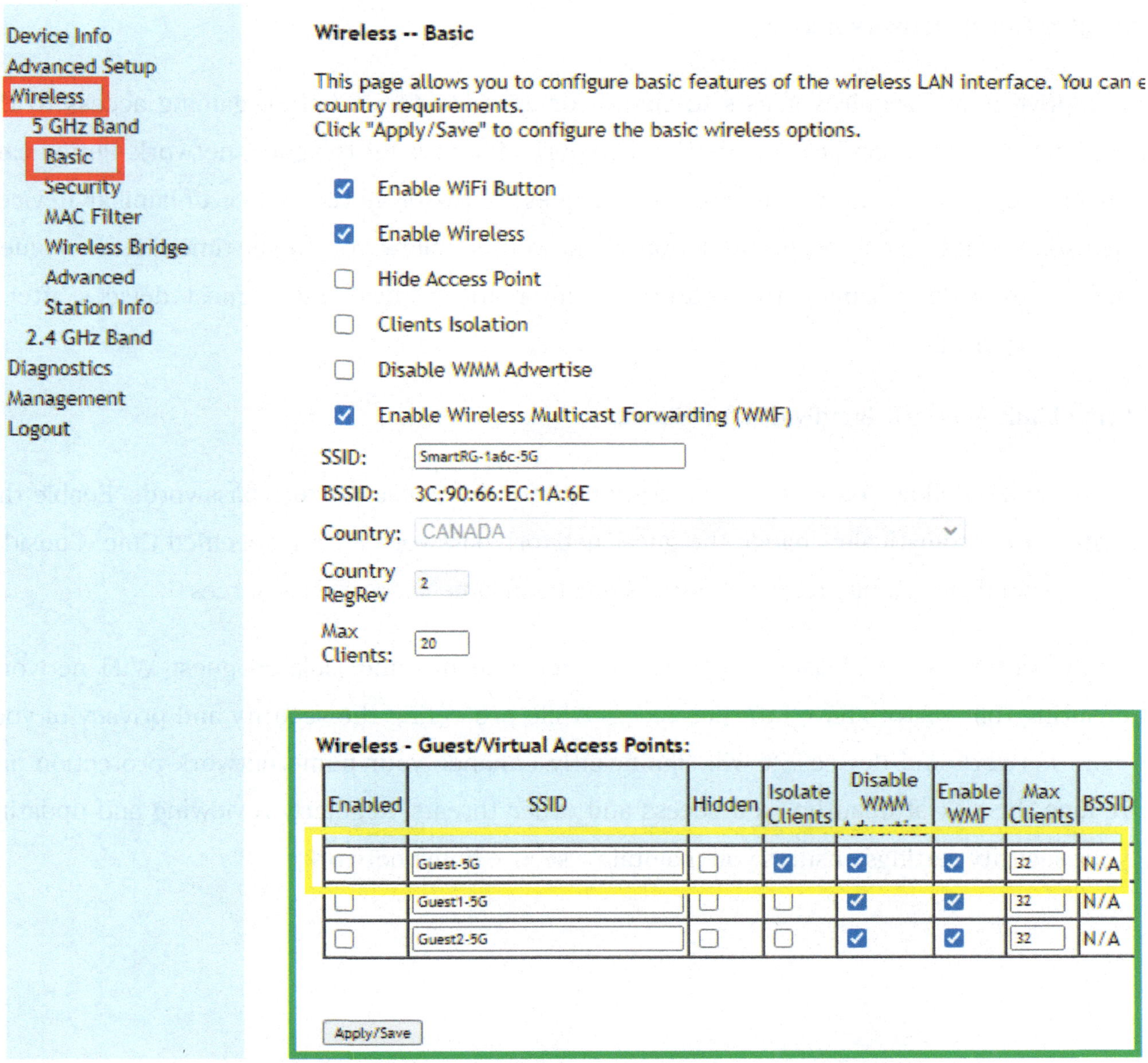
Device Info
Advanced Setup
Wireless
5 GHz Band
Basic
Security
MAC Filter
Wireless Bridge
Advanced
Station Info
2.4 GHz Band
Diagnostics
Management
Logout
Wireless -- Basic
This page allows you to configure basic features of the wireless LAN interface. You can
country requirements.
Click "Apply/Save" to configure the basic wireless options.
Enable WiFi Button
Enable Wireless
Hide Access Point
Clients Isolation
Disable WMM Advertise
Enable Wireless Multicast Forwarding (WMF)
SSID:
SmartRG-1a6c-5G
BSSID:
3C:90:66:EC:1A:6E
Country:
CANADA
Country RegRev
2
Max Clients:
20
Wireless - Guest/Virtual Access Points:
Enabled
SSID
Hidden
Isolate Clients
Disable WMM
Enable WMF
Max Clients
BSSID
Guest-5G
32
N/A
Guest1-5G
32
N/A
Guest2-5G
32
N/A
Apply/Save

Monitor Guest Network Activity

A captive portal requires guests to sign in or agree to terms before gaining access to the internet. Some routers have built-in captive portal features for the guest network. Periodically check the list of devices connected to the guest network. If you notice unfamiliar devices, investigate and take appropriate action. Some routers allow you to set time limits for guest access. Consider enabling this feature to automatically disconnect guest devices after a specified period.

Time Limit Access & Bandwidth for Guests

Some routers allow you to set an expiration period for guest network passwords. Enable this feature to automatically change the guest network password after a specified time. Consider setting bandwidth limits to ensure guests don't consume excessive resources.

Implementing these measures, you can create a secure and isolated guest WiFi network, ensuring that visitors have internet access while protecting the security and privacy of your main network and devices. It will significantly enhance your home network protection and reduce the risk of unauthorized access and cyber threats. Regularly reviewing and updating your security settings ensures you maintain a secure home network.

Chapter 10: Securing Your Devices

Shannon loved the convenience of shopping and banking on her mobile phone. With just a few taps, she could order groceries, pay bills, or transfer money to friends. However, lately, she felt a nagging worry about doing these transactions over public Wi-Fi. She often used the café down the street or the library's internet to save on data, never thinking twice about the potential risks.

One afternoon, while scrolling through social media, she stumbled upon a post from a friend who had recently discovered that her Amazon account had been hacked. It shocked Shannon to learn that the hackers had gained access through her friend's unprotected use of public Wi-Fi. This revelation hit close to home, igniting a sense of urgency within her.

Determined to take action, Shannon gathered her family in the living room that evening. She began by sharing her concerns about using public networks for financial transactions without a Virtual Private Network (VPN).

"It's a significant risk," she explained, her voice steady but firm. "We can't afford to be careless."

But Shannon knew there was more to their digital safety than just avoiding public Wi-Fi. She turned the conversation towards another critical topic: the importance of regular software updates. "Keeping our devices up to date is fundamental for security," she said, pacing slightly as she spoke. "Software vulnerabilities are like open doors for hackers. If we don't update our apps and operating systems, we're leaving ourselves exposed."

As she talked, Shannon shared her own experiences. "I once received an email that looked like a legitimate update notification, complete with a company logo and perfect spelling. It was so convincing I almost clicked on it. We can't fall for those traps. Always close pop-ups and go directly to the vendor's website for updates."

Her family listened intently, realizing how easily they could be misled. Shannon emphasized, "Updates not only fix bugs but also enhance security features. Developers are constantly working to patch vulnerabilities, so we must keep our devices updated."

To make it practical, she explained how they could set their devices to accept updates automatically. "And if you're ever unsure, check the vendor's website or contact their support desk.

It's always better to be safe than sorry."

By the end of the conversation, Shannon had not only raised awareness about the dangers of unsecured networks but also empowered her family to take control of their online safety. Together, they agreed to establish routines for checking updates and using VPNs whenever they accessed public Wi-Fi. It was a small but significant step toward a more secure digital life.

Here are the key reasons that software updates are crucial for security:*

1. Importance of Timely Software Updates

Software updates often include patches that address known vulnerabilities and security issues. Cybercriminals actively exploit outdated software, and timely updates protect against these exploits.

2. Protection Against Malware and Exploits

Cyber attackers use software vulnerabilities to deliver malware, including ransomware. Regular updates close these vulnerabilities, reducing the risk of infections and ransomware attacks. Updates also allow developers to respond quickly to new threats, providing users with timely protection.

3. Enhanced Security Features and Data Protection

Updates introduce new security features or improve existing ones, better protection against evolving cyber threats. They also enhance data encryption, privacy settings, and other measures to safeguard sensitive information from unauthorized access.

4. Mitigation of Vulnerabilities

Updates often fix both known and unknown vulnerabilities, including zero-day exploits and software bugs. Regular updates reduce the chances of vulnerabilities being exploited.

5. System Stability and Reliability

In addition, security updates improve software stability, preventing crashes or glitches that attackers could exploit.

6. Mobile and Network Security

Software updates address vulnerabilities, improve performance, and add new security features on mobile devices. Vulnerable software can also compromise entire networks, so updating software helps maintain overall network security.

Neglecting updates increases the risk of security breaches, data compromises, and other cyber threats. Therefore, individuals and families should prioritize regular software updates as part of their cybersecurity strategy.

Anti-virus and Anti-malware Software

AV (AntiVirus) software falls into the category called endpoint protection. Endpoint protection is a class of software installed to protect devices the end user touches. Any device on a network that will connect to the internet, other computers, mobile devices, or tablets should have an AV installed.

Antivirus software runs in the background, checking every file you open and comparing it to known viruses and other types of malware; this helps prevent infection. The software also runs system scans to ensure no viruses are dormant on your computer, smartphone, or tablet. If your antivirus software comes across a signature for a virus or other malware, it will stop that file from running and put it into quarantine.

Installing anti-virus software is the easiest way to protect your computer. There are different classes of antivirus software, each with its limitations:

- **Signature-based detection** involves scanning files for known virus signatures. When the antivirus software detects a file with a known virus signature, it takes appropriate action to remove or quarantine the infected file.
- **Behavior-based** detection looks for suspicious behavior that may indicate the presence of malware or viruses. This method is particularly useful in detecting zero-day threats, which are newly discovered and previously unknown forms of malware.
- **Heuristics-based** detection is a more advanced method that analyzes the behavior of files to determine whether they are potentially malicious. This method is particularly effective in detecting new and unknown threats that do not have a known signature.

Anti-virus software that relies on signatures can only detect malware that has known characteristics. It is important to keep these signatures up-to-date. You will still be susceptible to malware that circulates before the anti-virus vendors add their signatures, so continue to take other safety precautions as well. Many antivirus programs integrate with email, so they scan attachments, strip undesirable attachments, and disable any links embedded in the message.

Here are key reasons why antivirus software is important for security.

Detection and Prevention of Malware & Exploits

Antivirus software is designed to detect and prevent various types of malware, including viruses, worms, Trojans, ransomware, spyware, and more. They can identify and block attempts by attackers to exploit weaknesses in operating systems or applications. They often include features to protect against software vulnerabilities and exploits. Antivirus defends against malicious software that can compromise the integrity and functionality of systems.

Scans Data Using Behavioral Analysis & Signature-Based Detection

Many antivirus solutions provide real-time scanning capabilities, constantly monitoring files, downloads, and system activities to identify and block potential threats as they occur. Antivirus software employs behavioral analysis to detect suspicious activities that may indicate the presence of malware. This proactive approach helps identify new and unknown threats. Antivirus programs use signature-based detection to identify known malware by comparing file signatures against a database of known threats. This helps quickly identify and quarantine or remove malicious files.

Protects Sensitive Data & Removes Infected Files

Antivirus programs help protect personal and sensitive data from being accessed or stolen by malware. This is crucial for safeguarding financial information, login credentials, and other confidential data. When malware is detected, antivirus software can take action to quarantine or remove infected files, preventing further spread and damage.

Prevents System Disruption & Botnet Infections

Malware, such as ransomware, can disrupt the normal operation of systems and networks. Antivirus (AV) software helps prevent disruptions by neutralizing ransomware and other malware. Good AV prevents systems from becoming part of botnets–networks of compromised devices controlled by attackers. Botnets are often used for malicious activities, such as launching DDoS attacks.

Email/Web Protection & Compliance

Antivirus solutions often include features to scan email attachments and block malicious links. They also provide web protection, blocking access to malicious websites that may distribute malware. In many industries and organizations, compliance standards mandate the use of antivirus software as a basic security measure. Adhering to these standards is essential for legal and regulatory compliance.

Mitigate Phishing Threats Across Multiple Platforms

Antivirus solutions are available for various operating systems, including Windows, macOS, and Linux, providing protection across different platforms and devices. Some antivirus programs include features to detect and block phishing attempts, protecting users from deceptive emails and websites designed to steal login credentials or other sensitive information.

Automatic Updates

Regular updates to antivirus databases and software ensure that the protection measures remain effective against the latest threats. Automatic updates are crucial for staying ahead of evolving malware.

Choosing An AntiVirus

Windows

Every Windows system is pre-installed with Defender AntiVirus. If you have another antivirus app installed and turned on, Microsoft Defender Antivirus will turn off automatically. If you uninstall the other app, Microsoft Defender Antivirus will turn back on automatically.

Windows Defender AntiVirus has come a long way since its inception. Here are the main features of basic Windows Defender:

1. **Real-Time Protection**: Actively scans files, programs, and processes to detect malware, ransomware, spyware, and other threats in real-time.
2. **Cloud-Based Protection**: Uses Microsoft's cloud to analyze suspicious files and detect emerging threats quickly, leveraging Microsoft's global threat intelligence.
3. **Automatic Updates**: Regularly receives updates from Microsoft to keep virus definitions and threat detection algorithms current without user intervention.
4. **Firewall and Network Protection**: Integrates with Windows Firewall to monitor network traffic and block unauthorized access, protecting against network-based attacks.
5. **Threat & Vulnerability Management**: Scans for potential vulnerabilities and configurations that could expose the system to threats, offering recommendations to improve security.
6. **Controlled Folder Access**: Provides ransomware protection by preventing unauthorized apps from accessing and modifying files in protected folders.
7. **Exploit Protection**: Built-in tools to guard against specific types of attacks, like code injection and memory exploits, protecting key system processes.
8. **Parental Controls**: Allows parents to set restrictions on app usage, set screen time limits, and monitor online activity for child accounts.
9. **Device Health Monitoring**: Monitors system health and performance, alerting users to issues with storage, battery, and software updates.
10. **Application and Browser Control**: Uses SmartScreen to block malicious websites, warn against suspicious downloads, and prevent harmful apps from running.

Windows Defender is effective for basic security needs, providing a strong foundation for users without requiring third-party antivirus software. For the average individual, it is sufficient protection for day-to-day tasks.

MacOSX

macOS uses a variety of built-in security features that provide some protection against malware, though it is not the same as a full-featured antivirus solution. Here are some of the main security components in macOS:

1. **XProtect**: A basic malware detection and removal tool that scans files for known malware signatures when they are downloaded or opened. It's updated periodically by Apple but lacks the extensive features of a traditional antivirus.

2. **Gatekeeper**: Designed to ensure that only trusted software (from the App Store or identified developers) is installed, adding an extra layer of security against unauthorized applications.

3. **System Integrity Protection (SIP)**: Protects core system files and processes from being modified by unauthorized applications, helping prevent rootkits and other deep-level malware from taking control.

4. **Notarization**: Apple requires apps distributed outside the App Store to go through a notarization process, where they are scanned for malicious content before being allowed to run on macOS.

While these features offer some baseline protection, they don't provide the same comprehensive defense as a full antivirus suite.

Ubuntu Linux

Ubuntu Linux does not come with a preinstalled antivirus program like Windows Defender. By default, Ubuntu and other Linux distributions rely on user permissions, software repositories, and community oversight to provide security. However, there are a few built-in and optional security features:

1. **User and File Permissions**: Ubuntu's user permission model limits the potential damage that malware can inflict. Only the root (administrator) user has the ability to make system-wide changes, so a compromised non-root account usually has limited impact.

2. **AppArmor**: Ubuntu includes AppArmor, a mandatory access control (MAC) system that restricts programs' capabilities, preventing unauthorized access to system resources even if a program is compromised.

3. **APT Repositories and Digital Signatures**: Software downloaded from Ubuntu's official repositories is signed and verified, reducing the risk of installing malicious software.

4. **Automatic Security Updates**: Ubuntu regularly provides security patches and updates that can be automatically installed, which helps to keep the system secure.

While Linux is generally less targeted by malware, there are still antivirus options available.

Highly Rated Antivirus Software

BitDefender

Bitdefender Antivirus Plus is a feature-packed antivirus solution designed primarily for Windows users but has a MacOS version. Core features include:

1. **Real-Time Protection**: Defends against a wide range of malware, including viruses, ransomware, spyware, and phishing attacks.

2. **Vulnerability Assessment**: Scans for system vulnerabilities, such as missing patches and outdated software, to help prevent exploitation.

3. **Privacy Tools**: Includes a secure password manager, a file shredder to permanently delete files, and a basic VPN (limited to 200 MB per day) for safer browsing.

4. **Web Protection**: Safeguards online transactions with anti-phishing technology and a secure browser for sensitive activities like online banking.

Bitdefender Antivirus Plus also offers an optional Rescue Environment for cleaning up more advanced infections and preventing damage from persistent malware.

While this package covers essentials, advanced features such as a firewall, parental controls, and support for Mac or mobile devices require an upgrade to Bitdefender Internet Security or Total Security plans.

Price: $14.99 per year for one device

Download: https://www.bitdefender.com/en-us/consumer/free-antivirus

Sophos Home

Sophos Home Premium offers a variety of security features tailored for families, with the option for remote management across multiple devices, making it useful for households. Key features include:

- **Malware and Ransomware Protection:** Sophos Home Premium provides AI-based real-time malware detection of common threats like viruses, spyware, and ransomware.
- **Web and Banking Protection:** Sophos includes web protection to block malicious websites and phishing. Banking protection helps secure online transactions.
- **Parental Controls and Webcam Protection:** Basic parental website filtering and webcam protection help to protect vulnerable family members.
- **Remote Management:** Users can manage and monitor security settings for multiple devices from a single web-based dashboard.

It is a cost-effective solution for users who need solid protection and value remote management but don't require additional features like a VPN or password manager included in other antivirus packages at this price point.

Price: $59.99 per year for up to 10 computers

Download: https://home.sophos.com/en-us/download-pc-security

AVG Antivirus Free

AVG AntiVirus Free is a basic, free option offering a solid range of features to protect against malware and online threats. It includes:

- malware scanning
- real-time updates
- ransomware protection
- phishing protection

and a file shredder for permanently deleting files. AVG also has a dark web monitor, a secure browser, and a rescue disk feature for emergency system repairs. However, the free version lacks features such as a firewall, webcam protection, and advanced ransomware tools, which are available in AVG's paid tiers.

AVG Internet Security, priced at $39.99 a year for 10 devices, adds enhanced ransomware protection, an advanced firewall, and webcam protection.

Download: https://www.avg.com/en-us/free-antivirus-download#pc

ClamAV

ClamAV is a free, open-source antivirus solution originally developed for Linux. It is primarily used for detecting and removing malware across different operating systems, including Linux, macOS, and Windows.

Its key features include:

- real-time scanning
- email scanning
- heuristic analysis
- customizable scans

and quarantine management. Although ClamAV does not offer real-time protection, it is suitable for scanning archives, emails, and other files, making it a solid option for periodic checks rather than continuous protection.

There are free third-party GUI options, like ClamTK for Linux, ClamWin for Windows, and ClamXAV for macOS, which improve accessibility. Despite the powerful detection engine, ClamAV's support is limited to community resources such as forums, email lists, and a Discord server.

Paid solutions based on ClamAV's engine, such as ClamXAV for macOS, are available through third parties, which offer additional support and features if needed.

Download: https://www.clamav.net/downloads

The list of Antivirus Software listed in this guide is by no means exhaustive. The best thing to do is take a deep dive into product reviews. Take a look at the needs of your family in order to match them with a product and price point that suits those needs.

Computer Firewall Configuration

A firewall is included in every computer's operating system. It is one of the most important pieces of security software available to all. There is no need for us to become firewall experts. A rudimentary understanding of the firewall settings that will keep your system safe is all you need. Once the firewall has been turned on and basic security is set up, there is no need to touch it again. The only time it will need to be touched will be to allow communication in and out of the computer for a special application or service.

Basic Windows Firewall Configuration

Configuring the Windows Firewall is an essential step in securing your Windows system. Here's a simple but safe configuration for the Windows Firewall that balances security and usability

1. Enable the Windows Firewall
2. Ensure that the Windows Firewall is enabled. This is the default setting in most cases.
3. How to Check: Go to "Control Panel" > "System and Security" > "Windows Defender Firewall." Ensure that the firewall is turned on.

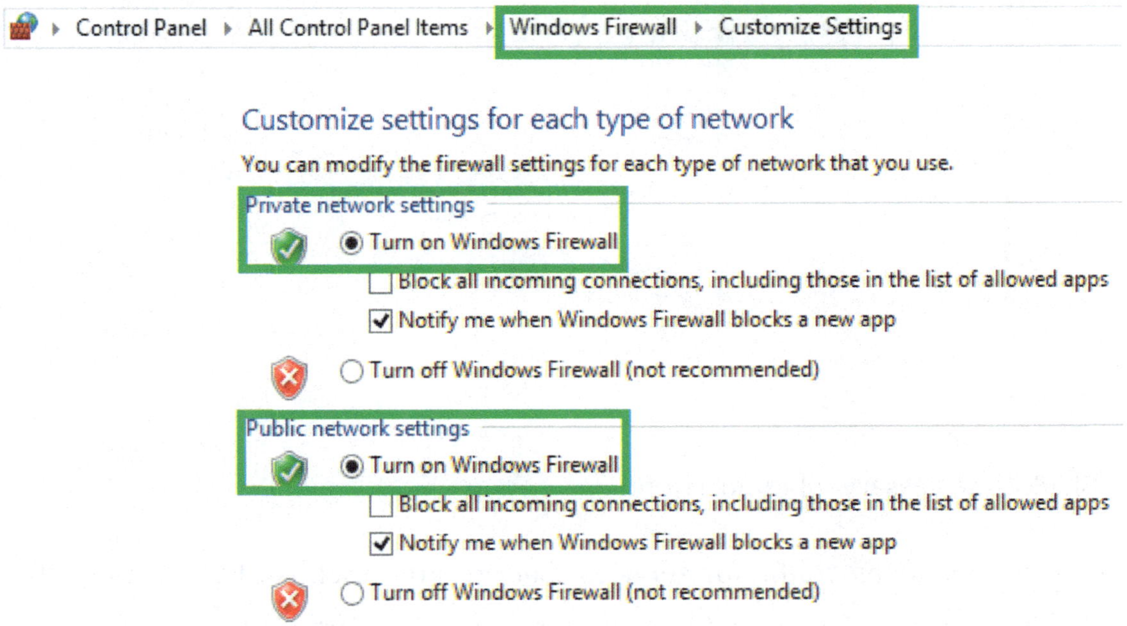

4. UseDefault Settings for Outbound Connections

5. The default outbound connection settings in the Windows Firewall are generally secure. Avoid making unnecessary changes to outbound rules unless you have specific requirements.

6. Allow Essential Inbound Traffic

7. Create rules to allow inbound traffic for essential services only. For example, Allow incoming traffic on port 80 (HTTP) for web servers.

8. Allow incoming traffic on port 443 (HTTPS) for secure web servers.

How to Add Inbound Rules

Go to "Windows Defender Firewall with Advanced Security." Right-click on "Inbound Rules" and choose "New Rule." Follow the wizard to create rules for specific ports or programs.

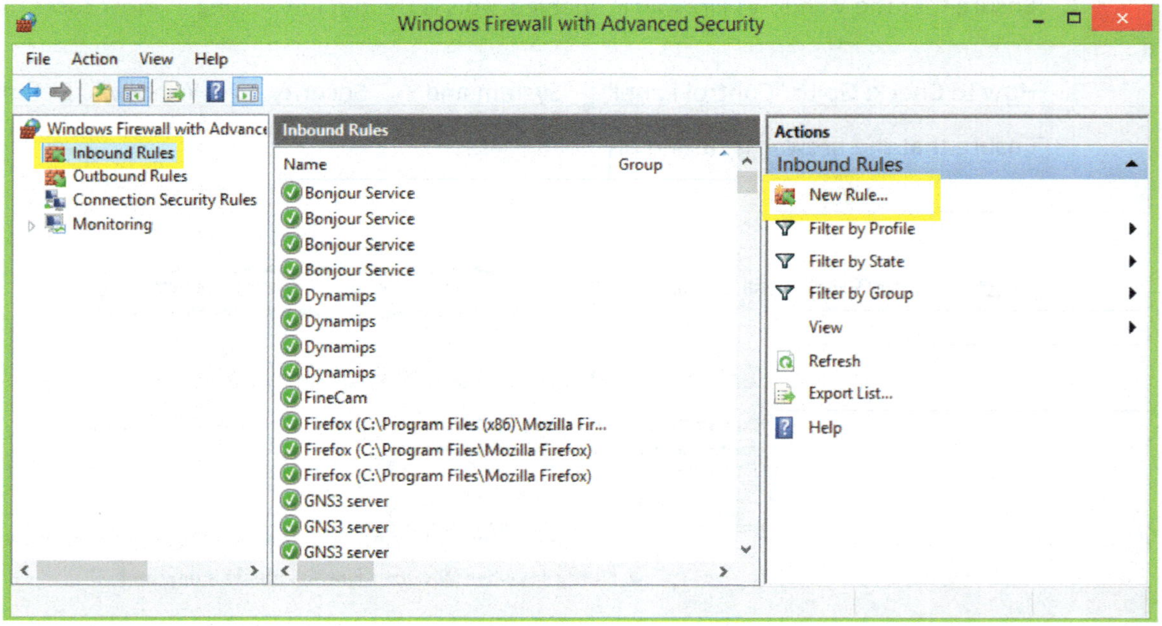

1. Block Unnecessary Inbound Traffic

- Block incoming traffic for services that are not essential. For example, if you are not running a specific server, block the corresponding port. How to Add Inbound Rules.

- Go to "Windows Defender Firewall with Advanced Security."
- Right-click on "Inbound Rules" and choose "New Rule."
- Follow the wizard to block specific ports or programs. Usually, this will be a port range.

2. Allow Remote Desktop (if needed). If you use Remote Desktop to connect to your Windows machine, create a specific rule to allow this traffic.

3. How to Add Remote Desktop Rule

- Go to "Windows Defender Firewall with Advanced Security."
- Right-click on "Inbound Rules" and choose "New Rule."
- Choose "Predefined" and select "Remote Desktop" from the list.

4. Enable Logging (Optional)

- Consider enabling logging for blocked and allowed traffic. This can help you monitor firewall activity.
- How to Enable Logging
- In "Windows Defender Firewall with Advanced Security," click on "Properties."
- Under the "Logging" tab, choose to log successful and blocked connections.

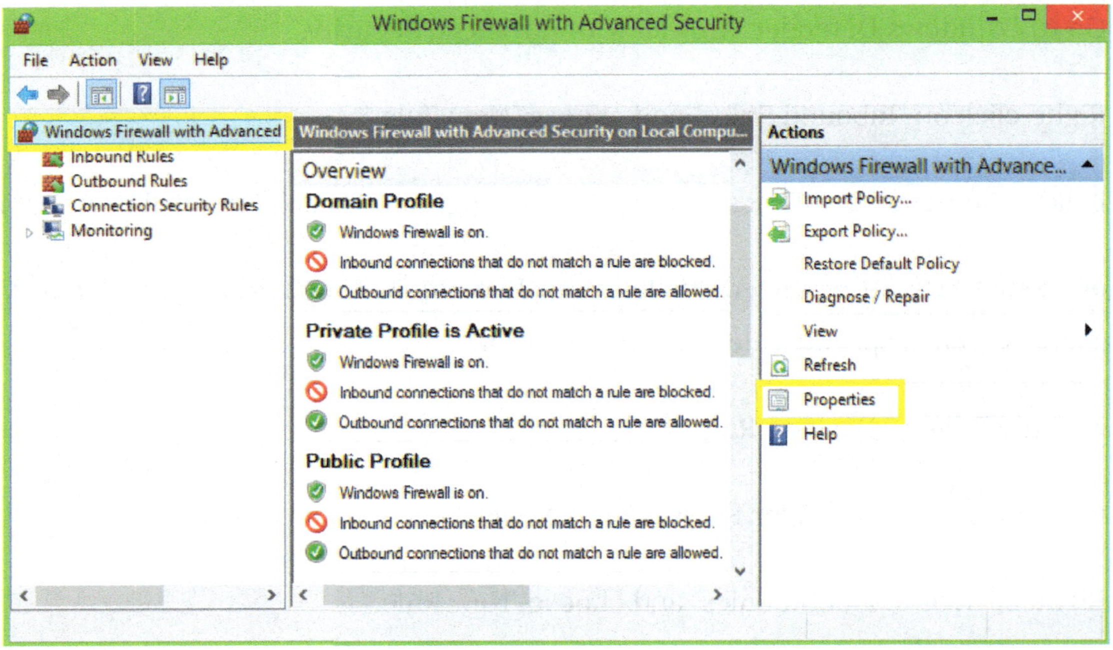
Windows Firewall with Advanced Security
File Action View Help
Windows Firewall with Advanced
Inbound Rules
Outbound Rules
Connection Security Rules
Monitoring
Windows Firewall with Advanced Security on Local Compu...
Overview
Domain Profile
Windows Firewall is on.
Inbound connections that do not match a rule are blocked.
Outbound connections that do not match a rule are allowed.
Private Profile is Active
Windows Firewall is on.
Inbound connections that do not match a rule are blocked.
Outbound connections that do not match a rule are allowed.
Public Profile
Windows Firewall is on.
Inbound connections that do not match a rule are blocked.
Outbound connections that do not match a rule are allowed.
Actions
Windows Firewall with Advance...
Import Policy...
Export Policy...
Restore Default Policy
Diagnose / Repair
View
Refresh
Properties
Help

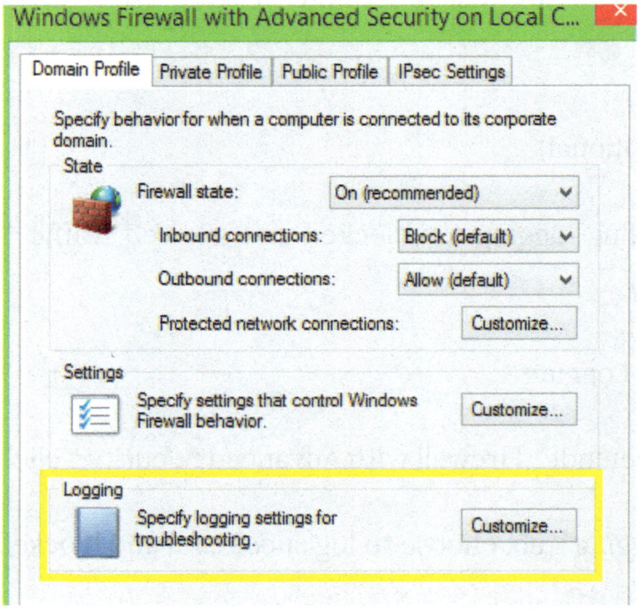
Windows Firewall with Advanced Security on Local C...
Domain Profile
Private Profile
Public Profile
IPsec Settings
Specify behavior for when a computer is connected to its corporate domain.
State
Firewall state:
On (recommended)
Inbound connections:
Block (default)
Outbound connections:
Allow (default)
Protected network connections:
Customize...
Settings
Specify settings that control Windows Firewall behavior.
Customize...
Logging
Specify logging settings for troubleshooting.
Customize...

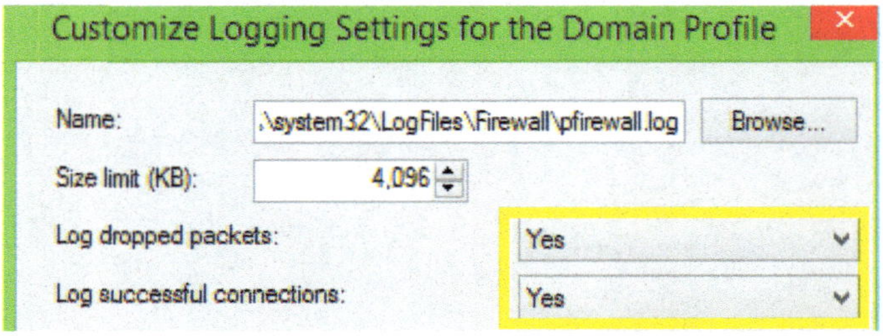
Customize Logging Settings for the Domain Profile
Name:
.\system32\LogFiles\Firewall\pfirewall.log
Browse...
Size limit (KB):
4,096
Log dropped packets:
Yes
Log successful connections:
Yes

Sample Configuration

Here's a simplified example configuration for a Windows Firewall

- Inbound Rules
- Allow HTTP (Port 80), HTTPS (Port 443)
- Block Unused or unnecessary ports
- Outbound Rules
- Use default settings for outbound connections.
- Advanced Settings

- Enable logging for both allowed and blocked traffic if monitoring is desired.

Remember to customize these rules based on your specific needs and the applications running on your system. Regularly review and update your firewall rules to adapt to network environment changes and address emerging security threats.

Basic MACOS Firewall Configuration

Configuring the macOS firewall is an essential step in securing your Mac system. Here's a simple but safe configuration for the macOS firewall that balances security and usability

1. Enable the macOS Firewall.

Ensure that the built-in firewall on macOS is enabled. It is typically enabled by default. To Check:

Go to "System Preferences" > "Security & Privacy" > "Firewall."

Click the lock icon and enter your administrator password.

Make sure the firewall is turned on.

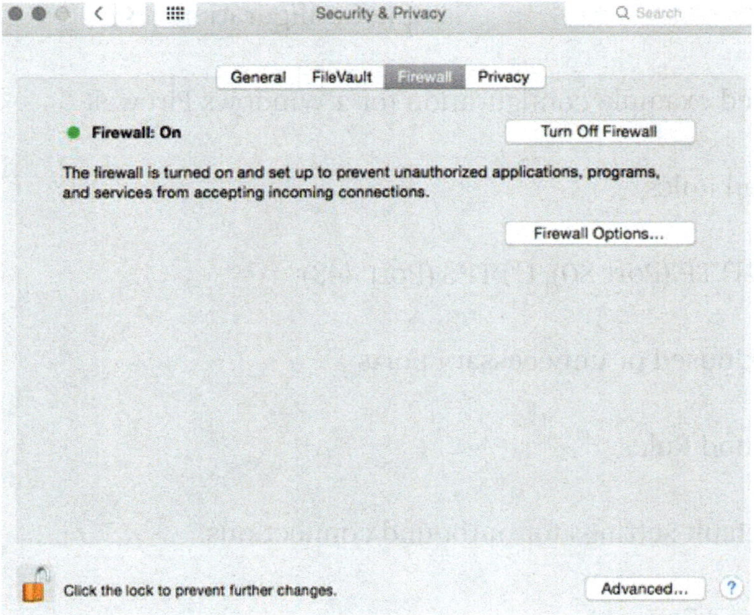
Security & Privacy
Search
General
FileVault
Firewall
Privacy
Firewall: On
Turn Off Firewall
The firewall is turned on and set up to prevent unauthorized applications, programs, and services from accepting incoming connections.
Firewall Options...
Click the lock to prevent further changes.
Advanced...
?

2. Use Default Settings for Outbound Connections

The default settings for outbound connections in the macOS firewall are generally secure. Avoid making unnecessary changes to outbound rules unless you have specific requirements.

3. Allow Essential Inbound Traffic

Create rules to allow inbound traffic for essential services only. For example, Allow incoming traffic on port 80 (HTTP) for web servers.

Allow incoming traffic on port 443 (HTTPS) for secure web servers.

How to Add Inbound Rules

In the "Firewall" tab of "Security & Privacy," click on "Firewall Options."

Click the "+" icon to add a new rule and choose the application or port you want to allow.

4. Block Unnecessary Inbound Traffic

Block incoming traffic for services that are not essential. For example, if you are not running a specific server, block the corresponding port.

How to Add Inbound Rules

In the "Firewall" tab of "Security & Privacy," click on "Firewall Options."

Click the "+" icon to add a new rule, and choose the application or port you want to block.

5. Enable Stealth Mode

Enable Stealth Mode to make your Mac more resistant to network reconnaissance. This prevents your Mac from responding to probing requests.

How to Enable Stealth Mode

In the "Firewall" tab of "Security & Privacy," click on "Firewall Options." Check the box for "Enable stealth mode."

6. Log Blocked Traffic (Optional)

Consider enabling logging for blocked traffic. This can help you monitor firewall activity.

How to Enable Logging

In the "Firewall" tab of "Security & Privacy," click on "Firewall Options." Check the box for "Enable logging."

Sample Configuration

Here's a simplified example configuration for the macOS firewall

Firewall Status

- Ensure that the firewall is turned on.

Inbound Rules

- Allow HTTP (Port 80), HTTPS (Port 443)
- Block Unused or unnecessary ports

Outbound Rules

- Use default settings for outbound connections

Stealth Mode

- Enable stealth mode to make your Mac less visible to network scans

Logging

- Optionally, enable logging for blocked traffic

Android Mobile Phone Security

Android mobile security settings are crucial for protecting your data, apps, and personal information from unauthorized access. Here's a guide to enhance your Android security:

1. Screen Lock

- Password, PIN, or Pattern: Set a secure screen lock (Password or PIN).
- Biometrics (Fingerprint or Face Unlock): Use biometrics for quick, secure access.

2. Encryption

- Device Encryption: Encrypts all data stored on the device. Most modern Android phones come with encryption enabled by default.
- SD Card Encryption: Some Android devices allow you to encrypt data on external SD cards, protecting any sensitive information stored externally.

3. Two-Factor Authentication (2FA)

- Enable 2FA for all accounts and apps that support it. Google prompts, Authenticator apps, and SMS-based codes add an extra layer of security.

4. Google Play Protect

- Automatically scans your device and apps for malicious activity. Ensure it is enabled by going to Settings > Security > Google Play Protect.
- Regularly update all apps. Updates often include security patches.

5. App Permissions

- Limit apps' access to sensitive data like location, camera, microphone, and contacts. Review and manage app permissions regularly via Settings > Apps & notifications > App permissions.
- Only download apps from trusted sources

6. Find My Device

- Enable Find My Device under Settings > Security > Find My Device. It helps track, lock, or wipe your phone if lost or stolen.

7. Secure Network Usage

- Avoid using public Wi-Fi for sensitive transactions (like online banking). If you must, use a VPN to secure your connection.
- Turn off Bluetooth and NFC when not in use to avoid unwanted connections.

8. System Updates

- Regularly update your Android OS to the latest version, as security vulnerabilities are often patched in new updates. Go to Settings > System > System update.

9. Lock Specific Apps

- Use app lock features, either built-in or through third-party apps, to add a layer of security for individual apps like banking or social media.

10. Backup and Restore

- Enable regular backups of your phone's data to Google Cloud or another service, ensuring you can recover your information if your device is compromised.

11. SIM Lock

- Set a PIN for your SIM card to prevent someone from using it on another device. You can find this option under Settings > Security > SIM card lock.

12. Disable Smart Lock

- Smart Lock keeps your phone unlocked in trusted locations, but it could be a risk if your phone falls into the wrong hands. Disable this or manage it carefully.

13. Trusted Devices

- Disable or limit trusted devices that can keep your phone unlocked, such as smartwatches or Bluetooth speakers.

Securing Android App Permissions

Securing your Android app permissions is crucial to protecting your privacy and safeguarding sensitive data. Many apps request permissions they don't need, which can pose security risks. Here's a guide on how to manage and secure Android app permissions:

1. Review and Manage App Permissions

Regularly review the permissions apps have access to and revoke any unnecessary ones.

Step 1: Open Settings.

Step 2: Go to Privacy or Apps & Notifications (depending on your device).

Step 3: Tap on Permission manager or App permissions.

Step 4: Review permissions like Location, Camera, Microphone, Contacts, and others.

Step 5: Revoke access for apps that don't need these permissions.
Tip: Apps that don't require constant access to your location, camera, or contacts should not have these permissions enabled.

2. Use Permission Prompts on Android 11+

From Android 11 onwards, you can grant temporary, one-time permissions for sensitive access (like camera, microphone, and location). The app will lose access once you close it.

Step 1: When an app requests sensitive permissions, select Only this time for one-time access.

3. Auto-Reset App Permissions

Android 11+ also has an auto-reset feature that revokes permissions for apps you haven't used in a while.

Step 1: Open Settings.
Step 2: Go to Apps & notifications.
Step 3: Tap on Unused apps or App permissions.
Step 4: Enable Remove permissions if the app isn't used. This automatically revokes permissions if you don't use the app for a few months.

4. Check Background App Activity

Some apps may use permissions like location or access data in the background, even when they are not in use.

Step 1: Open Settings.
Step 2: Tap on Apps & notifications.
Step 3: Select an app, then go to Permissions.
Step 4: Disable the option for the app to use the permission in the background.

Tip: Ensure apps don't have unnecessary background access to sensitive features like location or microphone.

5. Restrict Special Permissions

Certain permissions like Draw over other apps or Modify system settings can be risky, as they allow apps to change how your phone behaves.

Step 1: Go to Settings.
Step 2: Scroll to Special app access (or search for it in the settings menu).
Step 3: Review sensitive permissions such as Installing unknown apps, Modifying system settings, and Drawing over other apps.
Step 4: Disable these permissions for apps that don't require them.

6. Disable "Install Unknown Apps"

Prevent apps from installing other apps or APKs outside the Google Play Store.

Step 1: Go to Settings.
Step 2: Tap Apps & notifications.
Step 3: Select Special app access.
Step 4: Tap Install unknown apps.
Step 5: Ensure this permission is off for all apps except trusted ones (like Google Chrome if you need to sideload apps safely).

7. Check App Privacy Reports (Android 12+)

Android 12 introduced a Privacy Dashboard that gives you an overview of how often apps are using sensitive permissions.

Step 1: Go to Settings.
Step 2: Tap on Privacy.
Step 3: Select Privacy Dashboard.
Step 4: Review the usage of Location, Camera, Microphone, etc., over the past 24 hours, and adjust permissions if needed.

8. Limit App Access to Location

For apps that require location access, consider limiting them to precise or approximate locations.

Step 1: Go to Settings.
Step 2: Tap on Location.

Step 3: Select an app, and choose between Precise location (for navigation apps) or Approximate location (for apps that don't need exact location).

9. Disable Permissions for Default Apps

Some default apps (pre-installed apps) may have unnecessary permissions enabled by default.

Step 1: Go to Settings > Apps & notifications.
Step 2: Tap on the See all apps option.
Step 3: Select the default app and tap Permissions.
Step 4: Revoke permissions that aren't necessary for the app's functionality.

Best Practices for Securing App Permissions:

1. Only grant permissions when necessary: If an app doesn't need access to your contacts, camera, or location, deny those permissions.
2. Keep apps updated: Regular updates can fix security vulnerabilities and remove unnecessary permissions.
3. Uninstall unused apps: If you have apps you rarely use, uninstall them to prevent them from accessing your data.
4. Download apps from trusted sources: Always use the Google Play Store or trusted APK providers to minimize the risk of malware.

By managing app permissions carefully, you can significantly enhance your Android device's privacy and security.

Android Antivirus Options

Kaspersky Mobile Antivirus

Pros:

- Excellent malware detection.
- Includes anti-theft tools, call blocking, and a strong privacy audit.
- Minimal performance impact.

- No ads in the free version.

Cons:

Some advanced features like real-time web protection and app lock are locked behind a paywall.

Ideal for: Users who want solid, free antivirus protection without being bombarded by ads.

Sophos Intercept X for Mobile

Pros:

- Excellent malware protection (no ads or premium version needed).
- Web filtering, malware detection, and privacy advisor.
- Includes additional tools like a QR code scanner and Wi-Fi security scanner.
- Free to use with no in-app purchases or ads.

Cons:

- Interface is more complex and technical compared to other antivirus apps.
- Lacks anti-theft features in the free version.

Ideal for: Users who want a completely free, no-ads antivirus solution with solid protection and web filtering.

Bitdefender Mobile Security

Pros:

- Strong malware detection and real-time protection.
- Minimal impact on performance.
- Anti-theft features (locate, lock, or wipe device remotely).
- VPN included (with limited data).
- Web protection against malicious websites.

Cons:

- VPN has a 200MB daily limit (unless upgraded).

Ideal for: Users looking for excellent protection with minimal resource consumption.

Android VPN Options

ProtonVPN

Pros:

- Unlimited data (rare for free VPNs).
- Strong security features and a strict no-logs policy.
- Based in Switzerland, which has strong privacy laws.
- No ads in the free version.

Cons:

- Free users are limited to servers in three countries (US, Netherlands, Japan).
- Speeds can be slower due to limited free servers.

Ideal for: Users looking for a secure, free VPN with unlimited data for browsing or basic usage.

Hide.me

Pros:

- 10GB of free data per month.
- No ads, no-logs policy, and strong encryption.
- 5 server locations are available in the free version (Canada, Singapore, Netherlands, US East, US West).
- Fast speeds compared to other free VPNs.

Cons:

- 10GB monthly limit.
- Only one connection is allowed at a time on the free plan.

Ideal for: Users who want a secure, free VPN with no ads and relatively fast speeds.

Opera VPN (Built into Opera Browser)

Pros:

- Free with no data limit.
- Built directly into the Opera browser (no need to install a separate app)
- Easy to use and doesn't require registration.

Cons:

- Works only within the Opera browser (not for other apps on your device).
- Limited to three virtual locations (Europe, Americas, Asia).
- Not as secure as other dedicated VPNs

Each of these VPNs offers different benefits depending on your specific needs (e.g., data limits, server options, or usage simplicity). For basic browsing and occasional streaming, these free VPNs provide solid security and privacy without a subscription.

iPhone Mobile Security

Securing your iPhone is essential to protect your data, privacy, and personal information from various threats. Apple is known for its strong security features, but taking additional steps can further enhance your device's security. Here's a guide on how to secure your iPhone:

1. Set a Strong Passcode

A strong passcode is your first line of defense against unauthorized access to your iPhone.

- Step 1: Open Settings.
- Step 2: Tap Face ID & Passcode (or Touch ID & Passcode).
- Step 3: Enter your current passcode, then tap Change Passcode.
- Step 4: Choose a 6-digit code or tap Passcode Options to set a custom alphanumeric code

(more secure).

Tip: Avoid simple codes like "123456" or "0000." Use a combination of numbers, letters, and symbols for maximum security.

2. Enable Face ID or Touch ID

Use biometric authentication (Face ID or Touch ID) for a quick and secure way to unlock your iPhone and authorize purchases.

- Step 1: Go to Settings.
- Step 2: Tap Face ID & Passcode or Touch ID & Passcode.
- Step 3: Follow the prompts to set up Face ID or Touch ID.

Tip: Face ID is more secure than a passcode alone, but both add an extra layer of protection.

3. Use Two-Factor Authentication for Apple ID

Two-factor authentication (2FA) makes it harder for someone to access your Apple ID by requiring both a password and a code sent to your trusted device.

- Step 1: Go to Settings.
- Step 2: Tap your name at the top, then go to Password & Security.
- Step 3: Enable Two-Factor Authentication.
  Tip: Always use trusted phone numbers and email addresses for recovery.

4. Enable Find My iPhone

If your iPhone is lost or stolen, Find My iPhone helps you locate, lock, or erase your device remotely.

- Step 1: Go to Settings.
- Step 2: Tap your name at the top, then select Find My.
- Step 3: Enable Find My iPhone and turn on Send Last Location.

Tip: This feature also allows you to remotely wipe your phone if needed, protecting your data if the device is unrecoverable.

5. Turn on Automatic Updates

Regular iOS updates provide important security patches that protect your device from the latest threats.

- Step 1: Go to Settings.
- Step 2: Tap General and then Software Update.
- Step 3: Enable Automatic Updates.

Tip: You can manually check for updates under Software Update to ensure you always have the latest security patches.

6. Use a VPN on Public Wi-Fi

Public Wi-Fi networks are often unsecured and can expose your data to hackers. A Virtual Private Network (VPN) encrypts your internet connection for secure browsing.

- Step 1: Download a trusted VPN app (like ProtonVPN, Windscribe, or NordVPN) from the App Store.
- Step 2: Set up the VPN and use it whenever you're on public Wi-Fi.

Tip: Always be cautious when connecting to free or public Wi-Fi, even with a VPN.

7. Limit App Permissions

Review and control the data that apps can access, such as your location, contacts, and camera.

- Step 1: Go to Settings.
- Step 2: Tap Privacy & Security.
- Step 3: Review permissions for Location Services, Camera, Microphone, Contacts, etc.
- Step 4: Disable unnecessary permissions for apps that don't need them.

Tip: Set location services to While Using the App rather than Always for most apps.

8. Turn on iCloud Backup Encryption

iCloud automatically backs up your data, but you can enable end-to-end encryption for sensitive data like passwords, health data, and messages.

- Step 1: Go to Settings.
- Step 2: Tap iCloud, then select iCloud Backup.
- Step 3: Ensure iCloud Backup is turned on and encrypted.

Tip: Use a strong password for your iCloud account to maximize security.

9. Enable Privacy Features (iOS 14 and later)

iOS includes several privacy features, such as:

- Recording indicators: A green dot (camera) or orange dot (microphone) shows when an app is accessing these features.
- App tracking transparency: Apps must ask permission to track you for advertising purposes.
- Step 1: Go to Settings.
- Step 2: Tap Privacy & Security, then review Tracking settings and permissions.
- Step 3: Disable app tracking for apps that don't need it.

Tip: Pay attention to the indicators and review app behavior if you notice unusual activity.

10. Use Secure Browsing and Messaging Apps

For safer browsing and communication, use apps that offer built-in encryption:

- Safari: Turn on Fraudulent Website Warning to avoid phishing sites. Go to Settings > Safari > Privacy & Security.
- Messages: Apple's iMessage uses end-to-end encryption for secure messaging.
- Third-party apps: Use apps like Signal or WhatsApp for encrypted communication.

11. Disable USB Accessories When Locked

Prevent unauthorized access via the Lightning port by disabling USB accessories when your phone is locked.

- Step 1: Go to Settings.
- Step 2: Tap Face ID & Passcode or Touch ID & Passcode.
- Step 3: Scroll to USB Accessories and ensure it is toggled off.

Tip: This feature prevents USB-based attacks when your iPhone is locked.

12. Set Restrictions with Screen Time

Use Screen Time to set restrictions on app usage, purchases, and content to prevent unauthorized access.

- Step 1: Go to Settings.
- Step 2: Tap Screen Time.
- Step 3: Set a passcode for Screen Time and customize restrictions, such as App Limits and Content & Privacy Restrictions.

Best Practices for iPhone Security:

1. Download apps from trusted sources: Only use the App Store to download apps to minimize the risk of malware.

2. Review app permissions regularly: Some apps may request access to unnecessary data.

3. Avoid jailbreaking your iPhone: Jailbreaking can expose your phone to malware and weaken security.

4. Enable automatic backups: Back up your data to iCloud or a local device regularly to avoid data loss.

5. Monitor your account for suspicious activity: Regularly check your Apple ID for any unauthorized logins or activity.

By following these steps, you can enhance your iPhone's security, protect your personal information, and safeguard your device from unauthorized access and cyber threats.

Securing iPhone App Permissions

Securing your iPhone's app permissions is crucial to safeguarding your privacy and controlling how much access apps have to your personal data. Here's a guide to manage and secure your iPhone app permissions effectively:

1. Review App Permissions Regularly

Regularly check which permissions apps have and revoke any unnecessary access. Apple makes it easy to manage permissions for services like location, camera, microphone, and more.

Step 1: Go to Settings.
Step 2: Scroll down and select Privacy & Security.
Step 3: Tap on specific categories such as:

- Location Services
- Contacts
- Photos
- Camera
- Microphone
- Health
- Bluetooth
- Files and Folders
- Motion & Fitness

Step 4: Review each app's permissions and revoke any that seem unnecessary.

Tip: Be mindful of apps that request access to sensitive data like your contacts or location when they don't need it to function.

2. Limit Location Access

You can control when apps can access your location by limiting access to While Using the App or Never.

Step 1: Go to Settings > Privacy & Security > Location Services.
Step 2: Scroll through the list of apps and select an app to modify its location settings.
Step 3: Choose one of the following options:

- Never: The app cannot access your location.
- Ask Next Time: The app will prompt you for access when needed.
- While Using the App: The app can only access your location while you are using it.
- Always: Only allow this for essential apps like maps or navigation.

Tip: Apps rarely need Always access to your location. Using the App is usually sufficient.

3. Manage Camera and Microphone Access

Some apps may request access to your camera and microphone unnecessarily. You can control which apps have access to these features.

Step 1: Go to Settings > Privacy & Security > Camera.
Step 2: Review the list of apps with camera access and disable permissions for apps that don't need it.
Step 3: Do the same for Microphone under Settings > Privacy & Security > Microphone.

Tip: Social media, video chat, and camera apps need these permissions, but other apps often do not.

4. Control Photo Access

Instead of giving apps access to your entire photo library, iOS allows you to choose specific photos that an app can access.

Step 1: Go to Settings > Privacy & Security > Photos.
Step 2: Tap on an app and select:

- None: The app can't access your photos.
- Selected Photos: You choose specific photos the app can access.
- All Photos: The app has access to your entire photo library.

Tip: Use Selected Photos to only allow an app access to the photos it needs.

5. Control Bluetooth Permissions

Apps may request access to Bluetooth for reasons like connecting to accessories, but many don't actually need this access.

Step 1: Go to Settings > Privacy & Security > Bluetooth.
Step 2: Review the list of apps and toggle off Bluetooth access for apps that don't need it.

Tip: Avoid granting Bluetooth access to apps unless it's essential for their functionality (e.g., fitness apps connecting to wearables).

6. Limit Background App Refresh

Background App Refresh allows apps to update their content in the background, which can consume data and battery and may lead to unnecessary data access.

Step 1: Go to Settings > General > Background App Refresh.
Step 2: Turn off Background App Refresh for apps that don't need to update constantly.

Tip: You can disable this feature entirely or manage it on a per-app basis.

7. Check for Special Permissions

Some apps might request special permissions like access to your Health data or permission to track your activity for targeted ads.

Step 1: Go to Settings > Privacy & Security.
Step 2: Review sensitive permissions like:

- Health: Check which apps can read or write data from the Health app.
- Analytics & Improvements: Control whether your device shares analytics data with app developers or Apple.
- Tracking: Toggle off Allow Apps to Request to Track to prevent apps from tracking you across other apps and websites for advertising purposes.

Tip: Disable tracking for apps that don't require it for their core functionality.

8. Use Privacy Report (iOS 15+)

The App Privacy Report provides a detailed view of which apps are accessing sensitive data like your location, camera, microphone, and more, and how often they do so.

Step 1: Go to Settings > Privacy & Security > App Privacy Report.
Step 2: Enable the report and review which apps are accessing data over time.

Tip: Use this report to identify apps that access sensitive information more often than they need to and adjust their permissions accordingly.

9. Use One-Time Access (iOS 14+)

You can grant apps one-time access to your location, camera, or microphone, meaning they lose access once you close the app.

Step 1: When an app requests sensitive permissions, you will see an option to grant Only Once or Allow While Using the App.
Step 2: Select Only Once for apps that only need temporary access, like a weather app checking your location.

Tip: This feature is especially useful for apps that don't need long-term access.

10. Restrict Tracking (iOS 14.5+)

Apple's App Tracking Transparency feature requires apps to ask for your permission before tracking your activity across other apps and websites.

Step 1: Go to Settings > Privacy & Security > Tracking.
Step 2: Disable Allow Apps to Request to Track to prevent apps from tracking you without

your explicit consent.

Best Practices for Securing iPhone App Permissions

1. Review permissions frequently: Apps may request more permissions after updates, so check permissions regularly.
2. Grant minimal access: Only give apps the permissions they need for core functionality.
3. Be wary of new apps: Download apps from trusted sources and review their requested permissions carefully.
4. Use privacy features: Leverage tools like App Privacy Report and App Tracking Transparency to monitor app behavior.
5. Keep iOS updated: Regular updates often include privacy and security enhancements.

By managing and restricting app permissions, you can ensure that your data remains protected while still allowing your apps to function as intended.

iPhone Antivirus Options

iPhones are generally considered secure due to Apple's closed ecosystem and strong privacy protections, so traditional antivirus apps are less necessary than on Android or Windows platforms. However, using apps with privacy features, security monitoring, and VPN services can enhance protection, especially if you're concerned about phishing, unsafe Wi-Fi networks, or data leaks.

Here are some of the best free iPhone security and privacy apps to consider:

1. Avast Security & Privacy

Key Features:

- Wi-Fi security scanner to detect unsecured networks.
- Identity protection to check if your email or accounts have been compromised.
- Web shield to block malicious websites.
- Privacy tips and security alerts.

Free Version: Provides basic protection features like network scanning and identity checks.

Premium Version: Adds features like VPN and ad-blocking.

Why It's Good: Avast is a well-known name in security software and offers useful features like Wi-Fi protection and identity monitoring, even in the free version.

2. Avira Mobile Security

Key Features:

- Identity protection and data breach alerts.
- Device locator in case of loss.
- Anti-theft features.
- Call blocking to prevent unwanted or spam calls.

Free Version: Includes device security, identity protection, and anti-theft tools.

Premium Version: Offers enhanced web protection and VPN.

Why It's Good: Avira provides a robust set of free security features, including identity monitoring and anti-theft tools, making it a strong choice for iPhone users.

3. McAfee Mobile Security

Key Features:

- Anti-theft protection with a device locator.
- Media vault to protect your photos and files.
- Wi-Fi security analysis for safe internet use.
- System security scanner to ensure your device settings are secure.

Free Version: Includes anti-theft, Wi-Fi scanning, and basic security features.
Premium Version: Adds VPN protection and more advanced security features.

Why It's Good: McAfee offers good free features like anti-theft and Wi-Fi security, ideal for users who want additional protection for device and network safety.

4. Lookout Mobile Security

Key Features:

- System and app protection alerts.
- Identity protection features.
- Device locator for lost or stolen iPhones.
- Anti-theft alarm and remote lock.

Free Version: Provides basic device security and theft protection.
Premium Version: Adds identity theft protection and enhanced browsing protection.

Why It's Good: Lookout focuses on device security and privacy monitoring, offering reliable anti-theft features and basic security for free.

5. TotalAV Free Mobile Security

Key Features:

- Device security and performance monitoring.
- System scan to ensure no vulnerabilities.
- Photo manager to clear storage.
- Data breach checker for identity protection.

Free Version: Provides system security and identity protection features.
Premium Version: Includes advanced protection like VPN and real-time malware protection.

Why It's Good: TotalAV offers a solid set of features for free, including system scans and data breach monitoring, which are great for general security on an iPhone.

6. Kaspersky Security Cloud

Key Features:

- Password manager (limited in free version).
- VPN (200 MB/day free).
- Data leak checker.
- Home Wi-Fi security scanner.

Free Version: Offers a free VPN, Wi-Fi security, and data leak detection.

Premium Version: Adds advanced security monitoring and unlimited VPN.

Why It's Good: Kaspersky provides a good blend of privacy and security tools with features like VPN and identity monitoring in the free version, making it a strong all-rounder.

Why Traditional Antivirus Isn't Necessary on iPhone

Apple's iOS is designed with security in mind, using features like sandboxing (isolating apps from each other) and app vetting in the App Store to protect against malware. This makes it difficult for viruses to spread on iPhones. Instead of a traditional antivirus, iPhone users benefit more from:

Privacy Protection: Safeguarding personal data from phishing and data leaks.

Network Security: Ensuring safe Wi-Fi use with tools like VPNs and Wi-Fi scanners. Identity Monitoring: Detecting if personal accounts or data have been compromised. While iPhones don't generally need antivirus apps in the traditional sense, the apps listed above provide valuable privacy, security, and identity protection tools.

iPhone VPN Options

ProtonVPN

Key Features:

- Unlimited data (unlike many free VPNs).
- No logs and strong privacy protections.
- Secure connection with AES-256 encryption.
- Access to servers in three locations (US, Japan, Netherlands) for free users.

Limitations: Free version can have slower speeds and a limited number of servers. Why It's Great: ProtonVPN is known for its strong commitment to privacy and security. The fact that it offers unlimited data in its free tier makes it a top choice for those seeking continuous protection without a premium plan.

Hide.me

Key Features:

- 10 GB of free data per month.
- Access to five free server locations (CA, Singapore, Netherlands, US).
- No logs policy and AES-256 encryption for security.
- No ads in the free version.

Limitations: Limited server locations and data.

Why It's Great: Hide.me provides a 10 GB monthly data cap and strong security features, with no logging or ads. It's a reliable free VPN for iPhone users who prioritize privacy.

Windscribe

Key Features:

- 10 GB of free data per month.
- Access to servers in 10 countries (US, UK, Canada, France).
- Built-in ad-blocker and firewall.
- No logging of user activity.

Limitations: Limited to 10 GB of data per month on the free plan.

Why It's Great: Windscribe's 10 GB monthly data cap and access to a wide range of servers make it one of the better free VPNs for iPhone users. Its privacy tools, like the ad-blocker and firewall, are nice extras.

Chapter 11: Family and Child Safety Online

Hannibal and Margaret sat at the dining table, frustrated and worried. Earlier in the day, Margaret had clicked on an ad she saw on social media promoting a discounted health product. She entered her address and phone number to place an order, but something felt off when the product never arrived. To make matters worse, strange promotional texts and pop-up ads had started appearing on their devices. Unsure of what to do, they reached out to the family for help.

The following evening, the family gathered at home. Evan and Clarice sat with the grandparents while Shannon checked their tablet, scrolling through the suspicious sites. This time, they invited a family friend, Diego, who worked as a cybersecurity analyst.

Diego sat beside Margaret, patiently reviewing what had happened. He explained that these kinds of ads were often part of online scams designed to collect personal information. Hannibal and Margaret nodded, feeling more assured just knowing they weren't alone in navigating this new digital world.

Meanwhile, Aditsan, the youngest in the family, sat nearby on his tablet. He was reminded of the time he almost downloaded a fake game that looked just like one he played often. It dawned on him that staying safe online wasn't just something adults needed to do—it mattered for him, too, especially with games and apps.

As Diego continued, he highlighted the importance of being careful with unfamiliar apps and websites, especially those that asked for personal details or pressured users with limited-time offers. Shannon made a mental note to keep an eye out for similar issues on her parents' and grandparents' devices going forward.

By the end of the evening, Hannibal and Margaret felt less anxious. They realized that technology might be new to them, but they didn't have to figure it all out alone.

Parental Controls and Filters

Implementing parental controls for internet access is an important step in managing and regulating children's online activities. There are several types of parental controls, but their features include:

- content filters
- time limits
- privacy controls
- and online activity monitoring.

Here are some steps you can take to set up parental controls:

Understand Parental Control Options

Get familiar with the options available. These include:

1. Router-based controls
2. Operating system controls
3. and third-party software solutions.

Understand the features each option provides.

Router-Based Parental Controls

Many routers offer built-in parental control features. We access most router's settings through a web browser to find the options related to parental controls. Common features include website filtering, scheduling, and device-specific controls. We can use these features to implement parental controls on network devices and internet browsers. Most routers have features that restrict access to inappropriate content, set time limits, and monitor online activities.

The same router menu used to set time restrictions can be used to block unwanted websites. We can add the addresses of websites we wish to block from our network using URL (A URL is a website address) filter options.

Controlling devices at the router can be seen as network-level control. It is because changes made on your router apply to all devices connected to your home network. These controls can help you manage internet access for multiple devices. Regularly review and update the parental control settings based on your child's age, maturity, and changing needs. As your child grows, you will need to regularly update and test these controls.

Below is another example of a modern home router control panel interface. The parental controls section is clearly labeled:

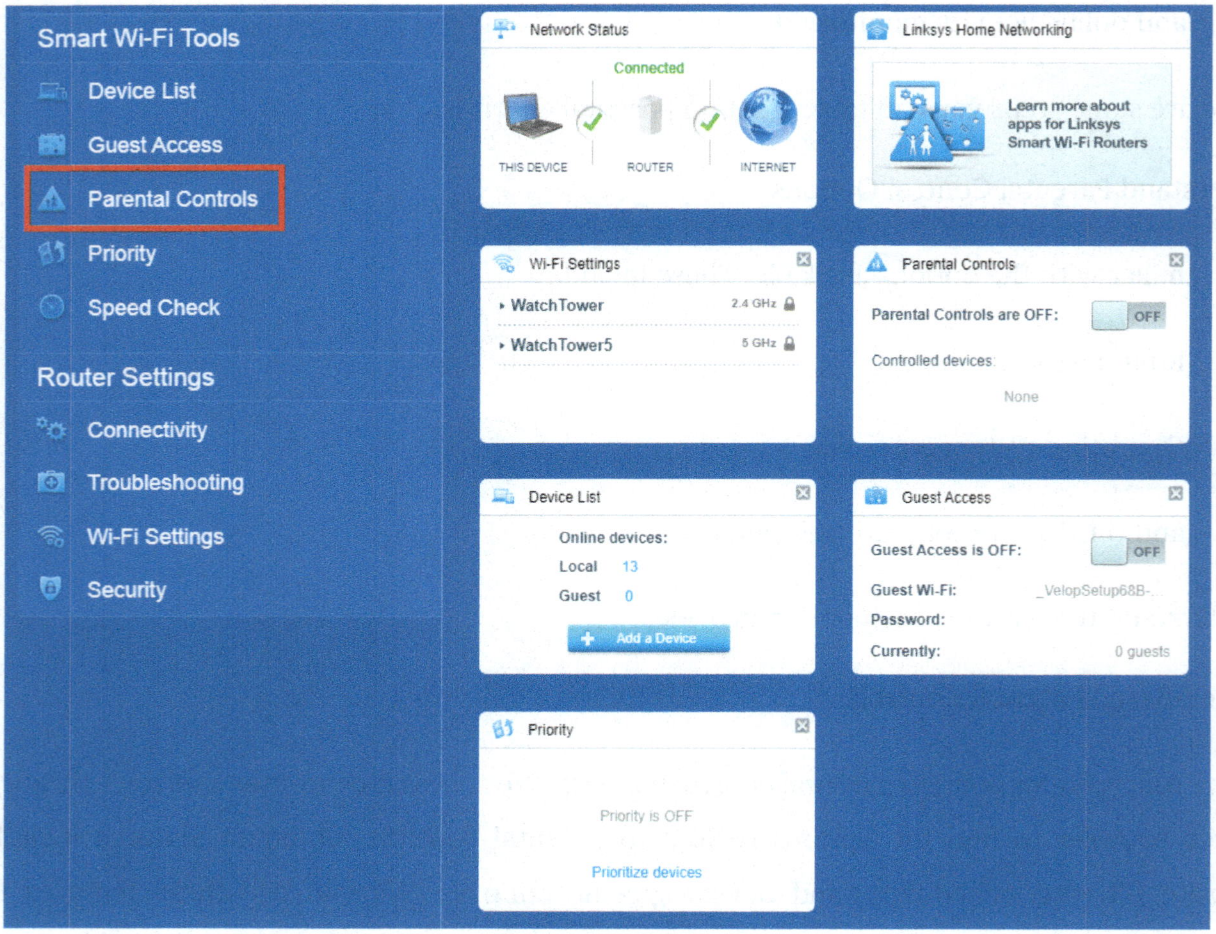

Clicking this menu option gives us access to the Parental Controls settings page:

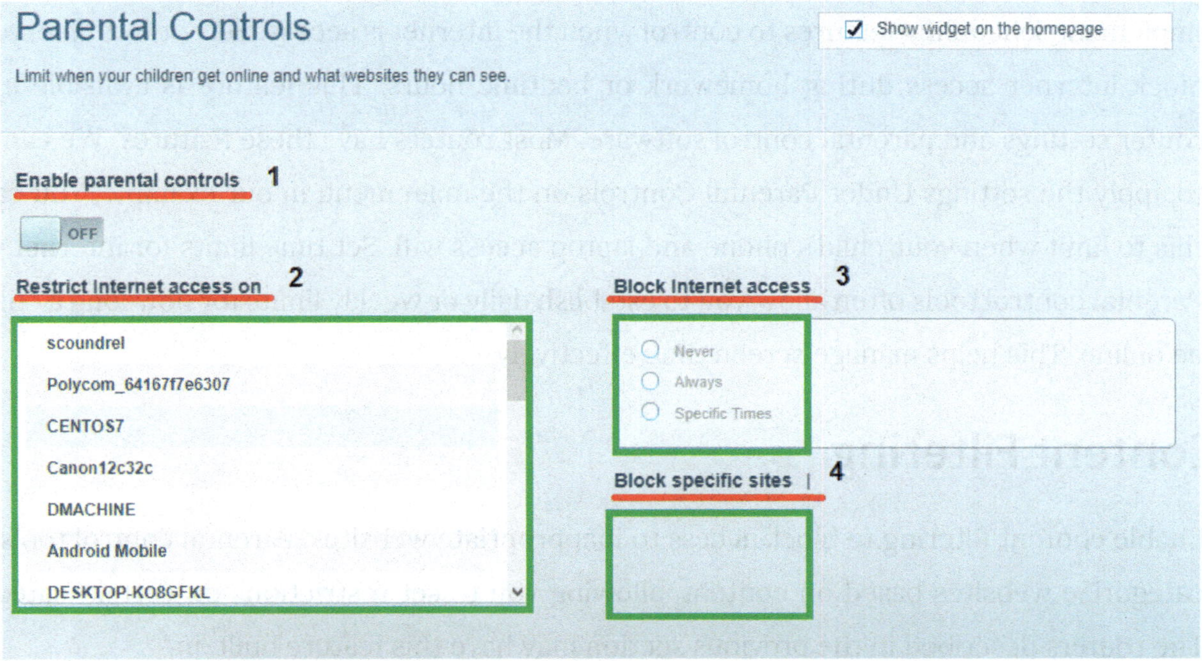

Option 1 is to turn the controls on.

Option 2 lists all of the devices on the network. You can choose any device on that list and restrict network access.

Option 3 Allows you to restrict internet access based on a time schedule.

Option 4 allows you to block specific content or websites.

Changes made here affect the entire network. To give a simple example if you add https://Youtube.com to your blocked sites list on the router. No device using your home network will be able to access the YouTube site.

Monitoring and Restrictions

Some parental control tools provide monitoring and reporting features. These features allow you to track your child's online activities, including the websites visited, search queries, and the time spent online. Use parental controls to restrict access to certain apps or games. This is particularly useful for mobile devices and gaming consoles where children may have access to various applications.

Scheduling & Time Limits

Implement scheduling features to control when the internet is accessible. For example, you can block internet access during homework or bedtime hours. This feature is available in both router settings and parental control software. Most routers have these features. We can log in to apply the settings Under Parental Controls on the main menu in our example. You can use this to limit when your child's phone and laptop access wifi. Set time limits for internet usage. Parental control tools often allow you to establish daily or weekly limits for how long a child can be online. This helps manage screen time effectively.

Content Filtering

Enable content filtering to block access to inappropriate websites. Parental control tools often categorize websites based on content, allowing you to set restrictions on certain categories. The routers described in the previous section may have this feature built-in.

Password Protect & Test

Password-protect the parental control settings to prevent children from circumventing the controls. Keep the password confidential and periodically update it. After implementing parental controls, test them to ensure they work as intended. Check that websites are appropriately filtered, time limits are enforced, and other settings are functioning correctly.

Password management will always be located somewhere under Router Settings. In our example it is in the connectivity panel.

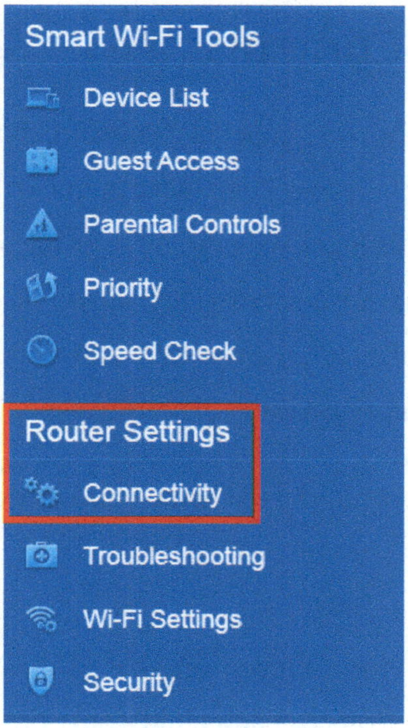

On the Connectivity page, the router password can be managed in 3 easy steps:

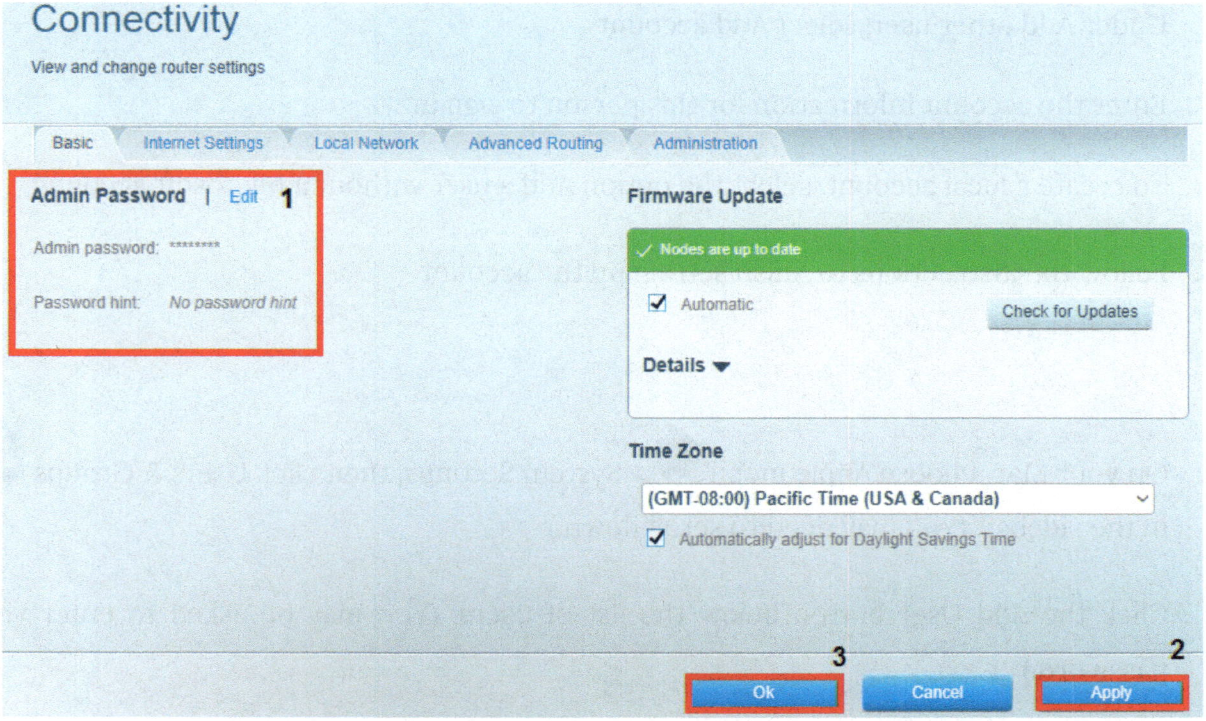

Operating System Controls

Most operating systems (Windows, macOS, Android, iOS) have built-in parental control features. These controls allow you to restrict access to certain apps, websites, and features. In order to establish control at this level, we employ user accounts. Separate user accounts must be created for children on shared devices. This allows us to apply different parental control settings for children and adults. It ensures that the child accounts have limited privileges. Familiarize yourself with the parental control settings specific to your operating system.

Controls applied at this level only apply to the specific device on which they are set.

Creating User Accounts

Create separate user accounts for children on shared devices. This allows you to apply age-appropriate settings and restrictions to each child's account.

Windows

1. In the Settings app on your Windows device, select Accounts > Other user
2. Under Add other user, select Add account
3. Enter the account information for this person to sign in:
4. To create a local account, select the option Add a user without a Microsoft account
5. Follow the instructions to finish setting up the account

Mac

1. On your Mac, choose Apple menu > System Settings, then click Users & Groups in the sidebar. (You may need to scroll down.)
2. Click the Add User button below the list of users. (You may be asked to enter your password.)
3. Click the pop-up menu next to New User, then choose a type of user.
4. Create a standard user account for your child.

Standard: <u>Standard</u> users are set up by an administrator. Standard users can install apps and change their own settings but can't add other users or change other users' settings.

Ubuntu Linux

1. Click the view applications button on the left corner of your home screen
2. Type settings in the search bar
3. Open Ubuntu Settings
4. Type users on the search bar
5. Click on the users option
6. click Unlock in the top right corner
7. Enter the root user password
8. click on the **Add User..** option
9. click on **Standard** to create a regular user

Third-Party Parental Control Software

We can implement parental control tools on devices our child uses. These tools often include features such as content filtering, time management, and activity monitoring. Choose tools that are age-appropriate and align with your monitoring goals. Consider using third-party parental control software. Numerous options provide advanced features such as content filtering, time management, and activity monitoring.

In this book, I would like to take a more agnostic approach without endorsing any specific brands. However, some popular choices include Norton Family, Qustodio, and Net Nanny. Without going into great detail, I encourage you to research 3rd party software options that meet your requirements.

Enable Safe Search Settings

Ensure that safe search settings are enabled on search engines your child uses. This helps filter out explicit content from search results and provides a safer online search experience. Most search engines have this feature. Enable safe search settings on popular search engines like Google, Bing, and Yahoo. This helps filter out explicit content from search results.

Google

Log into the Google account and then go to Google's homepage.

1. Click on Settings. You will find it in the right corner at the bottom.

2. In the popup window, click on Search Settings.

3. Click the box next to "Turn on SafeSearch."

4. Choose the SafeSearch level that you would like to use in the SafeSearch Filtering section:

- Strict filtering will filter sexually explicit images and videos from Google Search result pages and results that may link to explicit content.

- Moderate filtering will exclude sexually explicit videos and images from your Google Search result pages. However, it does not filter results that may link to other explicit content. Keep in mind that this is the default SafeSearch setting.

- No filtering will turn off SafeSearch filtering completely.

5. Now click on Save. You will find it in the blue box at the bottom of your screen.

6. Note that your search results will be filtered when the box next to "Turn on SafeSearch" has the checkmark. You will see all the search results when it doesn't have a checkmark.

7. If you would like to lock SafeSearch on a computer, click the words in blue, "Lock SafeSearch and then follow the prompts.

Locking SafeSearch

1. The top of the search results page will look different in two ways when the SafeSearch lock is on: “SafeSearch is locked” will be displayed below that search box, and you will see colored balls on the right.

2. Now, go to the Search settings page.

3. Click on Lock SafeSearch. You will find it below the filter levels.

4. You will be requested to sign in to your Google Account if you are not signed in.

5. Click on Lock SafeSearch when you sign in. This step will take a moment. This is because strict filtering is now being applied to all the Google domains.

6. When the lock is engaged, you will see a confirmation page.

Bing

SafeSearch is a Bing setting that filters out inappropriate web content. To change it:

1. Open a browser and go to Bing.com.

2. Select the icon in the upper right of the Bing.com window. Select Settings, and then select More.

3. Choose your SafeSearch preference: Strict, Moderate, or Off. Select Save at the bottom of the menu.

Duck Duck Go

With the dropdown box under the search box in our results pages (see screenshot below).

1. With the "Safe Search" option on the DuckDuckGo settings page (https://duckduckgo.com/settings).

2. By appending! Safe to your search (this uses our bang syntax).

3. By using safe.duckduckgo.com instead.

Yahoo

How to Turn Yahoo! SafeSearch On

1. Open Yahoo and perform a search.

2. Select the Menu icon.

3. Select Settings.

4. Select the SafeSearch drop-down menu, then select On - filter results.

5. Select Save.

6. Do a Yahoo search.

7. To revert these changes, follow the same steps but choose Off – do not filter results, then select Save.

Review Privacy Policies

When using third-party parental control tools, review their privacy policies. Ensure that the tools prioritize user privacy and do not compromise sensitive information. Stay informed about new technologies, apps, and websites that your child may encounter. Parental control tools may need updates or adjustments to address emerging online risks.

Teach About Risks & Privacy Protection

Instill the importance of privacy. Teach children to be cautious about sharing personal information online, such as full names, addresses, school names, and contact details. Ask them to think before clicking yes to the agreements required by services and games they wish to access. Establish clear rules and boundaries for internet use.

Keeping children safe online is a shared responsibility between parents, caregivers, and educators. Here are guidelines to help ensure a safe online environment for children:

Teach Digital Footprint Awareness

Explain the concept of a digital footprint. Help children understand that their online actions leave a trace and can impact their future. Teach them to be mindful of what they share and post online. Model responsible online behavior. Children often learn by observing, so demonstrate positive online habits, including respectful communication and appropriate content sharing. Instill good online etiquette or "netiquette." Teach children to be respectful, kind, and considerate when communicating online. Emphasize the importance of treating others as they would in person.

Teach Critical Thinking

Help children develop critical thinking skills to evaluate online information. Teach them to question the reliability of sources, recognize fake news, and think critically about online content. Encourage children to share their online friends with you. Monitor their friend lists and discuss the importance of connecting only with people they know in real life.

Address Cyberbullying & Social Media Usage

If your child uses social media, set age-appropriate restrictions and monitor their accounts. Discuss responsible social media behavior, including the implications of sharing photos and personal information. Discuss the concept of cyberbullying and teach children how to respond if they experience or witness it. Encourage them to report incidents and reassure them that seeking help is okay.

Create a Safe Environment

Designate a safe and visible space for internet use within your home. This allows you to monitor online activities and ensures that children feel comfortable seeking help if needed. Utilize online safety resources provided by reputable organizations. Websites like Common Sense Media https://www.commonsensemedia.org/, Stay Safe Online https://staysafeonline.org, and others offer valuable information and tips for parents.

Create a Family Media Plan with Educational Websites

Develop a family media plan that includes agreed-upon guidelines for screen time, device use, and online activities. Involve children in creating the plan to ensure they feel a sense of ownership. Introduce educational apps and websites that align with your child's interests.

Creating a family media plan that emphasizes educational websites is a great way for parents to guide their children's media consumption. Here are some valuable online resources that can assist in this process:

HealthyChildren.org - https://www.healthychildren.org/English/Pages/default.aspx

This site offers a tool to create a personalized family media plan aligning priorities, values and educational goals.

The American Academy of Pediatrics - https://www.aap.org/

Resources for creating a family plan balancing media use with educational content.

Common Sense Media - https://www.commonsensemedia.org

This organization offers guides and workshops for parents. They focus on digital citizenship and provide practical tips for navigating media use in a way that supports learning.

MediaSmarts: https://mediasmarts.ca/

Provides guides and tips to help parents support children through various digital issues, including how to choose educational content.

Turning Life On: https://www.turninglifeon.org

These resources have spent years researching and evaluating family media plans, offering extensive and customizable options for families to consider:

Digital Citizenship - https://www.commonsense.org/education/digital-citizenship

Digital Parenting -
https://www.ccrce.ca/parents_guardians/parent_resources/online_canadian_resources_for_digital_parenting

There are many resources available to provide digital citizenship advice, helping families engage with media in a responsible and educational manner. These resources can help parents create a comprehensive family media plan that prioritizes educational content while ensuring a balanced approach to media use. Be aware of the age appropriateness and potential risks of the apps and games used by your child. Understanding their content will provide a safer online environment.

Monitoring Online Activities

Monitoring your child's online activities is important for ensuring their safety and promoting responsible internet use. Periodically check your child's devices, including smartphones, tablets, and computers. Review their browsing history, installed apps, and any downloaded content. Be transparent with your child about this process. If your child has social media accounts, monitor their activity on these platforms. Many social media platforms have privacy settings that allow you to follow or friend your child to keep an eye on their posts and interactions.

Here are steps and tools you can use to monitor your child's online activities:

Communicate Expectations

Establish open communication with your child by letting them know you will monitor their online activities to ensure their safety and well-being. Encourage them to share their online experiences with you. If your child uses email or messaging apps, periodically check their messages. Understand who they are communicating with and the nature of their conversations. Discuss the importance of online communication etiquette. Clearly defining expectations regarding online behavior, time limits, and the types of websites or apps they are allowed to use ensures your child understands the rules and consequences for not following them.

Review Privacy Settings, App Usage & Streaming

Help your child review and adjust privacy settings on their online accounts. Teach them how to control who can see their information and posts, and encourage them to use strong, unique passwords. Review the apps and games your child is using. Understand their content, age appropriateness, and potential risks. Some parental control tools provide insights into app and game usage. Keep an eye on the video and streaming platforms your child uses. Review their viewing history and discuss appropriate content choices. Set guidelines for age-appropriate viewing.

Teach Offline Consequences

Help your child understand that online actions have offline consequences. Discuss scenarios where inappropriate online behavior can impact their real-world relationships, school, or future opportunities. If your child is engaged in online education platforms or virtual classrooms, stay involved. Attend virtual parent-teacher meetings, review learning materials, and ensure a safe online learning environment.

Promote Screen-Free Activities

Encourage a balance between online and offline activities. Promote screen-free time for physical activities, hobbies, and face-to-face interactions with friends and family.

Chapter 12: IoT Security

Risks Associated with Smart Devices

The sun was setting as Evan and Clarice entered the living room for a family discussion. The news had recently reported a security breach involving their neighbor's smart surveillance cameras. This incident sparked a wave of concern within the family about their own smart devices at home.

Just then, their neighbors, the Parkers, knocked on the door and came in. They were close friends, often sharing meals and stories together. Mrs. Parker looked worried as she sat down.

"I can't believe what happened to us," she said. "Our security cameras were hacked last week. We had no idea it could happen!"

Mr. Parker nodded in agreement. "We thought our cameras were safe because they were from a well-known brand. But now we're not so sure. It made us rethink all our smart devices."

Evan exchanged worried glances with Clarice. They had their own smart devices in the house and hadn't considered the risks.

"Maybe we should look into keeping our smart appliances off the internet when we don't need them connected," Evan suggested thoughtfully.

Mrs. Parker leaned forward. "That's a good idea. We didn't realize how exposed we were until it was too late."

"What about updates? Have you checked if your devices need new software?" asked Clarice.

"Oh, absolutely," Mr. Parker replied. "We need to stay on top of those. It seems like every device we own has a way to collect data, and we don't always know what they're doing with it."

The grandparents, Margaret and Hannibal, sat quietly listening, their expressions thoughtful. They understood the importance of keeping their home secure but were glad to hear the younger generation discussing these issues.

"Let's all make sure our devices are secure and up to date. We can't afford to take risks with our privacy," said Evan.

The Parkers nodded, and the family agreed to take action together, knowing they had to be vigilant with their smart home devices. It was evident that staying informed about potential risks was just as important as enjoying these devices' convenience.

Smart devices offer convenience and advanced functionality but also introduce risks and security concerns. Any Internet-connected device, such as those in the Internet of Things (IoT), can exchange sensitive data and become a target for hackers. As the family's discussion showed, understanding these risks is crucial to protecting both privacy and security.

Understanding the connected devices in your home is the first step in securing your IoT infrastructure. The challenge with many IoT devices is that they often lack the computing, memory, or storage capacity to support security software. Additionally, manufacturers may configure these devices to collect more data than necessary and transmit it back to their servers-commonly referred to as "phoning home." Without knowing it, many users give away more data than intended, exposing themselves to unnecessary risks.

Data transmission from smart devices to manufacturers expands your network's "attack surface," raising privacy concerns. IoT devices collect vast amounts of data, including location, shopping behavior, and browsing habits. This prompts the question: Is all this data collection essential for the device to function? The family wondered whether connected devices were always worth the trade-off, especially given how much data these appliances collected.

For example, does a smart fridge need to reorder groceries to keep food cold? Can we disable some data collection and still enjoy its basic features? Similarly, home security systems store video on cloud servers for remote access, and personal assistants like Alexa, Siri, or Google Assistant may transmit conversations to vendors, potentially enabling targeted advertising. Each device brings its own risks and benefits, making it important to think carefully about which features are necessary.

Since all IoT devices connect to Wi-Fi, collect private data, and may listen to conversations, it's important to decide which devices truly need to be IoT-enabled. The impact of a baby monitor being hacked is far more serious than that of a bird feeder breach. Choosing carefully which devices to connect helps manage both security and privacy risks.

IoT devices store, analyze, and transmit data across global networks; it's crucial to understand how a vendor will handle your data before bringing such devices into your home. Ultimately, as Evan, Clarice, and the Parkers realized, protecting their privacy meant staying vigilant, informed, and selective with their use of smart technology.

Here are some of the key risks associated with using smart devices:

Privacy Concerns

Smart devices often collect and process personal data to provide personalized services. This data may include information about your habits, preferences, and even sensitive details. This information could be vulnerable to unauthorized access or misuse if not adequately protected.

Data Breaches

Smart devices are potential targets for cybercriminals seeking to exploit vulnerabilities and gain unauthorized access to sensitive data. A data breach in a smart device could expose personal information, compromising your privacy and security.

Insecure Network Communication

Many smart devices communicate over Wi-Fi or other networks. If these communications are not properly secured, they could be intercepted by malicious actors, leading to eavesdropping, data manipulation, or unauthorized access to the device.

Vendor and Supply Chain Risks

The security of smart devices depends on the practices of the manufacturers and the entire supply chain. If manufacturers do not prioritize security or if there are vulnerabilities in the supply chain, devices may be at risk. Some smart devices may not receive regular security updates or patches from manufacturers. This can leave devices vulnerable to known exploits and increase the risk of security breaches over time.

Default or Weak Passwords

Many smart devices come with default usernames and passwords that users may not change. Additionally, some users may choose weak passwords, making it easier for attackers to gain unauthorized access to the device.

Smart Appliances

Examples: Smart refrigerators, ovens, washing machines
These connect to the internet and can be controlled with apps or voice assistants, helping with things like tracking food, adjusting settings, and scheduling maintenance.

Risks:

1. **IoT Botnets:** Hackers can take control of appliances and use them for cyberattacks (like DDoS).
2. **Data Privacy Issues:** Appliances collect information on how you use them, and if not protected, others could access this data.

How to Stay Safe:

- **Change Default Passwords:** Set new, strong ones.
- **Update Firmware Regularly:** Install updates to fix security issues.
- **Network Segmentation:** Keep smart devices on a separate Wi-Fi network to limit what they can access.

Voice Assistants

Examples: Alexa, Google Assistant, Siri
Voice assistants help control devices, answer questions, and do tasks by listening to voice commands.

Risks:

1. **Eavesdropping:** They are always listening for their wake word, which can sometimes lead to accidentally recording conversations.
2. **Unauthorized Commands:** Someone with a similar voice could control your devices.

How to Stay Safe:

- **Voice Profiles:** Set up user-specific voice profiles so only recognized users can give commands.
- **Check Privacy Settings:** Review what data is collected and adjust privacy settings.
- **Mute When Not Using:** Mute the device or disconnect it from the internet if privacy is a concern.

Home Automation Systems

Examples: Smart lighting, security cameras, thermostats

These systems link multiple smart devices through a central hub or app, letting you control them easily.

Risks:

1. **Central Hub Vulnerability:** If the hub or app is hacked, the entire system could be compromised.
2. **Communication Risks:** Hackers could intercept data between devices if the system isn't well-protected.

How to Stay Safe:

- **Secure the Hub:** Use strong passwords, enable two-factor authentication, and update software regularly.
- **Encrypt Communication:** Make sure the system encrypts data between devices to stop hackers.
- **Review Devices Regularly:** Check which devices are connected to ensure no unauthorized ones have been added.

IoT Botnets and Cyber Attacks

Smart devices are susceptible to being hijacked and recruited into botnets. Cybercriminals can exploit vulnerabilities to compromise multiple devices and use them for large-scale attacks, such as Distributed Denial of Service (DDoS) attacks.

Physical Security Concerns

In some cases, physical security risks exist. For example, smart home cameras or baby monitors could be hacked, allowing unauthorized individuals to spy on your home.

Standardization & Integration Challenges

The lack of standardized security protocols for smart devices can lead to inconsistencies in security measures. This makes it challenging for users to assess the security level of different devices and increases the overall risk of vulnerabilities. Smart devices often work within an ecosystem of interconnected devices and platforms. Poorly integrated systems can lead to security vulnerabilities, as weaknesses in one device may affect the overall security of the interconnected network.

Reliance On Cloud Services & Mobile Apps

Many smart devices rely on cloud services for storage and processing. If these cloud services experience downtime or are compromised, it can affect the functionality and security of connected devices. Smart devices often have associated mobile apps for remote control and management. If these apps lack security measures, such as encryption and secure authentication, they become potential targets for attackers.

Legal and Ethical Concerns

Users may not be fully aware of the security risks associated with smart devices. This lack of awareness can lead to unsafe practices, such as neglecting to update firmware or using default credentials. The use of smart devices raises legal and ethical questions about data ownership, consent, and the sharing of personal information. Regulations and laws regarding smart device security and data privacy may vary, adding complexity to the landscape.

Securing Smart Home Devices

Now that we are aware of IoT risks, securing smart devices improves the security of your home network. Many of the strategies employed when securing smart home devices are a review of the techniques discussed in the previous chapter, 9: Securing Network Devices. Technically, an IoT device is just another network device or endpoint. Having an inventory of all the IoT devices in your home is extremely important. The manufacturer often configures these devices to communicate via the Internet by default.

Inventory IoT & Change Default Passwords

Regularly audit the list of connected IoT devices on your network to ensure that only authorized devices are connected. Check your inventory and disconnect any unauthorized or unknown devices from your network. Change your smart devices' default usernames and passwords, especially on cameras, routers, and other devices that connect directly to the internet. Use strong, unique passwords for each device.

Enable & Check For Firmware Updates

Set a schedule to manually check for firmware updates on your smart devices. This can be done weekly or monthly, depending on the frequency of updates released by the manufacturer. Manufacturers often release updates to address security vulnerabilities and enhance device performance. Check if your smart devices have an automatic update feature. If available, enable it to ensure that your devices receive updates as soon as the manufacturer releases them. Regularly visit the official website of each smart device manufacturer. Look for a "Support" or "Downloads" section where you can find the latest firmware updates for your specific device.

Use the Official Mobile App & Check Permissions

Many smart devices come with official mobile apps that facilitate firmware updates. Install the official app on your smartphone or tablet, and use it to check for and install firmware updates for your devices. Review and adjust app permissions associated with your smart devices. Limit unnecessary access to features or data to minimize potential security risks.

Use Vendor-Specific Software & Check Notifications

Some smart devices may require the use of vendor-specific software on your computer to update firmware. Check if your device manufacturer provides such software and use it to perform updates. Some smart devices may display in-app notifications when a new firmware update is available. Monitor these notifications and follow the prompts to initiate the update.

Enable MFA & Strong Encryption

If your smart devices or associated apps support two-factor authentication, enable it. This adds an extra layer of security by requiring a second form of verification in addition to a password. Ensure that your Wi-Fi network is secured with strong encryption, such as WPA3. Use a strong, unique passphrase for your Wi-Fi password, and avoid using default credentials.

Implement Network Segmentation & Backups

Segment your home network using features like VLANs to isolate smart devices from other critical devices, such as computers or storage devices. Before performing a firmware update, consider backing up your device settings, configurations, or any critical data. This ensures that you can restore your preferred settings if needed. Place IoT devices on a guest network. All routers support this feature. We can configure Guest Access from the main menu:

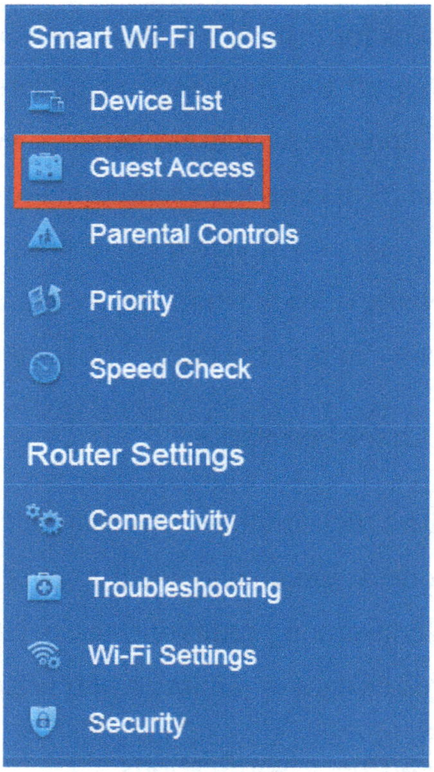

On the Guest Access page, it explains that all devices connecting via this network will be segregated from devices on your home network. It must be turned on then given a network name and password:

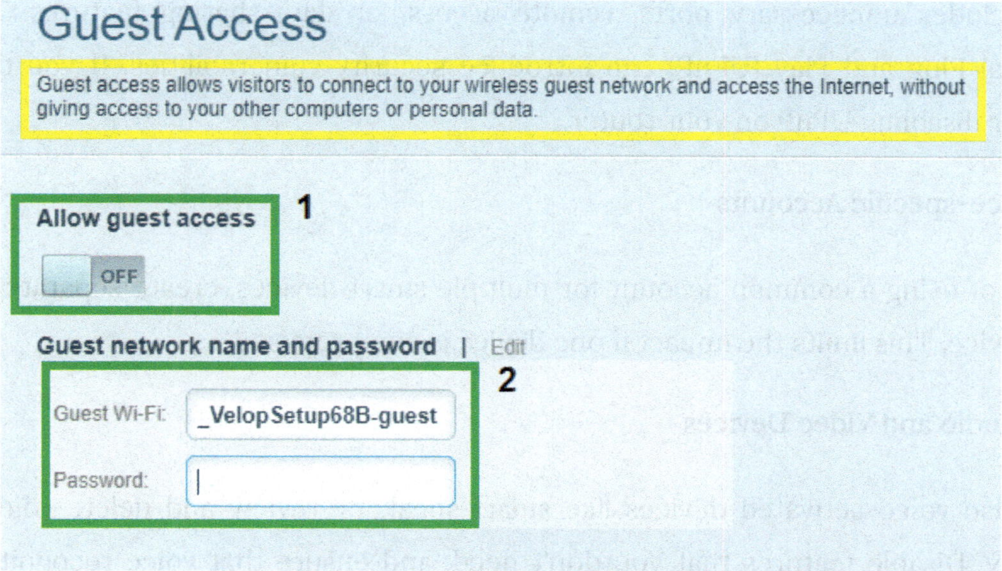

Disable Unused Features and Services

Review the settings on each smart device and disable any features or services you do not need. This includes unnecessary ports, remote access, or data-sharing features. Features like Universal Plug and Play (UPnP) can introduce security vulnerabilities. If you don't need it, consider disabling UPnP on your router.

Use Device-specific Accounts

Instead of using a common account for multiple smart devices, create separate accounts for each device. This limits the impact if one device is compromised.

Secure Audio and Video Devices

If you use voice-activated devices like smart speakers, review and delete voice recordings regularly. Disable features that you don't need, and ensure that voice recognition is set up securely. Place smart cameras strategically to avoid capturing sensitive areas of your home. Regularly check and update the camera's firmware for security improvements.

Choose Reputable Manufacturers & Register Your Devices

Choose smart devices from reputable manufacturers with a history of providing security updates and support. Research user reviews and security practices before purchasing. They may announce updates for registered products. Register your smart devices with the manufacturer, if applicable. Some manufacturers provide update notifications and support services to registered users. Some manufacturers provide newsletters or notifications for firmware updates. Subscribe to these services to receive timely alerts about new updates and security patches.

Secure Devices & Monitor Activity

If you have smart devices outdoors, such as smart locks or cameras, ensure they are weatherproof and secure against tampering. Regularly check their functionality and update their firmware. Periodically review the activity logs or usage history of your smart devices. Look for any unusual or unauthorized activities that may indicate a security issue.

Community Forums and Support

Participate in community forums or support groups related to your smart devices. Sometimes, fellow users share information about firmware updates and troubleshooting tips. Review the user manuals provided with your smart devices. Explore Cloud-Based Updates Some smart devices receive firmware updates through cloud services. Check if your devices have this capability and ensure that they are connected to the internet to receive updates. They often include information on how to update firmware and any specific requirements or precautions.

Warranty and Service Life

Older smart devices may no longer receive updates or support from manufacturers, leaving them more susceptible to security vulnerabilities as time passes. Be aware of the product life cycle of your smart devices. Some manufacturers may announce end-of-life for certain models, indicating that they will no longer receive firmware updates. If you encounter any issues during or after a firmware update, report them to the manufacturer's support. This helps the manufacturer identify and address potential bugs or glitches.

Consider Professional Assistance

If you are unsure about how to update the firmware or encounter difficulties, seek assistance from the manufacturer's customer support or consult professional services. Educate everyone in your household about the importance of smart device security. Ensure that all users follow best practices for securing devices and networks.

Chapter 13: Incident Response and Recovery

Recognizing a Security Incident

After the recent challenges—Clarice's stolen purse, Evan's ransomware scare, and the confusion faced by Margaret and Hannibal over online scams—the family gathered to discuss how to improve their internet safety.

They acknowledged that many people fall victim to phishing and hacking due to weak passwords and falling for suspicious emails. Clarice realized how easily her old passwords could have put her finances at risk, while Idris noted the signs of malware, such as slow performance or strange pop-ups.

As the conversation progressed, they understood that recognizing a security incident is crucial for taking prompt action to protect their digital assets. They learned about two main types of incidents:

- **Third-Party Breaches**: When services like Facebook or Equifax report data leaks, it means their credentials could be compromised. They knew that if they received such a notification, they needed to change their passwords immediately and consider implementing multi-factor authentication.

- **Personal Incidents**: If a family member's computer showed signs of malware—like sluggishness, intrusive pop-ups, or changes to the browser homepage—it indicated a direct threat.

To respond effectively, the family decided on a plan. If a third-party account was compromised, they would first reset the password and then review all accounts using those credentials, ensuring they had a complete inventory of their online services.

For personal incidents, they understood the importance of isolating the infected device by disconnecting it from the network. They planned to run security scans and, if necessary, consult a professional for virus removal. They also discussed the need for data backups, deciding that, in severe cases, formatting the hard drive and reinstalling the operating system might be necessary.

Here are common signs that may indicate a cybersecurity incident at home:

Social Media and Email Anomalies

- Monitor for unauthorized posts, friend requests, or privacy changes on social media.
- Look for suspicious emails, unexpected password reset requests, and failed login attempts.

Unusual Device Behavior

- Devices may slow down, crash, or behave oddly (e.g., apps opening/closing on their own).
- Check for unfamiliar software, processes, or unexpected installations.

Changes in Browser or System Settings

- Be cautious of unexplained changes in browser settings (homepage, search engine).
- Unauthorized system configuration changes (security settings, firewall, updates) are warning signs.

Unexpected Pop-ups, Ads, and Software Installs

- Intrusive pop-ups or redirects to strange websites may indicate adware or malware.
- Watch out for unauthorized software installations.

Security Software Issues

- Frequent antivirus alerts or unexpected disabling of security software may signal malware.

Device or Account Lockouts and Unauthorized Access

- Repeated lockouts or password reset requests might mean someone is trying to gain access.
- Monitor accounts for unusual activities like unrecognized logins or transactions.

Unusual Financial or Network Activity

- Regularly review financial statements for unauthorized transactions.
- Check for strange network traffic patterns and unfamiliar devices on your home network.

Ransomware Messages or Abnormal Resource Usage

- Files encrypted with demands for ransom are a clear red flag.
- Monitor system resources for unusual spikes in CPU, memory, or disk usage.

Steps to Take in the Event of a Breach

1. **Stay Calm and Follow Your Plan**
   Panic can lead to mistakes. You have a plan—now is the time to act methodically.

2. **Isolate-Affected Devices and Networks**
   Disconnect compromised devices from the network to prevent the spread of malware. Update Wi-Fi passwords to block unauthorized access.

3. **Run Security Scans and Update Software**
   - Use antivirus and anti-malware software to detect and remove threats.
   - Update operating systems, browsers, and all applications to close security vulnerabilities.

4. **Secure Accounts and Enable Multi-Factor Authentication (MFA)**
   - Change passwords for all critical accounts (email, banking, social media).
   - Use unique, strong passwords for each account and enable MFA wherever possible.

5. **Review for Suspicious Activity and Notify Contacts**
   - Monitor your online accounts and financial statements for unusual activities.
   - Alert your contacts if your email or social media accounts were compromised to prevent phishing.

6. **Restore Data from Backups**

- If files are corrupted or lost, restore them from backups stored offline.

7. **Report the Incident**

- Inform relevant authorities (cybersecurity agency, law enforcement) and your Internet Service Provider (ISP).
- Your ISP may help identify unusual activity and recommend further actions.

8. **Alert Credit Bureaus and Monitor Financial Activity**

- Consider placing a fraud alert or credit freeze with major credit bureaus to prevent identity theft.
- Review your financial statements for unauthorized transactions and contact your bank if needed.

9. **Scan for Phishing Attempts**

- Be wary of phishing messages related to the breach. Verify any suspicious communication.

10. **Consult with Cybersecurity Professionals**

- If you suspect a sophisticated attack or need additional help, seek professional assistance to secure your systems.

11. **Adopt Stronger Security Practices**

- Regularly update software, improve password management, and monitor your online presence to prevent future breaches.

Learning from Security Incidents

Experiencing a home cyber breach can be a challenging and concerning event, but it also provides valuable learning opportunities. Here are some key lessons that can be learned from a home cyber breach:

The Importance of Regular Backups

A cyber breach highlights the significance of regular backups. Having up-to-date backups of your important data ensures that you can recover it in the event of data loss or ransomware attacks.

The Need for Complex Passwords & Multi-Factor Authentication (MFA)

Passwords play a crucial role in online security. A breach underscores the vulnerability of weak or reused passwords. Learning to create and manage strong, unique passwords is essential for securing online accounts. Implementing MFA adds an extra layer of security to your accounts. Use MFA wherever possible to enhance account protection.

The Significance of Network Security & Software Updates

Strengthening network security, including using secure Wi-Fi passwords and configuring routers securely, becomes a priority. Understanding the fundamentals of home network security helps prevent unauthorized access. Outdated software often contains vulnerabilities that cybercriminals can exploit. Regularly updating your operating system, applications, and security software is critical for maintaining a secure digital environment.

Importance of Incident Response and Monitoring

Having a well-defined incident response plan is crucial. Being prepared with a set of actions to take in the event of a breach can minimize the impact and speed up recovery efforts. Regularly monitoring your online accounts for suspicious activities helps detect unauthorized access early. Being vigilant about account security contributes to a proactive defense against cyber threats.

Understanding the Impact of Social Engineering

Social engineering tactics, such as manipulating individuals to disclose sensitive information, may be involved in a breach. Awareness of social engineering techniques is key to avoid falling victim to such attacks. A breach may occur through phishing attempts. Recognizing and avoiding phishing emails and messages is crucial for preventing unauthorized access to accounts and sensitive information.

Promoting a Cybersecurity Mindset

Developing a cybersecurity mindset involves adopting a proactive and cautious approach to online activities. This mindset helps individuals anticipate potential risks and take preventive measures to protect their digital autonomy. A breach serves as a catalyst for fostering a security-conscious environment at home. Prioritizing security becomes a shared goal, creating a safer digital space for everyone. Understanding the responsibilities associated with digital citizenship, including respecting the privacy of others, reporting suspicious activities, and using technology ethically, is crucial in a connected world. Sharing responsibility for cybersecurity among family members ensures that everyone plays a role in maintaining a secure digital environment. A cyber breach underscores the importance of ongoing cybersecurity education. Staying informed about the latest threats, best practices, and emerging technologies helps families make informed decisions about online security.

Acknowledging the Value of Prevention

Prevention is a key aspect of cybersecurity. Recognizing the value of proactive measures, such as regular updates, secure practices, and a culture of security, reinforces the importance of preventing breaches before they occur. Cyber threats are constantly evolving. A breach underscores the dynamic nature of cybersecurity risks, emphasizing the need for ongoing vigilance and adaptability to new and emerging threats.

Seeking Professional Help When Necessary

Understanding when to seek professional help is important. In certain situations, consulting with cybersecurity professionals can provide expert guidance in addressing and mitigating the impact of a breach.

Conclusion

Essential Home Cybersecurity Tips

Manage Your Digital Footprint

Here are a few ways we can manage our digital footprint:

- Close old or unused email accounts
- Browse the internet in incognito mode to avoid cookies
- Unsubscribe from unwanted email newsletters
- Limit the information you share on social media
- Keep your personal email address private
- Regularly update your browser and privacy settings
- Use virtual private networks (VPN) to stop web browsers from accessing your IP address and other data
- Set age-based internet safety restrictions for children;
- Regularly update passwords used online.

It is now standard practice for employers, universities, and government agencies to check an individual's digital footprint prior to making hiring, admission, and application approval decisions.

It is much easier to prudently limit the data you share than to go back and try to scrub it from the internet.

Create a Backup Strategy

Understand that having an offline backup is the ultimate solution to any cybersecurity breach. With a verified backup, you can restore your systems and data to a pre-incident state. It will give you the confidence to move forward and keep you from becoming another extortion victim of threat actors.

Install Software Updates

Keeping your operating system and application software up to date plugs security holes. Security deficiencies are found in software every day. Manufacturers patch these vulnerabilities by issuing updates. Make sure these updates are applied to your systems to keep them secure.

Secure All Layers of the Network

Refer to the Defense in Depth Diagram presented in the introduction. Start from your Router/Firewall on the perimeter of your network, then move to the computers and devices living inside your network. Each layer has security controls.

- The default Router configuration must be changed.
- Passwords used must be complex.
- The firewall feature on the router must be enabled.
- Firewalls on individual computers must be turned on.
- Guest wireless and IOT devices must not be allowed to communicate with each other or the family network.

Secure Your Online Accounts

Use a password manager. Make sure that your email and social media account passwords are complex and secure. Enable 2FA on all of your accounts and devices whenever feasible.

Drill into the security settings for your social media accounts:

- Facebook
- Instagram
- Linked In
- TikTok
- Twitter

All of these platforms have security settings that allow you to limit the amount of content that you share publicly. They also allow you to limit the amount of data being collected by the platforms themselves. Choose the settings that reflect your preferences and only share what makes you comfortable.

Secure Your Browser

Use up-to-date browser software. Modern browsers have security features that warn users about potentially harmful websites. Set your browser to use https as the default. Pay attention to browser warnings and take them seriously.

Be Proactive

Adopt a Cybersecurity Mindset

Cyber security is a mindset that requires you to be present, aware, vigilant, and creative. Armed with awareness, we are less vulnerable to tactics being used to compromise our freedom, safety, and security. Teaching our children critical thinking at an early age will allow them to assess information with a healthy skepticism that will help keep them safe. Being vigilant is the opposite of being fearful. Vigilance empowers us to be present when doing things on the internet. In a world full of multi-tasking and instant gratification, it reminds us to breathe before clicking the next button labeled I Accept or I Agree. Stay informed about the latest online trends, challenges, and apps popular among children. This knowledge helps you anticipate potential concerns and engage in relevant conversations.

Consult Experts

Don't be afraid to ask for help. If you're unsure about how to proceed or suspect a sophisticated attack, consult with cybersecurity professionals. They can assess the situation, provide guidance, and help secure your digital environment.

Continuously Learn and Adapt

A cyber breach underscores the importance of ongoing education. Staying informed about the latest threats, best practices, and emerging technologies helps us all make informed decisions about online security.

Learn about phishing and educate others in your family or community. Training and awareness are effective tools for preventing phishing attacks. Stay informed about the latest phishing techniques and scams. Criminals continually adapt their tactics, so stay updated.

Remember that phishing attacks can take various forms, including emails, text messages, phone calls, or even messages on social media. Always exercise caution and verify the legitimacy of communications, especially when dealing with sensitive information or unexpected requests.

If in doubt, contact the supposed sender through official channels before taking any action. Staying vigilant and using a combination of the above tips will help you identify and avoid suspicious websites, reducing the risk of falling victim to online scams or malware.

Stay informed about new technologies, apps, and websites. Parental control tools for children and the elderly may need updates or adjustments to address emerging online risks.

Appendix 1: Chapter Summaries

Chapter 1 Summary: Understanding Your Digital Footprint

This chapter introduces the idea of a **digital footprint**—the trail of data created by everything we do online. It blends a family story with practical cybersecurity concepts to show why managing personal information matters.

Key Themes

1. What a Digital Footprint Is

Your digital footprint is the collection of data you leave behind online.

It comes in two forms:

- **Active footprint** – information you intentionally share
- (posts, photos, online banking, newsletters, app sign-ups)
- **Passive footprint** – information collected without your awareness
- (IP address, browsing habits, location data, cookies, app tracking)

The chapter uses Clarice's purse theft to illustrate how quickly personal data can be misused once it falls into the wrong hands.

Managing Your Digital Footprint

The chapter provides a comprehensive list of strategies to reduce exposure:

- Close unused accounts
- Use incognito mode
- Limit social media sharing
- Keep email private
- Update privacy settings regularly
- Use VPNs
- Set parental controls
- Update passwords and use a password manager
- Avoid unencrypted websites
- Remove metadata from photos
- Review what search engines reveal about you
- Reduce data shared with third-party sites
- Avoid logging into apps using Facebook or similar accounts
- Be cautious on public Wi-Fi
- Review app permissions and mobile security

The message is clear: **prevention is easier than cleanup**.

Risks of Oversharing

Oversharing online can expose you to:

- Phishing and identity theft
- Location tracking and loss of privacy
- Harassment, stalking, cyberbullying
- Social engineering attacks
- Damage to employment or reputation
- Targeted advertising and profiling
- Data breaches

The chapter emphasizes intentional, cautious online behavior to reduce these risks.

Importance of Privacy Settings

Privacy settings are framed as essential tools for:

- Controlling who sees your information
- Reducing exposure to scams and harassment
- Limiting data collection
- Protecting children online
- Managing your online reputation
- Preventing unwanted solicitations

The chapter encourages reviewing and customizing privacy settings across all platforms.

Overall Message

Your digital footprint is constantly evolving.

Managing it requires awareness, intentional choices, and regular maintenance.

By understanding how data is created and shared—and by using tools like privacy settings, strong passwords, and VPNs—you can protect your identity and maintain a safer online presence.

Chapter 2 Summary: Common Cyber Threats

This chapter shifts from understanding digital footprints to recognizing the **real-world dangers** that threaten both individuals and organizations. It uses Evan's workplace ransomware incident as a practical example of how quickly things can go wrong when cybersecurity is neglected.

The Wake-Up Call: Evan's Company Gets Hit

Evan arrives at work to find the company paralyzed by a **ransomware attack**.

A single employee clicked a phishing email, allowing attackers to encrypt company data and demand payment.

The fallout revealed several weaknesses:

- Weak, reused passwords
- No two-factor authentication
- Outdated security protocols
- No reliable backup system

The company had to bring in cybersecurity experts to rebuild defenses. For Evan, it was a personal reminder that **cybersecurity is everyone's responsibility**, not just IT's.

Major Cyber Threats Explained

1. Social Engineering & Phishing

Attackers manipulate people into revealing sensitive information by:

- Sending deceptive emails or messages
- Pretending to be trusted contacts
- Exploiting personal details found on social media

These attacks rely on **human error**, not technical flaws.

2. Malware & Ransomware

Malicious software can:

- Steal data
- Spy on activity
- Lock files until a ransom is paid

Ransomware is especially destructive because it **encrypts everything**, often halting entire organizations.

3. Identity Theft & Data Breaches

Cybercriminals may:

- Steal personal data
- Open accounts in your name
- Access financial information
- Commit fraud

Large-scale breaches expose millions of users at once.

4. Password Attacks

Attackers exploit weak or reused passwords through:

- Brute force (guessing every combination)
- Credential stuffing (using leaked passwords from other sites)
- Password spraying (trying common passwords across many accounts)

5. Unsecured Wi-Fi & Device Vulnerabilities

Weak Wi-Fi security or outdated software allows attackers to:

- Intercept data
- Access devices
- Exploit unpatched vulnerabilities

Regular updates and strong encryption are essential.

6. Online Scams & Social Media Threats

Common scams include:

- Fake shopping sites
- Lottery or prize scams
- Tech support scams

Social media is often used to gather personal info or impersonate victims.

7. Online Predators & Eavesdropping

Children are especially vulnerable to:

- Manipulation
- Exploitation
- Grooming

Attackers may also use compromised devices to **listen in** or spy.

8. Insecure IoT Devices

Smart home devices with weak security can be hijacked, allowing attackers to:

- Access personal data
- Spy through cameras or microphones
- Control home systems

Core Message

Cyber threats are everywhere–at home, at work, and across every device we use.

This chapter emphasizes **cyber hygiene**, including:

- Strong, unique passwords
- Software updates
- Caution with emails and links
- Secured Wi-Fi
- Awareness of evolving threats

This chapter asks a foundational question:

Do you have a backup and restore strategy? Because even the best defenses can fail.

Chapter 3 Summary: Data Backup Strategies

Chapter 3 shifts from understanding cyber threats to **building resilience**—specifically through strong, reliable **data backup strategies**. The chapter uses Evan's workplace ransomware incident as the catalyst for exploring why backups matter and how both organizations and families can protect their data.

Why Backups Matter

After the ransomware attack at Evan's company, it became clear that **security tools alone aren't enough**. Without backups, encrypted or corrupted data can be permanently lost. Backups act as:

- Insurance against ransomware
- Protection from accidental deletion
- Recovery from hardware failure
- A safety net for software issues
- Peace of mind

Evan helps his coworkers understand that backups aren't just an IT responsibility–they're essential for everyone, at work and at home.

How to Choose a Backup Strategy

A good backup plan depends on:

- What data needs protection
- How often it changes
- How quickly it must be restored
- What tools and storage are available

The chapter outlines several backup types, each with strengths and trade-offs.

Backup Strategy Overview

Strategy	Description	Pros	Cons	Recovery Speed
Full Backup	Complete copy	Simple recovery	Slow, storage-heavy	Fast
Incremental	Only changes since last backup	Saves time & space	Slower recovery	Moderate-High
Differential	Changes since last full backup	Faster recovery than incremental	Grows larger over time	Moderate
Mirror	Exact real-time copy	Immediate access	No version history	Very fast

Recommended Home Strategy: The 3-2-1 Rule

A practical approach for families:

- **3** copies of your data
- **2** different storage types
- **1** copy stored **offline**

Suggested weekly routine:

- Full backup once per week
- Incremental backups on other days
- Rotate three external drives so one is always offline

System Recovery Methods (Windows)

The chapter also explains how to restore a system after failure:

- **System Restore** (roll back to a previous state)
- **Safe Mode** (diagnose and fix issues)
- **Startup Repair** (automatic troubleshooting)

Backup Procedures by Operating System

Windows

- Use **Backup and Restore (Windows 7)**
- Optionally use **Robocopy** for advanced or automated backups
- Supports scheduled backups, system images, and file-level restores

macOS

- Use **Time Machine**
- Supports hourly, daily, and weekly backups
- Allows full system recovery via macOS Recovery

Linux (Ubuntu)

Multiple free tools:

- **Deja Dup** (GUI, encrypted, scheduled)
- **Timeshift** (system snapshots)
- **Tar** (compressed archives)
- **rsync** (syncing and automation via cron)
- **rclone** (cloud backups)

Key Benefits of Backups

Backups protect against:

- Ransomware
- Human error
- Hardware failure
- Software corruption
- Natural disasters
- Data versioning needs

Ultimately, backups provide **continuity, security, and peace of mind.**

Chapter 4 Summary: Data Encryption

Chapter 4 dives into one of the most essential pillars of cybersecurity: **encryption**. It explains what encryption is, why it matters, and how to apply it across devices, files, and online communications using free, widely available tools.

What Encryption Is

Encryption transforms readable information (**plaintext**) into unreadable data (**ciphertext**) using algorithms and keys.

Only someone with the correct key can decrypt it.

This protects data even if it's stolen, intercepted, or accessed without permission.

Two Types of Encryption

1. Data at Rest

Data stored on devices or in the cloud.

Examples:

- **Full Disk Encryption (FDE)** – encrypts the entire drive
- **File-level encryption** – encrypts specific files/folders
- **Database encryption**

Purpose: Prevents unauthorized access if a device is lost, stolen, or compromised.

2. Data in Flight (Data in Transit)

Data moving across networks.

Examples:

- TLS / HTTPS
- SSH
- VPNs
- **Encrypted email protocols (S/MIME, PGP)**

Purpose: Protects against eavesdropping, man-in-the-middle attacks, and packet sniffing.

Encrypting Data on Windows

BitLocker (Drive Encryption)

- Encrypts entire drives
- Uses TPM or USB startup key
- Requires backing up a recovery key
- Supports different encryption modes (XTS-AES recommended)

EFS (Encrypting File System)

- Encrypts individual files/folders
- Works per-user
- Requires backing up the encryption certificate
- Only works on NTFS drives

Cross-Platform Encryption: VeraCrypt

Open-source tool for Windows, macOS, and Linux.

Capabilities:

- Encrypt entire drives or partitions
- Create encrypted containers
- Support for multiple algorithms (AES, Serpent, Twofish)
- Pre-boot authentication for system drive encryption
- Requires a Rescue Disk for recovery

File-Level Encryption Tools

7-Zip

- Creates encrypted archives (.7z)
- Uses AES-256
- Can encrypt file names
- Ideal for securely sharing or storing individual files

WinRAR

- Similar to 7-Zip
- Supports encrypted RAR or ZIP archives
- Also supports AES-256
- Can hide file names

Encrypting Online Traffic (Data in Transit)

HTTPS-Only Mode

Ensures your browser always uses encrypted connections.

Browsers:

- Chrome: "Always use secure connections"
- Firefox: "Enable HTTPS-Only Mode"
- Edge: "Automatic HTTPS"
- Safari: Enabled by default

Private Browsing

Reduces tracking and limits stored session data.

A VPN really is one of the quiet heroes in Chapter 4 – not because it's flashy, but because it solves a problem most people never notice until it's too late: your data is exposed every time it travels across the internet unless it's encrypted end-to-end.

A few things make VPNs especially important in the context of the chapter you're working through:

1. VPNs Encrypt Data in Transit

Even if your files are encrypted on your device (data at rest), they're vulnerable the moment they leave it.

A VPN wraps all outgoing traffic in an encrypted tunnel, protecting it from:

- Eavesdropping
- Packet sniffing
- Man-in-the-middle attacks
- Rogue Wi-Fi hotspots

This is why VPNs are emphasized alongside HTTPS, TLS, and secure browsers.

2. VPNs Protect You on Public Wi-Fi

Public networks are notoriously unsafe. Anyone sharing the network can potentially intercept:

Login credentials

- Emails
- Browsing activity
- Session cookies

A VPN neutralizes that risk by encrypting everything before it even touches the Wi-Fi network.

3. VPNs Hide Your IP Address

Your IP reveals:

- Your approximate location
- Your ISP
- Your device's network identity

Masking it helps reduce:

- Targeted attacks
- Tracking
- Profiling
- Location-based exploitation

This ties directly into the chapter's broader theme of reducing your digital footprint.

4. VPNs Add a Layer of Privacy Beyond HTTPS

HTTPS protects your connection to a specific website, but:

- Your ISP still sees which sites you visit
- DNS queries may still leak
- Not all sites enforce HTTPS
- Apps may transmit data insecurely

A VPN encrypts everything, not just browser traffic.

5. VPNs Complement Other Encryption Tools

The chapter covers BitLocker, EFS, VeraCrypt, 7-Zip, and more – all focused on data at rest.

A VPN is the natural counterpart: it protects data in motion.

Together, they create a full-spectrum defense.

Tor Browser

A privacy-focused browser that:

- Routes traffic through multiple encrypted relays
- Masks your IP address
- Helps bypass censorship
- Protects anonymity

Limitations:

- Slower speeds
- Not foolproof if you log into personal accounts
- Exit nodes can see unencrypted traffic
- Some sites block Tor

Proxy Servers

Intermediary servers that:

- Mask your IP
- Filter traffic
- Bypass geo-restrictions
- Cache content for performance
- Provide parental controls or enterprise monitoring

Public proxies exist but come with risks:

- No encryption
- Logging or data harvesting
- Slow speeds
- Unreliable uptime

Core Message

Encryption is a foundational defense that protects your data whether it's stored, shared, or transmitted.

By using built-in tools like BitLocker, EFS, Time Machine, VeraCrypt, 7-Zip, secure browsers and VPN's anyone can significantly strengthen their privacy and security.

Chapter 5 Summary: *Password Management*

Chapter 5 centers on one of the most fundamental pillars of personal cybersecurity: **creating, maintaining, and protecting strong passwords**. Through Clarice's experience, the chapter shows how weak or reused passwords can expose someone to serious risk–and how simple changes can dramatically improve security.

Clarice's Turning Point

After the burglary, Clarice realizes her long-standing habit of reusing simple passwords ("Clarice123") puts her online accounts in danger. She updates her passwords, strengthens them, and quickly discovers the challenge everyone faces: **how to remember dozens of complex credentials**.

This leads her to adopt:

- Strong, unique passwords
- Regular password rotation
- Two-factor authentication (2FA)
- A password manager

Her journey becomes the chapter's framework for teaching best practices.

How to Create Strong Passwords

The chapter outlines clear, practical rules:

- Length: At least 12 characters
- Complexity: Mix of uppercase, lowercase, numbers, symbols
- No personal info: Avoid names, birthdays, email fragments
- No dictionary words: Prevent easy brute-force attacks
- Use passphrases: Random word combinations are both strong and memorable
- Avoid patterns: No "12345," "password," or predictable sequences
- Never reuse passwords: Each account must have its own
- Update regularly: Rotate passwords to reduce long-term exposure
- Use a password manager: Let software generate and store secure passwords
- Enable 2FA/MFA: Add a second layer of protection
- Test password strength: Use reputable tools to evaluate weak passwords

Two-Factor Authentication (2FA/MFA)

2FA adds a second verification step based on:

- Something you know (password or passphrase)
- Something you are (biometrics)
- Something you have (authenticator app, hardware token)

Benefits include:

- Protection against password guessing
- Defense against password reuse attacks
- Security for sensitive transactions
- Stronger resistance to phishing and man-in-the-middle attacks
- Better security when using app-based authenticators instead of SMS

Password Managers

Password managers solve the biggest challenge: remembering dozens of unique, complex passwords.

Key benefits:

- Generate strong, random passwords
- Store them securely in an encrypted vault
- Autofill credentials to prevent phishing
- Protect against keyloggers
- Sync across devices
- Store secure notes, credit cards, and sensitive data
- Provide password strength analysis
- Offer secure sharing and recovery options

The chapter also emphasizes that **low-tech solutions**—like writing passwords in a notebook stored offline—can be surprisingly effective because they're unhackable.

Comparison of Leading Password Managers

The chapter reviews several major tools:

Zoho Vault

- Unlimited storage, MFA, autofill, offline access
- Integrates with Zoho ecosystem
- Starts at $1/user/month

Bitwarden

- Open-source, transparent, affordable
- Free plan available
- Premium: $3.33/month

LastPass

- Password storage, autofill, dark web monitoring
- Free and premium tiers
- Premium: $4.99/month

1Password

- Secure vaults, Travel Mode, Watchtower alerts
- Personal: $2.99/month

Dashlane

- Includes a built-in VPN
- Premium: $5.99/month

Keeper

- Strong security features, breach monitoring
- Premium: $3.75/month

Each option has strengths—pricing, transparency, features, or bundled tools—so the "best" choice depends on individual needs.

Overall Message

Password management is not just about creating strong passwords—it's about **maintaining them**, protecting them, and using tools that make good security habits sustainable. By combining:

- Strong, unique passwords
- Regular updates
- Multi-factor authentication
- A password manager
- Low-tech offline backups

...anyone can dramatically reduce their risk of account compromise.

Chapter 6 Summary: Social Media Security

Chapter 6 focuses on protecting yourself—and your family—from the risks that come with using social media. Through Idris's story, the chapter highlights how easily personal information can be exposed and how important it is to take control of privacy and security settings before they become a problem.

Idris's Wake-Up Call

As Idris prepares for college applications, he realizes how much of his life is publicly visible online. Old posts, photos, and comments could be misinterpreted or used against him. This prompts him to:

- Review his social media profiles
- Strengthen his passwords
- Enable multi-factor authentication
- Lock down privacy settings
- Limit what the public can see

His experience becomes a lesson in how oversharing can create long-term risks.

General Security Tips for All Platforms

The chapter outlines universal best practices that apply to every social media site:

1. Enable Multi-Factor Authentication (MFA)

Adds a second layer of protection beyond passwords.

2. Use Strong, Unique Passwords

Avoid reuse; use a password manager to generate and store them.

3. Limit Third-Party App Access

Remove apps you no longer use or don't trust.

4. Monitor Account Activity

Turn on login alerts and review suspicious activity.

5. Limit Personal Information

Avoid sharing details like your address, phone number, or travel plans.

6. Be Cautious With Links

Phishing attacks often spread through social media messages.

7. Stay Educated

Follow platform security updates and learn to recognize scams.

Why Privacy Settings Matter

Oversharing increases your "attack surface."

Every post reveals:

- Time and location
- Personal details
- Your network of friends
- Photos of you and your environment
- Behavioral patterns

Attackers can use this information for identity theft, social engineering, or targeted scams.

Deep Dive: Facebook Security

The chapter provides a detailed walkthrough of Facebook's security and privacy tools, including:

Password & Security

- Change password
- Enable 2FA
- Review login alerts
- Check where you're logged in
- Run a Security Checkup

Privacy Checkup

Guided wizards help you adjust:

- Who can see your posts
- How people find you
- Data permissions
- Ad preferences

Audience Settings

Control visibility of:

- Posts
- Stories
- Reels
- Tags
- Followers
- Profile details

Supervision Tools

Parents can monitor and support their children's accounts through Meta's Family Center.

Activity Log

Shows every action you take on Facebook–revealing how much data Meta collects.

Apps & Websites

Review and remove third-party apps connected to your account.

Data Management

Access, download, or delete your Facebook data.

Instagram Security

Because Instagram is also owned by Meta, many settings overlap. Key areas include:

- Account Privacy (public vs. private)
- Story controls
- Comment and message filtering
- Tagging and mention restrictions

Core Message

Social media is powerful–but risky when used carelessly.

The chapter emphasizes:

- Minimizing exposure
- Using platform security tools
- Controlling who sees your content
- Protecting children and elderly family members
- Reducing the data available to attackers

The goal is to help you enjoy social media while keeping your identity, privacy, and personal information safe.

Chapter 7 Summary: *Email Security*

This chapter uses Margaret and Hannibal's experience to illustrate how easily people—especially those newer to technology—can fall for email scams. It then builds a complete, practical guide to securing email accounts, recognizing fraudulent messages, and avoiding malicious attachments.

Why Email Security Matters

Email is one of the most common attack vectors for:

- Phishing
- Identity theft
- Malware and ransomware
- Account takeover

Because email often links to banking, cloud accounts, and password resets, a compromised inbox can lead to full identity compromise.

Spotting Email Scams

The chapter highlights common red flags:

- Too-good-to-be-true offers (prizes, winnings)
- Urgent warnings (account locked, payment overdue)
- Generic greetings ("Dear Customer")
- Poor grammar or spelling
- Suspicious sender addresses
- Links that don't match the sender's domain
- Requests for personal information or money

It emphasizes that scammers rely on fear, urgency, and curiosity.

Securing Your Email Account

The chapter provides step-by-step instructions for Gmail, Outlook, and Yahoo:

1. Enable Two-Factor Authentication (2FA/MFA)

Use an authenticator app rather than SMS when possible.

2. Set a Strong, Unique Password

At least 16 characters, complex, and not reused anywhere else.

3. Review Account Activity

Check for:

- Unknown devices
- Suspicious sign-ins
- Recent security events

4. Set Up Account Recovery

Add:

- A recovery email
- A recovery phone number
- Backup codes (for Gmail)

5. Review Third-Party App Access

Remove apps you don't recognize or no longer use.

How to Check Email Headers

The chapter explains how to view full headers in:

- Outlook Desktop
- Outlook Web
- Apple Mail
- Gmail

This helps identify spoofing, mismatched domains, and authentication failures (SPF, DKIM, DMARC).

Avoiding Malicious Attachments

Key practices include:

- Never open unexpected attachments
- Hover over links before clicking
- Verify the sender through another channel
- Use antivirus to scan attachments
- Be cautious with password-protected files
- Report suspicious emails to your provider

The chapter also explains how to **disable automatic image loading**, which prevents tracking pixels and malicious content from loading automatically.

Safe Email Practices

The chapter closes with a set of habits that significantly reduce risk:

- Don't click links in unsolicited emails
- Rotate strong passwords
- Use encrypted email services when possible
- Avoid checking email on public Wi-Fi unless using a VPN
- Back up important messages
- Maintain separate email accounts for different purposes
- Stay informed about phishing trends

Core Message

Email is both essential and vulnerable. By combining:

- Strong authentication
- Careful behavior
- Regular account maintenance
- Awareness of scam tactics

...anyone can dramatically reduce their exposure to email-based threats. The chapter empowers users—especially those less familiar with technology—to navigate email safely and confidently.

Chapter 8 Summary: Safe Browsing Habits

Chapter 8 focuses on helping users—especially children like Aditsan—navigate the internet safely. It blends practical cybersecurity guidance with real-world scenarios to show how easily online interactions can become risky and how to build strong, safe browsing habits.

Aditsan's Story: Why Safe Browsing Matters

Aditsan loves gaming and exploring the internet, but when he befriends someone online he has never met, his parents step in to explain the risks:

- People online may pretend to be someone they're not
- Catfishing, bullying, and manipulation are real dangers
- Children should talk to parents about online interactions

This sets the stage for the chapter's deeper dive into safe browsing practices.

Recognizing & Avoiding Phishing Attacks

Phishing remains one of the most common online threats. The chapter teaches users to look for:

- Suspicious or mismatched email domains
- Poor grammar or unusual tone
- Urgent or threatening language
- "Too good to be true" offers
- Links that don't match the sender's domain

Key defenses include:

- Using a password manager
- Monitoring financial statements
- Being cautious on social media
- Reporting phishing attempts
- Staying educated on evolving scam tactics

Identifying Suspicious Websites

The chapter provides a comprehensive checklist for evaluating website safety:

1. Verify Reputation

Use tools like:

- ScamAdviser
- Google Safe Browsing
- VirusTotal
- Trend Micro Site Safety
- URLVoid

2. Inspect the URL

Look for:

- Misspellings
- Extra characters
- Fake variations of real domains

3. Check for HTTPS & Padlock

HTTPS indicates encrypted communication, though it does *not* guarantee legitimacy.

4. Review Website Design

Poor layout, broken links, or inconsistent branding can signal a fake site.

5. Validate SSL Certificates

Click the padlock to confirm:

- Certificate matches the domain
- Issuer is reputable
- Certificate is valid

6. Verify Contact Information

Legitimate sites list:

- Physical address
- Customer support
- Clear privacy policies

7. Check Domain Age

Newly registered domains can be suspicious.

Using Browser Security Features

Modern browsers include built-in protections. The chapter walks through enabling them in:

- Chrome
- Firefox
- Edge
- Opera
- Bing (Edge)

Key settings include:

- Safe Browsing / SmartScreen
- HTTPS-Only Mode
- Secure DNS
- Blocking insecure content
- Enhanced tracking protection

Using HTTPS and Secure Connections

The chapter emphasizes:

- Enabling HTTPS-Only mode
- Understanding HSTS (HTTP Strict Transport Security)
- Blocking insecure content
- Avoiding login pages that lack HTTPS

Additional Safe Browsing Practices

The chapter recommends:

- Keeping browsers updated
- Using a VPN for encrypted connections
- Blocking cookies and disabling autofill
- Avoiding downloads from untrusted sites
- Using secure browsers like Brave, DuckDuckGo, Tor, Mullvad, Firefox, or Opera
- Using browser extensions that detect malicious sites

Core Message

Safe browsing is about awareness, caution, and using the tools built into modern browsers. By:

- Recognizing phishing
- Evaluating websites carefully
- Enforcing HTTPS
- Using secure browsers
- Staying updated
- Using VPNs and security features

...users can dramatically reduce their exposure to online threats.

Chapter 9 Home Network Security

Chapter 9 focuses on protecting the home network—the foundation that all devices, apps, and online activity rely on. If the network itself is insecure, every connected device becomes vulnerable. This chapter teaches how to secure routers, Wi-Fi, connected devices, and the overall digital environment inside the home.

Why Network Security Matters

A home network connects:

- Computers
- Phones
- Smart TVs
- IoT devices
- Security cameras
- Gaming consoles

If attackers gain access to the network, they can:

- Steal data
- Spy through cameras or microphones
- Install malware
- Hijack devices for botnets
- Intercept traffic
- Access personal accounts

Network security protects the entire digital household.

Securing Your Wi-Fi Network

1. Change Default Router Credentials

Default admin usernames and passwords are widely known and easily exploited.

The chapter emphasizes:

- Changing the router's admin password
- Using a strong, unique passphrase
- Avoiding default SSIDs that reveal the router brand

2. Use Strong Wi-Fi Encryption

Always use:

- WPA3 (best)
- WPA2-AES (acceptable if WPA3 unavailable)

Never use:

- WEP
- WPA-TKIP
- Open networks

3. Hide or Limit SSID Broadcasting

While not a security feature by itself, reducing visibility helps limit casual probing.

4. Create a Guest Network

Separate guests—and their potentially insecure devices—from your main network.

Router & Firewall Best Practices

1. Keep Firmware Updated

Routers often have vulnerabilities. Updates patch security flaws.

2. Disable Unnecessary Features

Turn off:

- WPS
- UPnP
- Remote administration
- Port forwarding (unless required)

These features are commonly exploited.

3. Enable the Router Firewall

Most routers include a built-in firewall—ensure it's enabled.

4. Use Network Segmentation

Separate IoT devices from personal devices to reduce risk.

Securing Connected Devices

The chapter highlights that IoT devices are often the weakest link.

Best practices include:

- Changing default passwords
- Updating firmware
- Disabling unused services
- Reviewing app permissions
- Avoiding cheap, untrusted brands
- Using strong Wi-Fi encryption for all devices

Monitoring Your Network

The chapter encourages regular checks:

- Review connected devices
- Look for unknown or suspicious connections
- Monitor bandwidth usage
- Use router logs or security apps
- Enable alerts for new device connections

Using a VPN

A VPN adds an encrypted tunnel for all outbound traffic, protecting:

- Browsing
- Email
- Online banking
- Public Wi-Fi usage

It prevents ISPs, attackers, and snoopers from seeing your activity.

Advanced Network Protections

1. DNS Filtering

Use secure DNS providers like:

- Cloudflare (1.1.1.1)
- Google DNS (8.8.8.8)
- Quad9 (9.9.9.9)

These block malicious domains.

2. Intrusion Detection / Prevention

Some routers support IDS/IPS features that detect suspicious traffic.

3. MAC Address Filtering

Not foolproof, but adds another layer of control.

4. VLANs

For advanced users, VLANs isolate devices into separate virtual networks.

Core Message

Network security is the backbone of digital safety. By securing the router, using strong encryption, monitoring connected devices, and applying layered defenses like VPNs and DNS filtering, families can dramatically reduce their exposure to cyber threats.

Chapter 10 Securing Your Devices

Chapter 10 focuses on protecting the devices we use every day—phones, laptops, tablets, and computers—because these devices are often the first targets for attackers. Through Shannon's story, the chapter highlights how easily people can overlook risks like public Wi-Fi, outdated software, and weak device protections.

Shannon's Wake-Up Call

Shannon frequently used public Wi-Fi for banking and shopping until she learned a friend's Amazon account was hacked through an unsecured network. This pushed her to:

- Use a VPN on public Wi-Fi
- Keep her devices updated
- Avoid clicking fake update pop-ups
- Teach her family about safe device habits

Her experience frames the chapter's deeper dive into device security.

Why Software Updates Matter

The chapter emphasizes that updates are one of the most important—and most ignored—security practices.

1. Patch Vulnerabilities

Updates fix known security flaws that attackers actively exploit.

2. Protect Against Malware

Outdated software is a common entry point for ransomware and other malware.

3. Improve Security Features

Updates often strengthen encryption, privacy controls, and system protections.

4. Fix Zero-Day Exploits

Developers patch newly discovered vulnerabilities quickly—if you don't update, you stay exposed.

5. Improve Stability

Updates reduce crashes and bugs that attackers can leverage.

6. Strengthen Mobile & Network Security

Phones and tablets rely heavily on updates to stay secure.

Antivirus & Anti-Malware Protection

The chapter explains how antivirus software works and why it's essential:

Detection Methods

- Signature-based: Matches known malware
- Behavior-based: Detects suspicious activity
- Heuristic analysis: Identifies new, unknown threats

What Antivirus Protects Against

- Malware infections
- Ransomware
- Spyware
- Botnet hijacking
- Phishing attempts
- Malicious downloads
- Exploits targeting software vulnerabilities

Why It Matters

Antivirus tools:

- Quarantine infected files
- Block malicious websites
- Scan email attachments
- Prevent system disruption
- Help meet compliance requirements

Choosing Antivirus Software

The chapter reviews several options:

Windows

- Windows Defender is built-in and provides strong baseline protection.

macOS

- Uses XProtect, Gatekeeper, SIP, and notarization for basic security.

Ubuntu Linux

- Relies on permissions, AppArmor, and secure repositories.

Recommended Antivirus Tools

- Bitdefender
- Sophos Home
- AVG Free
- ClamAV

Each has different strengths depending on budget, features, and family needs.

Firewall Configuration

Firewalls block unauthorized access and are essential for device security.

Windows Firewall

- Ensure it's turned on
- Allow only essential inbound traffic
- Use default outbound rules
- Enable logging for visibility
- Add rules only when necessary

macOS Firewall

- Enable the built-in firewall
- Allow only trusted apps
- Enable stealth mode
- Block unnecessary inbound connections
- Enable logging

Firewalls don't require deep expertise—just basic configuration and occasional review.

Core Message

Device security is a combination of:

- Keeping software updated
- Using antivirus protection
- Configuring firewalls
- Avoiding unsafe networks
- Using VPNs on public Wi-Fi
- Practicing safe browsing and download habits

By following these steps, families can dramatically reduce their exposure to malware, account compromise, and network attacks.

Chapter 11 Family and Child Safety Online

Chapter 11 focuses on protecting families—especially children and seniors—from online risks. Through real-world examples involving Margaret, Hannibal, and young Aditsan, the chapter highlights how easily people can fall for scams, download unsafe apps, or share personal information without realizing the consequences. It then provides a comprehensive guide to building a safer digital environment at home.

Why Family Online Safety Matters

Different family members face different risks:

- Seniors may fall for scams, fake ads, or phishing attempts
- Children may encounter predators, cyberbullying, or unsafe apps
- Adults may overlook privacy settings or trust unsafe websites

The chapter emphasizes that online safety is a shared responsibility and requires ongoing communication.

Recognizing Online Scams

Margaret's experience with a fake health-product ad illustrates how scammers:

- Use convincing websites and ads
- Collect personal information
- Trigger spam, pop-ups, and unwanted messages

Key lessons:

- Be skeptical of limited-time offers
- Avoid entering personal details on unfamiliar sites
- Verify legitimacy before purchasing anything online

Child Safety: Teaching Kids to Navigate the Internet

Aditsan's near-miss with a fake game shows how vulnerable children can be.

The chapter encourages parents to teach children:

- Not everyone online is who they claim to be
- Never share personal information
- Ask an adult before downloading apps or clicking links
- Report anything that feels uncomfortable or suspicious

It also stresses digital citizenship—kindness, respect, and awareness of digital footprints.

Parental Controls & Filters

The chapter provides a detailed overview of tools parents can use to protect children:

1. Router-Based Controls

- Block inappropriate websites
- Set time limits
- Restrict devices
- Apply network-wide filters

2. Operating System Controls

- Create separate child accounts
- Limit app access
- Restrict downloads
- Apply age-appropriate settings

3. Third-Party Parental Control Software

Tools like Qustodio, Net Nanny, and Norton Family offer:

- Activity monitoring
- Content filtering
- Screen-time management
- App blocking

Monitoring & Restrictions

Parents are encouraged to:

- Review browsing history
- Check installed apps
- Monitor social media activity
- Discuss online interactions openly
- Set clear rules and expectations

Transparency is key—children should understand *why* monitoring is happening.

Safe Search Settings

The chapter explains how to enable SafeSearch on:

- Google
- Bing
- DuckDuckGo
- Yahoo

This helps filter explicit content from search results.

Teaching Critical Thinking

Children should learn to:

- Evaluate online information
- Recognize fake news
- Question suspicious content
- Understand offline consequences of online behavior

Parents are encouraged to model good digital habits.

Creating a Family Media Plan

A structured plan helps balance screen time, learning, and entertainment. Recommended resources include:

- HealthyChildren.org
- Common Sense Media
- MediaSmarts
- Turning Life On

These tools help families set boundaries and choose age-appropriate content.

Core Message

Online safety is not a one-time setup–it's an ongoing process. By combining:

- Parental controls
- Safe search settings
- Open communication
- Critical thinking
- Monitoring and guidance
- Awareness of scams

...families can create a safer digital environment for children, seniors, and adults alike.

Chapter 12 IoT Security

Chapter 12 explores the growing risks associated with Internet-connected smart devices—everything from cameras and thermostats to voice assistants and appliances. Through the Parkers' experience with hacked security cameras, the chapter shows how easily IoT devices can become entry points for attackers if not properly secured.

Why IoT Security Matters

Smart devices collect, store, and transmit personal data. When compromised, they can expose:

- Private conversations
- Video footage
- Location data
- Household routines
- Account credentials

Because many IoT devices have limited processing power, they often lack strong built-in security, making them attractive targets for attackers.

Key IoT Security Risks

1. Privacy Concerns

Smart devices gather data about habits, schedules, and preferences. If mishandled or breached, this information can be misused.

2. Data Breaches

Weak security or outdated firmware can allow attackers to access sensitive data stored on or transmitted by the device.

3. Insecure Network Communication

Unencrypted Wi-Fi traffic can be intercepted, enabling eavesdropping or unauthorized control.

4. Vendor & Supply Chain Risks

Some manufacturers:

- Don't provide regular updates
- Collect excessive data
- Use insecure cloud services

This increases long-term vulnerability.

5. Default or Weak Passwords

Many devices ship with default credentials that attackers can easily guess or find online.

6. IoT Botnets

Compromised devices can be hijacked and used in large-scale cyberattacks (e.g., DDoS).

7. Physical Security Risks

Hacked cameras or baby monitors can allow strangers to spy inside the home.

8. Poor Standardization

Different devices use inconsistent security protocols, making it hard for consumers to evaluate safety.

Risks by Device Type

Smart Appliances

- Can be hijacked for botnets
- Collect usage data
- Mitigation: change passwords, update firmware, isolate on separate networks

Voice Assistants

- Always listening
- May record unintended audio
- Mitigation: enable voice profiles, review privacy settings, mute when not in use

Home Automation Systems

- Central hubs can be single points of failure
- Mitigation: secure the hub, enable MFA, ensure encrypted communication

How to Secure Smart Devices

1. Inventory All IoT Devices

Know what's connected to your network and remove anything unfamiliar.

2. Change Default Passwords

Use strong, unique passwords for every device.

3. Enable Firmware Updates

- Check for updates regularly
- Enable automatic updates when possible
- Use official apps or vendor tools

4. Review App Permissions

Limit access to microphones, cameras, location, or contacts.

5. Enable MFA

If the device or its app supports multi-factor authentication, turn it on.

6. Strengthen Wi-Fi Security

- Use WPA3
- Use a strong Wi-Fi passphrase
- Avoid default SSIDs

7. Network Segmentation

Place IoT devices on:

- A guest network
- A separate VLAN
- An isolated Wi-Fi SSID

This prevents compromised devices from reaching sensitive computers or storage.

8. Disable Unused Features

Turn off:

- UPnP
- Remote access
- Unnecessary ports
- Data-sharing features

9. Secure Audio & Video Devices

- Delete stored recordings
- Position cameras carefully
- Update firmware frequently

10. Choose Reputable Manufacturers

Look for vendors with:

- Strong security track records
- Regular updates
- Transparent privacy policies

11. Monitor Device Activity

Review logs and alerts for unusual behavior.

12. Replace Unsupported Devices

Older devices may no longer receive updates and should be retired.

Core Message

IoT devices bring convenience—but also expand the attack surface of the home. By staying informed, updating devices, using strong passwords, segmenting networks, and choosing reputable manufacturers, families can enjoy smart technology without sacrificing privacy or security.

Chapter 13 Summary: Incident Response and Recovery

Chapter 13 brings the entire HomeGuard journey full circle by teaching the family—and the reader—how to recognize, respond to, and recover from cybersecurity incidents. After experiencing stolen credentials, ransomware scares, and online scams, the family realizes that **being prepared** is just as important as prevention.

Recognizing a Security Incident

The chapter explains that incidents fall into two major categories:

1. Third-Party Breaches

When companies like Facebook, Equifax, or banks announce data leaks, your credentials may be exposed.

Key actions include:

- Changing passwords immediately
- Enabling MFA
- Reviewing all accounts that reused the same password

2. Personal Device Incidents

Signs your own device may be compromised:

- Slow performance or crashing
- Strange pop-ups or browser redirects
- Unauthorized software installations
- Antivirus warnings
- Unexpected password resets
- Unknown devices on your network
- Suspicious financial activity
- Ransomware messages

The family learns that early detection dramatically reduces damage.

Steps to Take During a Breach

1. Stay Calm

Panic leads to mistakes. Follow your plan step by step.

2. Isolate the Device

Disconnect from Wi-Fi or unplug the Ethernet cable to stop malware from spreading.

3. Run Security Scans

Use antivirus and anti-malware tools to identify and remove threats.

4. Update Everything

Install updates for:

- Operating systems
- Browsers
- Apps
- Security tools

5. Secure Your Accounts

- Change passwords
- Enable MFA
- Review login history
- Check for unauthorized activity

6. Notify Contacts

If your email or social media was compromised, warn others so they don't fall for follow-up scams.

7. Restore From Backups

Offline backups are the safest recovery method, especially after ransomware.

8. Report the Incident

Contact:

- Your ISP
- Relevant service providers
- Law enforcement (if identity theft or financial fraud occurred)

9. Monitor Financial Accounts

Consider a fraud alert or credit freeze if sensitive data was exposed.

10. Watch for Follow-Up Phishing

Attackers often send fake "security alerts" after a breach.

11. Seek Professional Help

If the attack is advanced or you're unsure how to proceed, consult a cybersecurity professional.

Lessons Learned From a Breach

1. Backups Are Essential

Offline backups are the ultimate safety net.

2. Strong Passwords & MFA Matter

Weak or reused passwords are a major cause of compromise.

3. Network Security Is Critical

Secure routers, strong Wi-Fi passwords, and updated devices reduce risk.

4. Updates Prevent Exploits

Outdated software is one of the most common attack vectors.

5. Monitoring Helps Catch Problems Early

Regularly checking accounts and devices helps detect unauthorized access.

6. Social Engineering Is a Real Threat

Phishing and manipulation are often more effective than technical attacks.

7. Cybersecurity Is a Shared Responsibility

Everyone in the household must participate in safe practices.

8. Prevention Is Better Than Recovery

A breach reinforces the value of proactive security habits.

Core Message

Incident response isn't just for businesses—it's essential for families too. By recognizing warning signs, acting quickly, maintaining backups, and adopting strong security habits, anyone can recover from a cyber incident and build a safer digital environment moving forward.

Appendix 2: Glossary of Terms

A

Account Activity Monitoring: Regularly checking email account logs to spot unauthorized access or suspicious behavior.

Accidental Deletion: The unintentional removal of data, often caused by human error. Regular backups allow for the recovery of data to a state before the deletion occurred.

Admin Interface: The web-based control panel used to configure and manage the router settings.

Antivirus Software (AV): A type of security software designed to detect, prevent, and remove malware from computers and other devices. It is a key component of cybersecurity, offering protection through various detection methods.

App and Game Restrictions: Parental control settings that restrict access to specific apps or games based on content ratings or other criteria.

App Usage: The behavior and patterns of how users interact with mobile applications, including data collected by apps and third-party services.

Apps and Websites: External applications or websites that are connected to a user's social media account, which may have access to the user's data.

Attack Surface: The sum of all possible points of entry that an attacker can use to gain access to personal information.

Authentication Factor: An element used to verify a user's identity in the authentication process. In two-factor authentication, one factor is typically something the user knows (like a password), and the other is something the user has (like a mobile authenticator app).

Autofill: A feature in password managers that automatically enters saved usernames and passwords into login fields on websites, enhancing convenience and reducing the likelihood of entering incorrect information.

Automated Backups: A process where backups are scheduled and performed automatically without manual intervention. This reduces the likelihood of human error and ensures that backups occur consistently.

B

Backdoor Access: Unauthorized access to a computer system through a hidden entry point is often created by exploiting a software vulnerability. Regular updates help close potential backdoors.

Backup Device Settings: The practice of saving current device configurations and settings to restore them if needed, especially before performing updates.

Backup Frequency: The regularity with which backups are performed. This can range from daily to monthly, depending on the importance and volatility of the data being backed up.

Backup Storage Location: The physical or virtual location where backup data is stored, such as local storage devices, external hard drives, network-attached storage (NAS), or cloud storage.

Backup Window: The specific time period during which backups are scheduled to occur. Backup windows are often set during low-activity periods to minimize disruption.

Baiting: A social engineering attack where the victim is lured into a trap with the promise of something enticing, such as free software or a prize.

Bandwidth Limiting: A feature that restricts the amount of data that can be transmitted or received by devices on a network, often used on guest networks to ensure fair distribution of available bandwidth.

Behavior-Based Detection: A method used by antivirus software to identify potential threats by analyzing the behavior of files or applications. This is particularly useful in detecting new or unknown forms of malware.

Biometric Authentication: A security process that uses an individual's unique biological characteristics, such as fingerprints or facial recognition, to verify identity and grant access.

Botnet: A network of private computers or devices infected with malicious software and controlled as a group without the owners' knowledge. Botnets are often used to perform distributed denial-of-service (DDoS) attacks.

Breaches: Security incidents where unauthorized access to personal data occurs, often leading to data theft or misuse.

Browser Extensions: Add-ons installed in web browsers to enhance functionality, such as ad-blockers or privacy tools.

Browser Security Settings: Configurations within a web browser that control privacy and security features, such as blocking insecure content or enabling HTTPS-only mode.

C

Captive Portal: A web page that users are redirected to before being granted broader access to a network, often used for guest networks to agree to terms or log in.

Cloud Security: Measures and controls designed to protect cloud-based systems, data, and infrastructure. Examples include enabling two-factor authentication (2FA) and configuring strict privacy settings on cloud-based accounts.

Cloud Services: Internet-based services that store, manage, and process data remotely, often used by smart devices for storage and functionality.

Cloud Storage: A service that allows data to be stored on remote servers accessed through the internet. It is often used for offsite backups, providing additional protection against local disasters.

Community Forums: Online platforms where users of smart devices share information, updates, and troubleshooting tips.

Connection Privacy: Settings that manage who can view a user's connections and follow them on platforms like LinkedIn.

Content Filters: Tools or software that restrict or control the content that a user is allowed to access, often used to ensure that children view age-appropriate content online.

Cookies: Small pieces of data stored by a web browser that track information such as browsing history and preferences. Disabling cookies can enhance online privacy.

Credential Compromise: When login details (username, password) are exposed during a breach, it is necessary to reset passwords and enable additional security measures like multi-factor authentication (MFA).

Credential Stuffing: A type of cyber attack where attackers use stolen username and password combinations from one site to try to gain access to other sites where the same credentials may have been reused.

Critical Thinking: The ability to analyze and evaluate information found online, particularly to discern between reliable sources and misleading or false content.

Cross-Device Synchronization: A feature offered by many password managers that allows users to access their passwords and sensitive information across multiple devices, ensuring consistency and accessibility.

Cyberbullying: The use of electronic communication to bully a person, typically by sending messages of an intimidating or threatening nature.

Cybersecurity: The practice of protecting systems, networks, and programs from digital attacks, theft, or damage. It involves implementing various security measures to safeguard personal information, financial data, and digital assets.

Cybersecurity Education: Ongoing learning about the latest threats, best practices, and technologies in cybersecurity to stay informed and prepared for potential incidents.

D

Data Backup: A copy of important files and data stored separately from the main system. Regular backups are essential for recovery in case of data loss or ransomware attacks.

Data Backup and Recovery: The process of creating and storing copies of data to protect against loss. Recovery plans ensure that data can be restored in the event of a cyberattack, hardware failure, or other data loss events.

Data Backup and Recovery Strategy: A comprehensive plan that outlines how data backups will be performed, stored, and restored. This strategy is crucial for ensuring data availability and integrity in case of data loss or corruption.

Data Breach: An incident where sensitive, protected, or confidential data is accessed or disclosed in an unauthorized fashion. Scammers often exploit such events by crafting phishing emails based on the stolen data.

Data Corruption: The unintended alteration or damage of data, often due to software errors or hardware failures. Regular backups allow for the restoration of uncorrupted data.

Data Encryption: The process of converting information or data into a code to prevent unauthorized access. Encryption is commonly used to protect sensitive data, such as financial information and personal communications.

Data Hygiene: The practice of maintaining and protecting personal data, including regularly updating passwords, monitoring accounts, and reviewing privacy settings.

Data Loss Prevention (DLP): A set of tools and processes used to ensure that sensitive data is not lost, misused, or accessed by unauthorized users. DLP tools monitor and control the flow of data within an organization.

Data Masking: A method used to protect sensitive information by replacing it with fictional data while maintaining the usability of the data. This is often used in non-production environments to protect data privacy.

Data Mining: The process of analyzing large sets of data to discover patterns or relationships. Often used by companies to gain insights into consumer behavior.

Data Versioning: The practice of saving multiple versions of files over time, allowing for the restoration of a specific version of a file in case of errors or unwanted changes.

DDoS Attack (Distributed Denial of Service): A cyberattack where multiple compromised devices are used to overwhelm a target system with traffic, rendering it unavailable.

Default Gateway: The IP address of a router that a device uses to send data to devices outside its local network.

Default Passwords: Pre-set usernames and passwords provided by manufacturers, often weak and easily guessable, posing a security risk if not changed.

Defense in Depth: A cybersecurity strategy that involves implementing multiple layers of security controls organization's infrastructure. This approach ensures that if one layer of defense is compromised, other layers can still provide protection.

Device Isolation: The act of disconnecting a compromised device from the network to prevent malware spread or unauthorized access to other devices.

Device Obsolescence: The condition where older smart devices no longer receive updates or support from manufacturers, making them more susceptible to security vulnerabilities.

Device-Specific Accounts: Unique user accounts created for each smart device to minimize the impact if one account is compromised.

Dictionary Attack: A method used by attackers to crack passwords by systematically trying every word in a dictionary or a pre-defined list of common words and phrases.

Digital Assets: Intangible assets that are stored in digital form, including family photos, videos, documents, and other valuable data.

Digital Citizenship: The responsible use of technology, including respecting privacy, reporting suspicious activities, and adhering to ethical standards online.

Digital Footprint: The record of a person's online activities, including the websites they visit, the content they post, and the data they share, can have long-term consequences.

Digital Footprint - Active: Data intentionally left by a user, such as social media posts, online banking transactions, or information provided during online registrations. Users are aware of this data being collected.

Digital Footprint - Passive: Data collected without the user's knowledge, such as website visits, search history, or location data. This data is often gathered without explicit consent, making it harder to track.

Digital Etiquette: The standards of conduct and behavior that individuals are expected to follow when interacting with others online.

Digital Identity: The collection of data points, including usernames, passwords, and other identifiers, that define a person's online presence.

Digital Identity Information: Personal identifiers used online, such as usernames, passwords, and device fingerprints.

Disaster Recovery: The process of restoring systems and data following a catastrophic event such as a natural disaster, hardware failure, or cyberattack. A robust backup plan is a critical component of disaster recovery.

Digital Identity: The online persona created through usernames, passwords, and other personal identifiers used across various platforms.

Disposable Email Addresses: Temporary email addresses are used to avoid sharing a primary email with potentially insecure websites or services.

E

Ease of Migration: The simplicity of transferring data from one system or device to another, often facilitated by having reliable backups that can be restored onto new hardware or platforms.

Educational Apps and Websites: Online resources that provide educational content and activities for children, often designed to be both informative and safe.

Email Communication: Includes email addresses, communication patterns, and content within emails. Emails can be a significant part of one's digital footprint.

Email Domain: The part of an email address that comes after the "@" symbol represents the organization or entity that owns the email service.

Email Headers: The part of an email that contains information about the sender, recipient, and email's path. Analyzing headers can help detect spoofing attempts.

Email Scams: Fraudulent schemes are carried out via email with the intent to deceive and steal personal information or money from the recipient.

Email Security Features: Tools provided by email services to protect against spam, phishing, and other malicious activities, such as spam filters, DKIM, SPF, and DMARC.

Email Spoofing: A technique used in phishing attacks where the attacker falsifies the sender's address to make it appear as if the email is from a legitimate source.

Email Signature: The block of text is automatically appended at the end of an email message, often including the sender's name, job title, and contact information. Inconsistent or missing signatures can indicate phishing.

Employment and Educational History: Professional and academic background information is shared on platforms like LinkedIn. This data is part of an individual's digital footprint.

Encrypted Email Services: Email services that protect messages by converting them into code to prevent unauthorized access.

Encrypted Sites: Websites that use encryption to protect user data. Identified by a URL that begins with "https://" and a padlock icon in the address bar, indicating a security certificate.

Encryption: The process of converting data into a coded form that is unreadable without a specific key or password. Used by password managers to secure stored passwords and sensitive information.

End-of-Life Announcements: Notifications from manufacturers indicating that a device will no longer receive updates or support, marking the end of its lifecycle.

Endpoint Security: Security measures designed to protect endpoint devices such as desktops, laptops, smartphones, and servers from cyber threats. This includes antivirus software, host-based intrusion detection systems (HIDS), and endpoint detection and response (EDR) tools.

Endpoint Protection: Security measures implemented on individual devices (endpoints) that connect to a network, such as computers, smartphones, and tablets. Antivirus software is a form of endpoint protection.

F

Fake Update Notifications: Deceptive messages that mimic legitimate update notifications, often used by attackers to trick users into downloading malicious software. Users should avoid clicking on such notifications and instead visit the vendor's official website for updates.

Family Media Plan: A set of agreed-upon guidelines within a family that outlines the rules and expectations for device use, screen time, and online activities.

Firewall: A network security device that monitors and controls incoming and outgoing network traffic based on predetermined security rules. Firewalls are used to protect networks from unauthorized access.

Firewall - macOS: A built-in firewall provided by the macOS operating system helps protect Mac computers by managing network traffic and preventing unauthorized access.

Firewall - Windows: A built-in firewall provided by the Windows operating system helps protect the system by filtering network traffic and blocking harmful communications.

Firmware: Permanent software programmed into a router that controls its hardware functions.

Footprinting: The process of gathering data about a system or user, often used by hackers to collect information for potential attacks.

Fraud Alert/Credit Freeze: A security measure placed with credit bureaus to prevent unauthorized access to credit information, often used after a breach involving financial data.

Full Backup: A backup method that involves copying all selected data in its entirety. Full backups are comprehensive but can be time-consuming and resource-intensive.

G

Generic Greetings: Non-specific salutations like "Dear Customer" or "Dear User" used in scam emails, lacking personalization typical of legitimate emails.

Gift Card Scams: Emails requesting urgent purchase of gift cards, often using emotional appeals or fabricated emergencies.

Guest Network: A separate network within a home that provides internet access to guests while isolating their devices from the main network. This prevents unauthorized access to the primary network and its connected devices.

H

Hardware Failure: The malfunction or breakdown of physical components in a computer or storage device leads to potential data loss. Backups protect against data loss due to hardware issues.

Heuristics-Based Detection: An advanced method of detecting malware by analyzing the behavior and characteristics of files to determine if they are potentially malicious, even if they do not match known virus signatures.

Host-Based Intrusion Detection System (HIDS): A security system that monitors and analyzes the internals of a computing system to detect and respond to suspicious activities or policy violations. Think of HIDS as a security camera and alarm system for an individual device. It watches for suspicious behavior, such as unauthorized changes to files or unusual system activity. If it detects something that looks like it could be a security threat, it alerts you or takes action to protect the device. This helps to ensure that even if a threat manages to bypass other defenses, it can still be detected and dealt with on the specific device.

Hover Over: The action of placing the cursor over a link without clicking allows the user to preview the actual URL to verify its legitimacy.

HSTS (HTTP Strict Transport Security): A web security policy that forces browsers to interact with websites over HTTPS, preventing certain types of attacks like protocol downgrade attacks.

HTTPS (Hypertext Transfer Protocol Secure): An extension of HTTP used for secure communication over a computer network. Websites with HTTPS encrypt data between the user and the server, protecting against interception.

I

Identity Theft: The fraudulent acquisition and use of a person's private identifying information, usually for financial gain.

Inbound Traffic: Data that is received by a computer system from an external source. Firewalls manage inbound traffic to ensure that only authorized communications are allowed.

Incident Response Plan: A predefined set of procedures to follow in the event of a security incident. Having an incident response plan helps minimize damage and expedite recovery.

IoT (Internet of Things): Refers to a network of physical devices, vehicles, appliances, and other items embedded with sensors, software, and connectivity, enabling them to collect and exchange data.

Impersonation: A social engineering tactic where the attacker pretends to be someone in a position of authority to gain the victim's trust and obtain sensitive information.

Incremental Backup: A backup method that only saves changes made since the last backup, whether it was a full or incremental backup. This approach saves storage space and reduces backup time.

Insecure Network Communication: The risk associated with unprotected data transmission between smart devices and networks, which can be intercepted by malicious actors.

Intrusion Prevention System (IPS): A network security tool that continually monitors network traffic to detect and prevent known threats, unlike intrusion detection systems (IDS), which only alert administrators of a potential threat, IPS actively blocks malicious traffic.

Internet of Things (IoT): A network of interconnected devices, such as smart home appliances, that communicate and exchange data with each other over the internet.

IP Address: A unique string of numbers that identifies each computer using the internet. IP addresses can be used to track online activities.

IP Address Range: The range of IP addresses that a router can assign to devices connected to the network.

J

Job Seeking Preferences: Privacy settings on LinkedIn allow users to manage who can see their job-seeking activities.

K

Keylogger: A type of malicious software that records keystrokes made by a user, potentially capturing sensitive information such as passwords. Password managers can help protect against keyloggers by using autofill features.

L

Legal and Ethical Concerns: Issues related to data ownership, consent, and the use of personal information by smart devices, often governed by varying regulations and laws.

Logging: The process of recording events or activities, such as blocked or allowed traffic, within a firewall. Logs are useful for monitoring and analyzing security incidents.

Location Sharing: A setting on social media platforms that controls whether a user's location is shared with others.

M

MAC Address (Media Access Control Address): A unique identifier assigned to network interfaces for communications on a physical network segment.

Malicious Redirects: Redirecting a user from a legitimate website to a malicious one to steal information or install malware.

Malware: Malicious software designed to harm, exploit, or otherwise compromise the security of a computer system. Phishing emails may contain malware in attachments or links.

Man-in-the-Middle Attack: A type of cyber attack where an attacker intercepts and potentially alters communication between two parties without their knowledge. Using tools like VPNs and Two-factor authentication help mitigate this risk.

Manufacturer Notifications: Alerts or newsletters from device manufacturers about firmware updates, security patches, or other important information.

Metadata: Data that provides information about other data, such as the date, time, and location stored in a photo file. Removing metadata before sharing can protect personal details.

Mismatched Email Address: An email address that closely resembles a legitimate one but includes subtle differences, such as misspellings or additional characters, often used by scammers to appear trustworthy.

Misspellings and Grammar Mistakes: Common in scam emails, these errors are indicators that the message may not be from a legitimate source.

Mobile Apps: Applications on smartphones or tablets used to control and manage smart devices. These apps must be secure to prevent unauthorized access.

Monitoring Device Activity: Regularly reviewing logs and usage history of smart devices to detect any unusual or unauthorized activities.

Monitoring and Reporting: Features in parental control tools that provide parents with reports on their child's online activities, including the websites visited, search queries made, and time spent on different activities.

Multi-Factor Authentication (MFA): A security process that requires multiple forms of verification before granting access to an account. It adds an extra layer of protection beyond just a password.

N

Natural Disasters: Events such as fires, floods, or earthquakes can physically damage infrastructure and storage devices. Offsite backups ensure data is protected even if the primary location is affected.

Network Access Control (NAC): A security solution that enforces policies on devices attempting to access a network, ensuring that only compliant and authorized devices are allowed to connect. Imagine it as a bouncer at a club who checks IDs and makes sure only the right people get in. NAC does something similar for your network: it verifies the identity and security status of devices (like computers, phones, or printers) before allowing them to connect. If a device doesn't meet the security requirements or is not recognized, NAC can block it or limit its access to sensitive parts of the network. This helps to keep your network safe from unauthorized access and potential threats.

Network Isolation: A security feature that prevents devices connected to the same network from communicating with each other.

Network-Level Controls: Parental controls implemented at the router level that apply to all devices connected to the home network, allowing for centralized management of internet access.

Network Segmentation: The practice of dividing a computer network into smaller segments or subnetworks to improve security and performance. This can be done using virtual LANs (VLANs) and guest networks.

Network Traffic Patterns: Observing and analyzing the flow of data in and out of a network. Unusual patterns may signal a cybersecurity threat or compromise.

O

Offsite Backups: Backups that are stored in a different physical location from the primary data source, often using cloud storage. This provides protection against localized disasters.

Offline Consequences: The real-world impact that online actions and behaviors can have on a child's relationships, education, or future opportunities.

Online Activity Monitoring: The process of tracking a child's online activities, including websites visited, apps used, and time spent online, to ensure safe internet use.

Online Etiquette (Netiquette): The code of polite behavior that children should follow when communicating online includes being respectful, avoiding cyberbullying, and being mindful of what they share.

Online Harassment: Unwanted behavior conducted through digital means, including social media, emails, or messaging platforms.

Online Purchases: Details of transactions made online, including items purchased, payment methods, and shipping information. Online shopping history contributes to a digital footprint.

Online Reputation: The perception of an individual based on their online activities and the information available about them on the internet.

Online Reviews and Ratings: Feedback provided on e-commerce platforms or services, contributing to an individual's digital footprint.

Online Subscriptions: Services or content that users subscribe to often involve the sharing of personal information. Managing subscriptions can help limit the data shared online.

Online Trends: The latest popular activities, challenges, apps, or games that children may engage with online can have both positive and negative implications.

Operating System Controls: Parental control features built into the operating systems of devices (such as Windows, macOS, Android, iOS) that allow parents to restrict access to certain content and features.

Oversharing: The act of sharing too much personal information online, which can lead to privacy risks such as identity theft or targeted cyberattacks.

Outbound Traffic: Data that is sent from a computer system to an external destination. Firewalls monitor and control outbound traffic to prevent unauthorized data leaks.

P

Parental Controls: Tools and settings that allow parents or guardians to manage and regulate the online activities of children, including restricting access to certain content, setting time limits, and monitoring online behavior.

Passphrase: A type of password that consists of a series of random words or a sentence. Passphrases are often easier to remember and can be more secure than traditional passwords due to their length.

Password: A secret combination of characters used to access accounts, systems, or networks. It acts as a primary defense mechanism against unauthorized access.

Password Auditing: The process of analyzing the strength and security of existing passwords, identifying weak, duplicated, or outdated passwords that need to be improved.

Password Manager: A software tool that securely stores, manages, and generates strong and unique passwords for different accounts, helping users maintain better security practices.

Password Master: The primary password used to access a password manager's vault contains all other passwords and sensitive information. This password is typically the only one a user needs to remember.

Password Offline Storage: A low-tech method of storing passwords, such as writing them down in a physical notebook. This approach is highly secure as it is not vulnerable to online hacking.

Password Recovery: Methods provided by password managers to help users regain access to their password vault if they forget their master password, ensuring they can still access their stored credentials.

Password Strong: A password that is difficult to guess or crack, typically characterized by a length of at least 12 characters and a mix of uppercase letters, lowercase letters, numbers, and special characters.

Password Strength Analysis: A feature in password managers that evaluates the complexity and security of a password, encouraging the use of stronger, more secure passwords.

Patch: A software update specifically designed to fix vulnerabilities or bugs in a program. Patches are crucial for securing software against emerging threats.

Personalization: The practice of addressing an email recipient by name or including specific details that are unique to the individual. Phishing emails often lack personalization, using generic greetings instead.

Personal Data: Information that can identify an individual, such as names, addresses, social security numbers, and more.

Personally Identifiable Information (PII): Any data that could potentially identify a specific individual, such as names, social security numbers, and financial information. Protecting PII is essential to preventing identity theft and fraud.

Phishing: A cyberattack in which a threat actor poses as a legitimate entity to deceive individuals into revealing sensitive information, such as passwords or financial details.

Phishing Attack: A type of cyber attack where attackers attempt to trick users into providing sensitive information, such as passwords, by masquerading as a legitimate entity.

Physical Security Concerns: Risks associated with the physical vulnerability of smart devices, such as cameras or baby monitors, being accessed by unauthorized individuals.

Psychological Manipulation: The use of tactics to influence a person's thoughts or behaviors for malicious purposes, often employed in social engineering attacks.

Pop-Ups: Unwanted advertisements or notifications that appear frequently and may indicate the presence of adware or other malicious software.

Pop-Up Form: A window that appears on a website, often unexpectedly, to request user input. Phishing websites may use pop-up forms to collect sensitive information.

Privacy Settings: Configurations in online accounts and devices that control the level of information shared and who can access it. Regularly reviewing and adjusting privacy settings enhances security.

Pretexting: A social engineering tactic where the attacker creates a fake scenario to trick the victim into giving away valuable information.

Profile Privacy: Settings on social media that control who can view a user's personal profile information.

Privacy Awareness: Understanding and taking steps to protect personal data online, including being cautious of what information is shared.

Privacy Concerns: Issues related to the unauthorized collection, use, and distribution of personal data by smart devices.

Privacy Controls: Settings that protect a child's personal information by limiting the visibility and sharing of data on websites, apps, and social media platforms.

Privacy Policies: Documents provided by companies that outline how they collect, use, and manage user data.

Made in United States
Orlando, FL
05 November 2026

90207813R00177